Exploring Sentencing Practice in England and Wales

Also by Julian V. Roberts

POPULAR PUNISHMENT: The Normative Significance of Public Opinion for Sentencing Theory and Practice (2014, *co-editor*)

SENTENCING GUIDELINES: Exploring the English Model (2013, *co-editor*)

SENTENCING FOR MURDER: Exploring the Mandatory Sentence of Life Imprisonment for Murder (2012, *co-author*)

PRINCIPLES AND VALUES IN CRIMINAL LAW AND CRIMINAL JUSTICE (2012, *co-editor*)

MITIGATION AND AGGRAVATION AT SENTENCING (2011, *editor*)

THE ROLE OF PREVIOUS CONVICTIONS AT SENTENCING: Theoretical and Applied Perspectives (2010, *co-editor*)

HEARING THE VICTIM: Adversarial Justice, Crime Victims, and the State (2010, *co-editor*)

PRINCIPLED SENTENCING (THIRD EDITION) (2009, *co-editor*)

PUNISHING PERSISTENT OFFENDERS: Community and Offender Perspectives on the Recidivist Sentencing Premium (2008, *author*)

UNDERSTANDING PUBLIC ATTITUDES TO CRIMINAL JUSTICE (2005, *co-author*)

THE VIRTUAL PRISON: Community Custody and the Evolution of Imprisonment (2004, *author*)

PENAL POPULISM AND PUBLIC OPINION (2003, *co-author*)

RESTORATIVE AND CRIMINAL JUSTICE (2003, *co-editor*)

CHANGING ATTITUDES TO PUNISHMENT: Public Opinion, Crime and Justice (2002, *co-editor*)

MAKING SENSE OF SENTENCING (1999) (*co-editor*)

PUBLIC OPINION, CRIME AND CRIMINAL JUSTICE (1997, *co-author*)

CONFRONTING SEXUAL ASSAULT (1994, *co-editor*)

EVALUATING JUSTICE (1993, *co-editor*)

Exploring Sentencing Practice in England and Wales

Edited by

Julian V. Roberts
University of Oxford

palgrave
macmillan

First published 2015 by
PALGRAVE MACMILLAN

Palgrave Macmillan in the UK is an imprint of Macmillan Publishers Limited, registered in England, company number 785998, of Houndsmills, Basingstoke, Hampshire, RG21 6XS

Palgrave Macmillan in the US is a division of St Martin's Press LLC, 175 Fifth Avenue, New York, NY 10010.

Palgrave Macmillan is the global academic imprint of the above companies and has companies and representatives throughout the world.

Palgrave® and Macmillan® are registered trademarks in the United States, the United Kingdom, Europe and other countries

ISBN: 978–1–137–39039–4

This book is printed on paper suitable for recycling and made from fully managed and sustained forest sources. Logging, pulping and manufacturing processes are expected to conform to the environmental regulations of the country of origin.

A catalogue record for this book is available from the British Library.

A catalog record for this book is available from the Library of Congress.

Contents

List of Figures

List of Tables

Foreword

Sentencing lies at the heart of the criminal justice process. Court-imposed judicial sanctions set the tone for the criminal justice system and attract widespread public and media attention. Given the number of criminal courts sitting all over the country, there is an inherent danger that sentencing practices could vary between different places. Our legal system has long recognised this danger and tried to manage it by a system of precedence and hierarchical decision-making. Despite these responses, the problem of differential judicial decision-making was repeatedly raised as a matter of concern in the last quarter of the twentieth century. In the words of the populist press, there were allegations of a 'postcode lottery' in criminal sentencing, supported by data that showed apparently identical offences receiving different sentences across the country. Whether these really were identical offences, or whether they were sufficiently different in their facts to warrant different sentences, was difficult to determine because the judicial statistics lacked the necessary detail (and occasionally the quality), and there was resistance to collecting the evidence needed for systematic research.

One response to this apparent lack of consistency was the creation, by the Criminal Justice Act, 2003, of the Sentencing Guidelines Council and its sister body, the Sentencing Advisory Panel, to provide guidelines for criminal sentencing. England and Wales thereby became one of the very few countries outside the United States to implement a national criminal sentencing guidelines system. The new body did important work in establishing that guidance could be provided to judges without impeding judicial discretion to such an extent that sentencing was reduced to a mechanical, formulaic process that denied substantive justice to both victims and offenders. However, this first attempt at creating a sentencing guidelines body had some weaknesses, and in late 2007, the Sentencing Commission Working Group, chaired by Lord Justice Gage, was set up to consider the existing arrangements and make recommendation for the future.[1]

The result was a new body – the Sentencing Council for England and Wales – created by the Coroners and Justice Act, 2009, with an enhanced remit as to the status of its guidelines and a simplified and strengthened analytic and research function. The new Council was also given a remit to increase public understanding of sentencing and to consult widely when drawing up its guidelines. From the beginning, the Council sought to lay out the logic of judicial sentencing in such a manner as to guide sentencers but also make the process of sentencing more transparent to the public.

As is so often the case with government reform, the new body was conceived at a time of plenty but came into being during a period of financial constraint. Nevertheless, the new Council implemented a key recommendation from the Gage Report and started collecting information about sentencing decisions in the Crown Court through the Crown Court Sentencing Survey (CCSS).[2] The CCSS has provided an important basis for the Council to make evidence-based decisions about its guidelines. In addition, since the Council has made the data available to researchers, scholars have a new source of data that relates directly to development and evaluation of sentencing guidelines.[3]

These changes in the provision of sentencing guidelines – greater transparency regarding sentencing, concern for public understanding, evidence-based guideline development, open consultation and new data collection – have led to a renewed interest in sentencing research. The present volume is evidence of this increased activity. In itself, this is an important outcome of the creation of the Council because, despite the centrality of sentencing to the criminal justice process, sentencing research has long been the Cinderella of criminal justice research. From the 1970s onwards, David Thomas, at Cambridge, opened up sentencing in England and Wales to academic scrutiny, but his work was legal rather than empirical. Andrew Ashworth, at Oxford, continued this work and extended it into empirical analysis, whilst later scholars, several of whom contribute to this volume, conducted studies on sentencing. This collection contains significant contributions on a range of important issues in sentencing. The authors report findings from the CCSS as well as other sources of data.

This new interest amongst the academic community is to be welcomed and will contribute to a more informed public debate about sentencing. Lack of public knowledge and analysis of sentencing has been unhealthy and has allowed uninformed criticism of sentencing to go unchallenged. The academic research community, of course, has its own responsibilities: namely to ensure its research represents the world truthfully and speak such truths openly. This research may be supportive of the judicial process – but not necessarily. The Sentencing Council was given a wide remit, ranging from promoting principled judicial consistency, to improving the position of victims in the sentencing process and to ensuring public confidence in sentencing. These are all worthy public goals, but in a time of shrinking public resources, difficult choices will have to be made for which the Council will be publicly accountable. Empirical research will help it make those choices (and fulfil its functions) but will also be a means to hold the Council accountable. This volume – the first collection of essays exploring empirical and normative issues in sentencing – represents a significant milestone towards the goal of understanding sentencing in England and Wales.

Paul Wiles

Notes

1. http://www.justice.gov.uk/docs/sentencing-guidelines-evolutionary-approach.pdf.
2. As a result of financial constraints upon the Council, data collection for the magistrates' courts has yet to be implemented.
3. For details of the CCSS data, see http://sentencingcouncil.judiciary.gov.uk/.

Acknowledgements

My primary debt is to the authors who have generously contributed to this volume. I am also grateful to Julia Willan, Harriet Barker and other colleagues at Palgrave Macmillan for their support and assistance, without which the publication of this volume would not have been possible. My thanks also to Binesh Hass for meticulous proofing and indexing.

Julian V. Roberts
Oxford
15 November, 2014

Notes on Contributors

Editor

Julian V. Roberts is Professor of Criminology at the University of Oxford. He has been conducting research in the area of sentencing since 1981. He is associate editor of *European Journal of Criminology* and *Canadian Journal of Criminology*. His books include *Punishing Persistent Offenders* (2008), *Mitigation and Aggravation at Sentencing* (2011), and *Understanding Public Attitudes to Criminal Justice* (2005, with Mike Hough). His most recent book is *Popular Punishment* (2014, edited with J. Ryberg).

The contributors

Rebecca Barnes has been Lecturer in Criminology at the University of Leicester since 2013. Her main area of research concerns domestic violence and abuse in lesbian, gay, bisexual and transgender relationships, and she has undertaken research on both the survivors and perpetrators of such abuse, as well as with prison, probation and third sector practitioners involved in the design and/or delivery of domestic abuse interventions.

Ian Belton is a PhD student and research assistant at Middlesex University. His research investigates the cognitive processes used by decision-makers in the legal domain, with a focus on criminal sentencing. He has authored publications on legal decision-making, and sentencing in particular. Ian is also a qualified solicitor with eight years' experience in the field of commercial litigation, both in London and in Brisbane, Australia.

Mandeep Dhami is Professor of Decision Psychology at Middlesex University. Her research focuses on human decision-making, particularly in the criminal justice system. She is the author of over 80 publications and lead editor of *Judgment and Decision-Making as a Skill: Learning, Development, and Evolution* (2011). Mandeep was an advisor to the Sentencing Council in England and Wales. She is a fellow of the Society for the Psychological Study of Social Issues (American Psychological Association).

Martina Feilzer is a senior lecturer in Criminology and Criminal Justice at Bangor University. Her main research interests are the relationship between public and criminal justice at local, national, and European levels; penal policy; and comparative and historical criminological research. She also has a strong interest in the use of mixed methods research and the secondary analysis and visualisation of existing datasets.

Loraine Gelsthorpe is Professor of Criminology and Criminal Justice at the Institute of Criminology, University of Cambridge. She is also director of the Cambridge ESRC Doctoral Training Centre and co-convenor of the Cambridge Migration Research Network – CAMMIGRES. Loraine has published widely on women, crime and criminal justice, youth justice, and community penalties in an international context, as well as on more general criminal justice topics. Recent research includes work on the criminalisation of migrant women. Recent publications include *A Restorative Justice Approach to Family Violence: Changing Tack* (2014, co-edited with A. Hayden, V. King and A. Morris). Loraine was made a fellow of the Royal Society of Arts in 2009 for distinguished contribution to criminal justice, and is the president of the British Society of Criminology (until July 2015).

Carol Hedderman has been Professor of Criminology at the University of Leicester since 2004. Her research interests include the comparative effectiveness of different approaches to securing compliance and enforcing court penalties, desistance and 'what works' in prison and probation, reconviction studies and the development of alternative measures of effectiveness, the treatment of women caught up in the criminal justice system, and the media reporting of probation.

Mike Hough is Professor of Criminal Policy at Birkbeck, University of London, and associate director at the Institute for Criminal Policy Research. Mike has published extensively, with around 250 publications to his name (see www.icpr.org.uk).

Max Lowenstein is a senior lecturer in Law at Bournemouth University. His research interests encompass sentencing law, comparative criminology and criminal justice.

Hannah Maslen is a research fellow in Ethics at the Oxford Uehiro Centre for Practical Ethics, University of Oxford. Her current research investigates the ethical, social and legal implications of brain intervention technologies. She also continues to work on topics in sentencing and is preparing a book on remorse and penal theory.

Shona Minson was called to the Bar of England and Wales and practised criminal and family law from 1 King's Bench Walk, London. Her professional experience has led to her research interest in the points of intersection between family and criminal law. Shona is pursuing ESRC-funded research at the Oxford Centre for Criminology on the impact of short-term maternal imprisonment on children, exploring the status of children of prisoners in English law. Her previous research examined the impact of motherhood as mitigation. She is part of the I-Hop Academic/workforce development task force – an initiative of Barnardo's and the Department of Education to bring together those with an interest in the children of prisoners.

Barry Mitchell is Professor of Criminal Law and Criminal Justice at Coventry University Law School, where he has long specialised in the law of murder and manslaughter and the punishment of offenders. He has published widely in these areas, and in pursuing his empirical research has worked with various government departments such as the Ministry of Justice, the Home Office, the Law Commission and the Crown Prosecution Service.

Thomas W. Perry is a postgraduate researcher at the University of Birmingham. He is currently completing a PhD in Education, funded by the ESRC. His research concerns statistical modelling approaches to measuring school effectiveness, such as the 'value-added' methodology. This research interest stems from his academic background in economics, in which he completed two degrees and five years' experience as a teacher.

Jose Pina-Sánchez is a fellow in Statistics at the London School of Economics and a part-time consultant to RAND Europe. His research interests encompass data quality issues such as measurement error and missing data, and other substantive topics such as consistency in sentencing and political decentralization.

Keir Irwin-Rogers is a postgraduate researcher at the University of Sheffield. His ESRC-funded doctoral research explores offenders' experiences and views of community sanctions. He has also conducted research for the Sentencing Council concerning the operationalisation of the principle of proportionality in sentencing guidelines.

Gillian Sharpe is a lecturer in Criminology at the University of Sheffield. Previous publications have examined criminalised young women (*Offending Girls*, 2012), the supervision of women lawbreakers, and persistent young offenders. Her current research focuses on transitions into adulthood amongst women criminalised as children.

Natalia Vibla is a postdoctoral researcher at the Centre of Penal Theory and Penal Ethics at the Institute of Criminology, University of Cambridge. Her PhD thesis was on sentencing in multiple offence cases, and her postdoctoral research is on sentencing theory and practice.

Paul Wiles has spent most of his career as an academic criminologist at various universities in the United Kingdom. From 1999 to 2010, he was chief scientific advisor at the Home Office and government chief social scientist. He has been an analytic advisor to the Sentencing Council since its inception.

1
Empirical Sentencing Research: Options and Opportunities

Julian V. Roberts and Mike Hough

Introduction

What do we know about the practice of sentencing in England and Wales? The answer, until relatively recently, was not very much. The explanation for this lack of knowledge lies primarily in the limited statistics and sporadic research record. Although empirical studies have been conducted for many decades now (e.g., Hood, 1962; 1972; 1992), over the decade between 1995 and 2005, only a handful of major empirical studies of sentencing were conducted (e.g., Tarling, 2006; Mason et al., 2007; Flood-Page and Mackie, 1998; Hough et al., 2003; for discussion and reviews of earlier empirical research in sentencing, see Ashworth, 2003; Roberts, 1988; Blumstein et al., 1983).

Most of this research has been conducted in the magistrates' courts (see Bottomley and Pease, 1986); as Ashworth observed in 2003, 'research into sentencing in the Crown Court has not been productive.' (p. 326). One reason for the focus on the magistrates' courts has been the limited access to the Crown Court until the 1990s (see Ashworth, 1984). The consequence of this limited research record is that answers to relatively elementary questions remain elusive, although several are now addressed in contributions to the present volume. What then, is needed to generate a comprehensive portrait of sentencing?

The most fundamental requirement is a comprehensive statistical database. Practitioners need to understand how the relevant statutes and sentencing guidelines affect the practice of the courts. Experienced advocates may be able to draw upon their own experiences representing clients in court, but there is no substitute for a database of sentences imposed. Knowing what the 'going rate' is for a range of offences, with offence and offender characteristics specified in a degree of detail, is a prerequisite for understanding a jurisdiction's approach to sentencing. Sentencers, too, are surely interested in the sentencing trends in their own area and across the country.

Beginning in 1991 the Home Office published an accessible 'Digest of Criminal Justice Statistics' (Barclay, 1991) and a series of digests were published over the next few years. These volumes provided informative graphics and text describing the relative frequencies of different disposals, the average custody rate, and other important indicators of sentencing practice. Unfortunately, the digests ceased publication with the fourth edition in 2003. Thereafter, the Ministry of Justice published an annual report ('Sentencing Statistics') containing a great deal of information in the form of statistical tables and accompanying text.

Professional researchers will have found these reports useful, albeit subject to some data limitations to which we return later in this chapter. However, as a resource for anyone beyond the small number of active researchers, the reports were unhelpful. More general audiences – such as policymakers or politicians – do not have the time to search through pages of tables in order to answer a specific query. In any event, the Ministry ceased publication of this annual publication; the last published edition contained data from 2009 (Ministry of Justice, 2010).[1] The report has been replaced by a series of Excel data tables which are updated periodically. The transition – from a research report to tables of data – is regrettable, and even these tables are hard to find on the Ministry of Justice website. (Some sentencing data are also available on the Open Justice website).[2]

It may be argued that the Sentencing Council has assumed the function of providing information about sentencing practices. This body, created in 2010 to replace the Sentencing Guidelines Council and the Sentencing Advisory Panel, has a statutory duty under Section 129(1) of the *Coroners and Justice Act 2009* to publish statistics on sentencing patterns from the magistrates' courts and Crown Court in local justice areas across the country. The Council has certainly published a great deal of information about sentencing patterns,[3] but it has not taken on (and, at least within its current resources, could not be expected to take on) the task of providing a comprehensive portrait of sentencing trends at both levels of court. The Council's research publications have to date focused on issues of direct relevance to its guidelines. These include the extent to which courts depart from the Council's guidelines, the likely impact of proposed new guidelines on prison places, and limited descriptive information on the use of mitigating and aggravating factors (see Sentencing Council, 2014). This information is helpful yet fails to fulfil the essential need of providing an annual comprehensive portrait of sentencing in the magistrates' courts and the Crown Court.

Resources permitting, the Sentencing Council could play a more significant role however. The Coroners and Justice Act 2009, which established the Council, assigned it powers to 'promote awareness of sentencing of offenders by courts ... including, in particular 'the sentences imposed by courts'. One way of promoting public and professional awareness of the sentences imposed by the courts is by publishing sentencing statistics in an accessible format. Sentencing commissions and councils in other jurisdictions include this activity as part of their mandate. The Sentencing Advisory Council in New South Wales is a model of good practice in this regard. In the ten years since its creation, this Council has published over 100 sentencing bulletins. These documents provide snapshots of current sentencing practice for a given offence or offence category (e.g., Sentencing Advisory Council, 2013).[4] They are widely used by the press and advocacy groups and are also cited by sentencers in their decisions.[5]

Research strategies[6]

In addition to an adequate database, research needs to draw upon both qualitative and quantitative approaches to research; no single approach or methodology will be sufficient to provide a comprehensive view of sentencing trends (see Merrall, Dhami and Bird, 2010). We identify a number of key elements and research approaches.

- *Court-based statistics*: Court records are used to produce an annual release of data, which provides high-level trends regarding key statistics such as the custody rate and the average custodial sentence length. This is the most common method of providing information about sentencing in other jurisdictions. Examples of publications drawing upon court records include Henham (2002); Turner (1992); Flood-Page and Mackie (1998); Bottomley and Pease (1986); Bottoms (1981). Findings from the latest national sentencing statistics are explored in more detail in Chapter 3 of this volume.
- *Statistics provided by those who make the sentencing decision*: In contrast to court records, data from sentencers can shed light on the factors actually influencing sentencing decisions – not simply those recorded in case files (we return to this point below). The Crown Court Sentencing Survey (described below) currently fulfils this function in England and Wales, although at present there is no comparable survey in the magistrates' courts.

- *Courtroom observational research*: This approach to research captures information about the case and the offender that will not appear in official court documents (e.g., Diamond, 1990; Ward, 2013; Jacobson et al., 2015). For example, the demeanour of the defendant or the reaction of the victim delivering an impact statement at sentencing cannot be captured by a record-based approach.
- *Experimental simulations*: This methodology permits the researcher to experimentally manipulate factors or to randomly assign judges to impose sentence in specific crimes in a way that is not possible using actual cases. It has been used in many other countries to measure disparity in sentencing outcomes. When judges sentence the same case, variation in outcomes can with confidence be attributed to characteristics of the judge rather than the case (e.g., Palys and Divorski, 1986; Corbett, 1987; Hood, 1972; Jacobson and Hough, 2007).[7]
- *'One-off' studies*: This method focuses on issues of specific interest which cannot be captured by other methods, such as research exploring the impact of sentencing on racial and ethnic minorities (e.g., Hood, 1992). This information cannot be derived from statistics collected from sentencers and may be misleading if drawn from court records.
- *Interviews, surveys and focus groups with key participants*: Sentencers, legal advisors, advocates, solicitors and other court workers can provide important insight into the sentencing process (e.g., Fielding, 2011; Raine and Dunstan, 2009; Hough et al., 2003; Jacobson and Hough, 2010, 2011; Millie, Tombs and Hough, 2007; Gilchrist and Blissett, 2002; Davies, Takala and Tyrer, 2002; Henham, 1990; Diamond, 1990; Fitzmaurice and Pease, 1986).
- *Interviews and focus groups with defendants and offenders*: This is the most neglected area of sentencing research. Offenders or ex-offenders could shed important light on questions such as whether increasing the magnitude of plea-based sentence reductions would elicit more guilty pleas – a very topical matter at present.[8] Interviews with ex-offenders would also improve our knowledge of issues such as the effectiveness of different disposals in reducing reoffending or promoting desistance (for examples, see Shute, Hood and Seemungal, 2005; Jacobson et al., 2015).

Since Dhami and Belton (this volume) discuss court records, we explore the other principal source of information: the Crown Court Sentencing Survey (CCSS). This is the most recent addition to the sentencing environment and has great potential to fill some of the analytic gaps.[9]

The Crown Court Sentencing Survey

When the Sentencing Council was created and charged with the duty of monitoring the impact of its own guidelines, it drew upon work conducted by the Sentencing Commission Working Group (2008a), which had proposed a survey of Crown Court centres. The Council set up and currently administers a Crown Court survey. Sentencers are asked to complete a return for each sentenced case; the survey therefore constitutes a *census* rather than a *sample* of sentencing decisions in the Crown Court. The CCSS return notes important elements of the offence and requires the sentencer to indicate which factors were taken into account at sentencing. The Sentencing Council then uses the data to develop and revise its guidelines and also to discharge its various statutory duties.

One sentencing expert has noted that the CCSS 'contains much useful information and is certainly an improvement upon the data which was available in the early days of producing guidelines' (Wasik, 2012, p. 571). Academic researchers also use the data since its release to the public domain[10] (e.g., Sentencing Council, 2014; Roberts, 2013; Maslen and Roberts, 2013; Pina-Sanchez and Linacre, 2013). However, the full significance of this new database may not immediately be apparent. If sentencing statistics have been compiled for years by the Ministry of Justice, what advantage is there of having a judge complete the form – rather than a court official? The Sentencing Council's survey offers unique insight into sentencing practices and goes beyond merely documenting the extent to which courts comply with the Council's guidelines. Information derived from the sentencer permits a much more accurate calibration of the influence of various factors upon sentence outcomes (subject to the limitations on the survey which we discuss later). We offer several illustrations of the contribution that such a database can make to our understanding of sentencing practices.[11]

(i) *Effect of previous convictions at sentencing*

It has been unclear for years how courts take previous convictions into account at sentencing (see Roberts, 2008). The Ministry of Justice statistics – and specific research projects – suggested that courts apply prior convictions in a relatively mechanical way. That is, the sentence simply becomes harsher – as seen in the fact that the custody rate increases in direct proportion to the number of prior convictions recorded against the defendant. Yet recent research reported in a later chapter of this volume demonstrates that courts adopt a more subtle approach to the use of prior convictions. Courts do not simply increase severity for each additional conviction.

One reason for the discrepancy between previous research and the latest trends from the Crown Court survey concerns the nature of the data collected. The Ministry of Justice statistics include *all* prior convictions recorded against the event that are noted in the case file. However, only some of these prior convictions will be relevant for the purposes of sentencing, and courts may use the previous convictions in complex ways. Merely counting the number of prior convictions generates a misleading portrait; what is needed is a database which includes only those priors which were legally relevant – and the CCSS serves this purpose. The story is told in detail in Chapter 9 of this book.

(ii) Sentence reductions for a guilty plea

The second illustration of the advantages of collecting data directly from sentencers concerns sentence reductions for a guilty plea. Defendants who plead guilty are rewarded with a sentence reduction. If the guilty plea is entered at the first reasonable opportunity, the recommended sentence length reduction is one-third. The size of the sentence reduction then diminishes the later the guilty plea is entered, and the defendant who changes his plea to guilty on the day the trial commences should receive a reduction of only 10% (Sentencing Guidelines Council, 2007).

To what extent do courts follow the definitive guidelines in terms of the magnitude of reductions awarded and the factors affecting these reductions? The annual sentencing statistics from England and Wales provided aggregate sentence length differentials between convictions following a contested trial and those following a guilty plea. These data suggest that the plea-based discount is higher than might be expected in light of the current guideline. Thus in 2011, the average sentence length in the Crown Court was more than twice as long for offenders convicted after trial compared to those pleading guilty (50 months compared to 22 months) – implying an average 56% reduction for a guilty plea (Ministry of Justice, 2012, Table A5.25). A discount of this magnitude is consistent with earlier research conducted in the 1990s using a database with similar limitations (Flood-Page and Mackie, 1998).

Uncorrected comparisons of sentence lengths imposed in convictions following a contested trial versus a guilty plea may overestimate the true levels of reductions. Cases in which the defendant pleaded not guilty may involve more serious crimes, and where offenders plead not guilty, they not only lose the discount for an early plea, but also forgo the possibility of claiming mitigating factors such as remorse (see Jacobson and Hough, 2007). For this reason, what is needed is a database such as the CCSS which permits researchers to control for the independent effect of all legally relevant case factors save the defendant's plea and which records the reduction specifically awarded for a guilty plea.

Drawing on the CCSS, Roberts and Bradford (2015) were able to provide a more accurate calibration of both the magnitude of reductions awarded and the degree of correspondence between the decisions of the courts and the reductions recommended by the guideline. Table 1.1, drawn from their research, summarises these trends. Two general conclusions may be drawn. First, reductions are more modest than suggested by court-based statistics. Second, the degree of 'fit' between the guideline and judicial practice is relatively close, although discrepancies do exist. For example, although the guideline recommends a one-tenth reduction for defendants who enter their plea on the day of trial, some defendants receive a significantly higher reduction (see Table 1.1 and discussion in Roberts and Bradford, 2015). The CCSS also permits researchers to conduct multivariate analyses to control for factors correlated with plea which may also affect sentence outcomes.

The link between this research and that on prior convictions is that existing court-based records provide a potentially misleading view of how important factors such as previous convictions or plea affect sentencing outcomes. Researchers using the CCSS data do not need to *infer* the relationship between a specific factor and sentence outcomes – the decision-maker provides direct evidence of impact.[12]

Table 1.1 Empirical and recommended sentence reductions for a guilty plea

	Greater than 1/3	1/3	21%–32%	11%–20%	1–10%	No Reduction Awarded	Guideline Recommended Reduction
Early Plea	9%	80%	9%	2%	<1%	<.05%	33%
Intermediate Plea (after first appearance but before day of trial)	3%	34%	34%	22%	6%	1%	25%
Late Plea	1%	11%	9%	24%	49%	6%	10%

Source: Roberts and Bradford (2015).

(iii) Effect and weight of sentencing factors

A survey of sentencing judges permits researchers to explore the impact of sentencing factors in a way that is impossible using court records alone. Consider remorse, an important mitigating factor at sentencing and also one cited in the definitive guidelines (Maslen and Roberts, 2013). Even if the court records state whether the offender was remorseful or not, this tells us nothing about its impact on sentence – or even whether the judge granted any remorse-related mitigation. It is possible the remorse was expressed in a formulaic way and had no effect. Alternatively, remorse may have made the difference between custody and a high-level community order. The CCSS makes it possible to address a range of questions about the role of remorse. For example, it is possible to compare sentences imposed in cases where remorse was taken into account with others where remorse was absent – having controlled for the influence of other correlated variables (such as previous convictions). In addition, it is possible to *quantify* the mitigating effect of remorse on sentencing – compared to other important mitigating factors such as whether the offender was a sole carer. Finally, it is also possible to see how remorse interacts with aggravating factors, and this question is addressed in Chapter 10 of this volume.

Limitations of the CCSS

All databases have their limitations, and the Crown Court sentencing survey is no exception. It is important to understand these limitations and their impact on the conclusions that may reasonably be drawn from research using this database. First, the CCSS has been operational only since 2011 and cannot therefore be used to explore historical trends – for these there is no substitute for the annual Ministry data. Second, the survey captures most but not all sentencing decisions. Response rates are variable: The response rate is in excess of 90% in some Crown Court locations; elsewhere it is significantly lower (see Sentencing Council, 2013, Chart 1.11). In 2013, the Council reported a completion rate across all Crown Court locations of 60%, although the response rate is now somewhat higher.

Missing data represent a potential threat to the validity of any survey. Sentencing Council researchers have addressed the non-response issue by comparing CCSS records to the Ministry of Justice CREST database,[13] which contains all Crown Court sentences (see Sentencing Council, 2013). These comparisons suggest that relatively robust conclusions may be drawn from data collected by the survey. If the current response rate were to decline, however, non-response would become an important threat to validity. If the sentencers with low response rates were different from those completing all returns, the CCSS would suffer from bias.

Third, the CCSS records the factors taken into account by Crown Court sentencers, but not necessarily *all* the factors affecting sentence. The form that sentencers are asked to complete lists all the guideline factors and provides respondents with the opportunity to note any other factors taken into account. Other factors which are not captured by the form may have influenced the sentence imposed. If the information is provided by the sentencer, the survey cannot detect the influence of extra-legal factors on the sentencing outcome – racial or ethnic status for example. This kind of information must be collected by alternative methodologies such as observational studies, qualitative research involving defendants and legal practitioners, or bespoke surveys (e.g., Hood, 1992). The most important limitation on the Crown Court Sentencing Survey, however, is that it collects data by definition in the Crown Court only. Since the vast majority of sentences – 92% in 2013 – are imposed in the magistrates' courts, this constitutes an important limitation on our awareness of sentencing.

Sentencing research priorities

In this concluding section, we offer some reflections on the emerging priorities for sentencing scholars in England and Wales, and also for the agencies such as the Ministry of Justice and the Sentencing Council who share an obligation to promote, conduct and disseminate research and statistics. We begin with some comments on the role of research in policy development.

The role of research in the evolution of sentencing policy

Absent a robust and comprehensive sentencing database, sentencing policy evolves in a vacuum. Solutions to the problems confronting sentencing will only emerge once there is a realistic appreciation of the nature and magnitude of those problems. We offer one example of what we mean. The sentencing trends presented in Chapter 3 of this volume reveal that the custody rate in England and Wales has been relatively stable over the past 15 years. Comparative analyses have for years demonstrated that England and Wales has one of the highest rates of incarceration in Western Europe. Sentencing scholars have been aware of this tendency for many years. Politicians and policymakers, however, appear oblivious.

The continued reliance on custody as a sanction is hard to understand in an era in which austerity has led to significant cuts throughout the public service sector. Two explanations may be offered: first, politicians have been indifferent to the results of research in the field of sentencing. The politics of penal populism in this country and elsewhere have demonstrated politicians' willingness to legislate in the field of sentencing without due regard to the consequences for the prison population. The second explanation relates to the low visibility of sentencing statistics, which demonstrate the comparatively high use of custody as a sanction. Only systematic research can establish whether this characterisation of sentencing in England and Wales is correct.

Helping to establish the custody threshold

There may be a lack of consensus about the appropriate length of sentence for various crimes, but there is agreement that custody should be reserved for the most serious offenders. This consensus is reflected in the custodial threshold found in the *Criminal Justice Act 2003*. Section 152(2) states that a court 'must not pass a custodial sentence unless it is of the opinion that the offence... was so serious that neither a fine alone nor a community sentence can be justified for the offence'. One view of the prison population is that all prisoners have been convicted of a crime for which only imprisonment was appropriate. Is this an accurate interpretation?

A useful research contribution to the debate about the use of short sentences would involve documenting the profile of admissions to custody with a focus on the prisoners serving short custodial terms. In an era of austerity with respect to public services, the search for economy should not overlook the criminal justice system. Within the realm of sentencing, austerity should generate a search to find disposals which fulfil the same objectives as prison terms, but which are cheaper. In all likelihood, this means replacing some of the shorter prison sentences with punitive community-based sentences. In addition, it might be reasonable to expect a greater use of fines as a sanction during a time of financial crisis.

The prison estate has not escaped the attention of the current (2014) coalition government, although not in a way that has been informed by research. Consider an analogy involving the medical rather than penal estate. A&E units in England and Wales are currently overburdened and in need of additional resources, both in terms of personnel and facilities. One way of reducing the costs of A&E would be to restrict the number of patients being treated in these facilities (rather than in community-based facilities).[14] Indeed, proposals have been made or implemented with this objective in mind. These include the creation of out-of-hours GP clinics and more effective use of telephone advice lines. The goal of these diversionary strategies is to ensure that A&E received only those patients who cannot be safely and effectively treated by primary care clinicians in alternate medical facilities. An alternative approach would be to let A&E units continue to silt up with thousands of cases which could be treated elsewhere, but to cut the costs of running the ward. No sane hospital administrator would advocate such an approach.

Yet this is the strategy adopted by the current coalition government with respect to the prison estate. The government proposes to reduce the costs of the prison estate by lowering the cost of imprisonment, rather than restricting the intake of prisoners. In 2014 the National Offender Management System announced plans to reduce the costs of incarceration by £2,200 per prison place.[15] Penal austerity has meant the introduction of larger, more cost-effective prisons and lower expenditures on prison facilities without attempting to restrict the number of offenders being committed to custody. The savings resulting from this approach will be minimal – compared to diverting the least serious cases away from prison. There appears to be a clear role here for research in terms of determining the most cost-effective ways of holding offenders accountable.

Using sentencing guidelines to manage the size of the prison population

In the first five years of its life, the Sentencing Council for England and Wales has set out to promote consistency in sentencing, to adjust sentencing for a small number of existing offences and to set guidelines for new offences. The consequence is that the overall severity of the sentencing system remains stable. This is an improvement on the uncontrolled upward drift in sentencing severity that characterised the 1990s and early 2000s. However, it is possible to use guidelines in a more dynamic way to ensure that expenditure on punishment falls within specified limits. This was a strategy that was considered by the Gage Committee (Sentencing Commission Working Group, 2008b) but not pursued thereafter, no doubt being regarded as too contentious. It would require quite extensive statistical research to lay the groundwork for this to become a reality. There would be a need for a comprehensive statistical model of the sentencing system that would provide quite precise answers to 'what if' questions relating to sentencing changes.

The Ministry of Justice already has some modelling capacity at present – but not enough to permit fine-tuning to guidelines that would control the size of the prison population.

Establishing public tolerance for non-custodial sentences

Part of the public's opposition to restricting admissions to custody is based upon the misperception that all prisoners have been convicted of a serious crime and all represent a serious threat to public security. Sentencing statistics have a role to play in refuting this assertion. If the public were aware of some of the cases being sent to prison – and this is a function of sentencing statistics and research – we believe they would be more interested in community penalties, if only to save funds. In fact, we have empirically demonstrated that when people are made aware of the costs of imprisonment, support for custody as a sanction declines (Roberts and Hough, 2012).

Although this research and studies by other researchers have laid the foundation for research on the relationship between sentence practice and public opinion (e.g., Roberts and Hough, 2005), much more needs to be done both at a conceptual and empirical level. It is intuitively persuasive that there are links between public tolerance of practice and the legitimacy of the courts and of the criminal law. However, the precise links between sentencing practice and the perceived legitimacy of sentencing is likely to be complex. Robinson and Darley (2007) argue that reference to public opinion is an acceptable way of making decisions about the relative severity of different types of offence. However, de Keijser (2014) has found that although the Dutch public themselves are tougher than judges when 'passing sentences' in sentencing exercises, they thought it right that judges should operate to different (and more lenient) criteria. There is a need for more research that will locate the drivers of the legitimacy of sentencing in a way that will allow the development of a more intelligent policy on issues relating to the role of public opinion.

Understanding defendants' experience of sentencing

Although defendants obviously occupy a central position in sentencing, little research has been done on how they experience both the court process and the outcome. The limited work (e.g., Jacobson et al., 2015) suggests that most tend to be passive and disengaged, often failing to appreciate the implications of what is happening to them. If sentencing is to have a more positive impact on defendants' lives, it is clearly important to find ways of ensuring that they are less marginalised in the process. There is a need for more research in the desistance tradition (e.g., Farrall et al., 2011), to examine the diverse routes that offenders take in their efforts to stop offending. An appreciation of the desistance process strikes us as a prerequisite for intelligent sentencing.

Surveying the magistrates' courts

As noted earlier, the Council's sentencer-based survey exists only in the Crown Court. However, there is no escaping the fact that most sentencing decisions are taken in the lower courts. Lay magistrates, who have a limited amount of training, impose almost all of these sentences. Due to their intermittent sittings, compared to Crown Court sentencers, magistrates have fewer occasions to become familiar with the increasingly complex guidelines being issued by the Sentencing Council. An important priority is therefore to launch some kind of data collection exercise in the magistrates' courts, even though it will require taking a sample of cases rather than a census of all decisions – due to the high volume of cases.

Effectiveness and cost-effectiveness of different disposals

Finally, we still need a great deal more research into the effectiveness – and especially the cost-effectiveness – of different sentencing options. The overall picture on variations in reconviction rates has changed little since the 1990s. Differences in outcomes for different sentences – controlling for relevant risk factors – remain small, although there are some consistent patterns in these marginal changes. Given that sentencers (and politicians) ought to have modest expectations about the impact of sentencing on people's lives, there is a strong case for robust and up-to-date information not just on effectiveness but on cost-effectiveness. A Crown Court judge sitting on a sentencing day may pass sentence on six to ten cases. As many of these typically result in custodial sentences, the judge may commit £0.5 million of public money in a single day. Sentencers need to know more precisely what benefits their decisions have bought the taxpayer, and at what cost.

Notes

1. The very useful sentencing volume for practitioners published by Banks and Harris (2014) contains tables of data derived from the Ministry data, but they are offence-specific, designed to inform a practitioner interested in the latest trends for a specific crime. They are not intended to provide a comprehensive portrait of sentencing patterns.
2. See http://open.justice.gov.uk.

3. See http://sentencingcouncil.judiciary.gov.uk/.
4. There is no equivalent publication in England and Wales, although the Sentencing Council publishes a sentencing practice bulletin as part of its consultation exercise prior to issuing a guideline.
5. The fact that the bulletins are read and cited by the courts is noteworthy; it suggests that sentencing statistics may also promote consistency in sentencing. Knowing about the distribution of sentences imposed for any given offence will mean that judges in that jurisdiction have a common context in which to determine sentence.
6. We restrict our discussion to court records, although other documentary sources of information exist. For example, presentence reports provide insight into decision-making at sentencing (see McNeill, 2002; Gelsthorpe and Raynor, 1995).
7. Palys and Divorski (1986) report one of the best-known of these studies. They provided a sample of judges with a set of cases to sentence. The researchers then examined the range of disposals imposed for each case, and the results were striking. In one case of robbery, the most lenient sentence was a suspended sentence, and the most severe was 13 years immediate custody.
8. The Sentencing Council has a statutory duty as per s. 120(3)(a) of the Coroners and Justice Act 2009 to prepare a guideline on the reduction in sentences for a guilty plea. The Council has indicated that a draft guideline will be issued for consultation in 2015.
9. It is also unique; no other jurisdiction routinely collects data directly from the sentencer.
10. The data are available on the Council's website.
11. Although it takes us beyond the domain of research, the CCSS may also contribute to the effectiveness of the guidelines. The survey form captures all the elements of the guideline including all the guideline factors. In completing the form a sentencer is therefore proceeding through the guideline, and this will increase his or her familiarity with the guidelines.
12. It may be argued that judges may misrecall the effect that a given factor has on their decision-making. There is a significant body of research in experimental social psychology which suggests that in a number of contexts, people lack insight into their own decision-making, and fail to recognise the influence of factors which affect their judgement. In our view, this experimental research has little significance for responses to the CCSS. At sentencing, legal professionals note the factors they took into account and record these factors on the forms – bearing in mind that their decision may be subject to appeal. We see little reason to suspect that errors of memory affect the outcomes.
13. This is the case management system used by Crown Courts to track case progression through the court system.
14. Hospital beds are (or should be) reserved for patients whose ailments cannot be adequately treated in a community outpatient clinic. Prison spaces should follow the same parsimonious approach – being reserved for those individuals for whom a community-based sanction is inadequate. There is clear evidence in England and Wales to suggest that the penal equivalent of hospital 'bed blocking' is occurring. Cases are sent to prison when they could be punished

in the community, and they spend longer inside than is necessary for the purposes of sentencing.

15. See 'Prisons Governors ordered to cut costs by £149m a year'. *Guardian*, 29 April 2014. http://www.theguardian.com/society/2014/apr/29/prisons-ordered-cust-costs-149-million-a-year.

References

Ashworth, A. et al. (1984) *Sentencing in the Crown Court*. Oxford: Centre for Criminological Research, University of Oxford.

Ashworth, A. (2003) Sentencing and sensitivity: a challenge for criminological research. In: L. Zedner and A. Ashworth (eds) *The Criminological Foundations of Penal Policy*. Oxford: Oxford University Press.

Ashworth, A. (2010) *Sentencing and Criminal Justice*. Fifth Edition. Cambridge: Cambridge University Press.

Banks, R. and Harris, L. (2014) *Banks on Sentence*. Ninth Edition. East Sussex: Banks.

Barclay, G. (ed.) (1991) *Digest. Information on the Criminal Justice System in England and Wales*. London: Home Office.

Blumstein, A., Cohen, J., Martin, S. and Tonry, M. (1983) *Research on Sentencing*. Washington, D.C.: National Academy Press.

Bottoms, A. (1991) The Suspended Sentence in England, 1967–1978. *British Journal of Criminology*, 21: 1–26.

Bottomley, K. and Pease, K. (1986) Sentencing trends and statistics of imprisonment. In: *Crime and Punishment. Interpreting the Data*. Milton Keynes: Open University Press.

Corbett, C. (1987) Magistrates' and court clerks' sentencing behaviour: an experimental study. In: D. Pennington and S. Lloyd-Bostock (eds) *The Psychology of Sentencing*. Oxford: Centre for SocioLegal Studies.

Davies, M., Takala, J.P. and Tyrer, J. (2002) Sentencing burglars in England and Finland: a pilot study. In: C. Tata and N. Hutton (eds) *Sentencing and Society. International Perspectives*. Aldershot: Ashgate.

De Keijser, J. (2014) Penal theory and popular opinion: the deficiencies of direct engagement. In: J. Ryberg and J.V. Roberts (eds) (2014) *Popular Punishment. The Normative Significance of Public Opinion for Sentencing Theory and Practice*. New York: Oxford University Press.

Diamond, S. (1990) Revising Images of Public Punitiveness: Sentencing by Lay and Professional English Magistrates. *Law and Social Inquiry*, 15: 191–221.

Farrall, S., Hough, M., Maruna, S. and Sparks, R. (eds) (2011) *Escape Routes: Contemporary Perspectives on Life After Punishment*. London: Routledge.

Fielding, N. (2011) Judges and Their Work. *Social and Legal Studies*, 20: 97–115.

Fitzmaurice, C. and Pease, K. (1986) *The Psychology of Judicial Sentencing*. Manchester: Manchester University Press.

Flood-Page, C. and Mackie, A. (1998) *Sentencing Practice: An Examination of Sentencing Decisions in the Magistrates' and the Crown Courts in the mid 1990s*. London: Home Office.

Gelsthorpe, L. and Raynor, P. (1995) Quality and Effectiveness in Probation Officers' Reports to Sentencers. *British Journal of Criminology*, 35: 188–200.

Gilchrist, E. and Blissett, J. (2002) Magistrates' Attitudes to Domestic Violence and Sentencing Options. *The Howard Journal*, 41: 348–363.

Hall, J. E. (1965) Sentencing in transition. In: T. Grygier, H. Jones and J. Spencer (eds) *Criminology in Transition*. London: Tavistock.
Henham, R. (1990) *Sentencing Principles and Magistrates' Sentencing Behaviour*. Aldershot: Avebury.
Henham, R. (2002) Sentencing policy and guilty plea discounts. In: C. Tata and N. Hutton (eds) *Sentencing and Society*. Aldershot: Ashgate.
Hood, R. (1962) *Sentencing in Magistrates' Courts*. London: Tavistock.
Hood, R. (1972) *Sentencing the Motoring Offender: A Study of Magistrates' Views and Practices*. London Heinemann.
Hood, R. (1992) *Race and Sentencing. A Study in the Crown Court*. Oxford: Oxford University Press.
Hough, M., Jacobson, J., and Millie. A. (2003) *The Decision to Imprison: Sentencing and the Prison Population*. London: Prison Reform Trust.
Jacobson, J. and Hough, M. (2007) *Mitigation: The Role of Personal Factors at Sentencing*. London: Prison Reform Trust.
Jacobson, J. and Hough, M. (2010) *Unjust Deserts: Imprisonment for Public Protection*. London: Prison Reform Trust.
Jacobson, J. and Hough, M. (2011) Personal Mitigation: An Empirical Analysis in England and Wales. In: J.V. Roberts (ed.) *Mitigation and Aggravation at Sentencing. Cambridge Studies in Law and Society*. Cambridge: Cambridge University Press.
Jacobson, J., Hunter, G. and Kirby, A. (2015) *Inside Crown Court: Personal Experiences and Questions of Legitimacy*, Bristol: Policy Press.
Maslen, H. and Roberts, J.V (2013) The role of remorse at sentencing: an analysis of guidelines and empirical practice. In: A. Ashworth and J.V. Roberts (eds) *Sentencing Guidelines*. Oxford: Oxford University Press.
Mason, T., de Silva, N., Sharma, N., Brown, D. and Harper, G. (2007) *Local Variation in Sentencing in England and Wales*. London: Ministry of Justice.
McNeill, F. (2002) Assisting sentencing, promoting justice? In: C. Tata and N. Hutton (eds) *Sentencing and Society*. Aldershot: Ashgate.
Merrall, E., Dhami. M. and Bird, S. (2010) Exploring Methods to Investigate Sentencing Decisions. *Evaluation Review*, 34: 185–219.
Millie, A., Tombs, J. and Hough, M. (2007) Borderline Sentencing: A Comparison of Sentencers' Decision-Making in England and Wales, and Scotland. *Criminology and Criminal Justice*, 7: 243–267.
Ministry of Justice (2011) *Sentencing Statistics: England and Wales 2010*. London: Ministry of Justice. Available at: www.justice.gov.uk. Table A5.25.
Ministry of Justice (2012) *Judicial and Court Statistics, 2011*. London: Ministry of Justice. Available at: www.justice.gov.uk.
Palys, T. and Divorski, S. (1986) Explaining Sentence Disparity. *Canadian Journal of Criminology*, 28: 347–361.
Pina-Sanchez, J. and Linacre, R. (2013) Sentence Consistency in England and Wales. Evidence from the Crown Court Sentencing Survey. *British Journal of Criminology*, 53: 1118–1138.
Raine, J. and Dunstan, E. (2009) How Well Do Sentencing Guidelines Work: Equity, Proportionality and Consistency in the Determination of Fine Levels in the Magistrates' Courts of England and Wales. *The Howard Journal*, 48: *13–36*.
Roberts, J.V. (1988) *Empirical Research on Sentencing*. Ottawa: Department of Justice Canada.

Roberts, J.V. (2008) *Punishing Persistent Offenders. Community and Offender Perspectives on the Recidivist Sentencing Premium*. Oxford: Oxford University Press.
Roberts, J.V. (2013) Sentencing patterns in England and Wales: findings from the Crown Court Sentencing Survey. In: A. Ashworth and J.V. Roberts (eds) *Sentencing Guidelines: Exploring the English Model*. Oxford: Oxford University Press.
Roberts, J.V. and Bradford, B. (2015) Sentence Reductions for a Guilty Plea: New Empirical Evidence from England and Wales. *Journal of Empirical Legal Studies*, in press.
Roberts, J.V. and Hough, M. (2005) *Understanding Public Attitudes to Criminal Justice*. Maidenhead: Open University Press.
Robinson, P.H., & Darley, J.M. (2007) Intuitions of Justice: Implications for Criminal Law and Justice Policy. *Southern California Review*, 81: 1–67.
Sentencing Advisory Council (2013) *Arson. Sentencing Snapshot*. Melbourne: Sentencing Advisory Council.
Sentencing Commission Working Group (2008a) *Crown Court Sentencing Survey*. London: Sentencing Commission Working Group.
Sentencing Commission Working Group (2008b) *Sentencing Guidelines in England and Wales: An Evolutionary Approach*. London: Sentencing Commission Working Group.
Sentencing Council (2013) *Guide to Crown Court Sentencing Statistics*. London: Sentencing Council of England and Wales.
Sentencing Council (2014) *Crown Court Sentencing Survey*. London: Sentencing Council of England and Wales.
Sentencing Guidelines Council (2007) *Reduction in Sentence for a Guilty Plea. Definitive Guideline. Revised*. London: Sentencing Guidelines Council.
Shute, S., Hood, R., and Seemungal, F. (2005) *A Fair Hearing? Ethnic Minorities in the criminal courts*. Cullompton: Willan.
Tarling, R. (2006) Sentencing Practice in Magistrates' Courts Revisited. *The Howard Journal*, 45: 29–41.
Turner, A. (1992) Sentencing in the magistrates' court. In: C. Munro and M. Wasik (eds) *Sentencing, Judicial Discretion and Training*. London: Sweet and Maxwell.
Ward, J. (2013) Punishing Drug Possession in the Magistrates' Courts: Time for a Rethink. *European Journal of Criminal Policy and Research*, 19: 289–307.
Wasik, M. (2012) The Crown Court Sentencing Survey. *Criminal Law Review*, 8: 569–571.

2

Using Court Records for Sentencing Research: Pitfalls and Possibilities

Mandeep Dhami and Ian Belton

Sentencing in England and Wales

Between June 2011 and June 2012, over 1.25 million offenders were sentenced in England and Wales (Ministry of Justice, 2012). The vast majority (92%) of sentences were passed by the magistrates' courts, where sentencing powers are limited to a maximum of 6 months in custody for a single offence. The remaining minority of sentences were passed in the Crown Court, which does not have such restraints. Two-thirds (66%) of the sentences imposed were fines. Community sentences/orders comprised 13% of sentences passed, followed by custodial sentences (12%; where 4% were suspended and the average length was 15 months). Finally, conditional or absolute discharges represented approximately 7% of sentences (Ministry of Justice, 2012).

When passing sentence, sentencers are required to consider what they aim to achieve (i.e., retribution, deterrence, rehabilitation, incapacitation, and/or reparation). Following this, and working within certain constraints such as fixed maximum and minimum sentences as well as sentencing guidelines, sentencers are expected to apply legal factors (e.g., offence seriousness and the defendant's criminal history), and to take into account any aggravating and mitigating factors (e.g., vulnerability of the victim and provocation of the offender, respectively). Sentencers may also be obliged to consider sentencing recommendations provided in a pre-sentence report from a probation officer who assesses the potential impact of the sentence on the offender (and victim or society). Finally, sentencers must consider if they wish to give a reduction for a guilty plea, and consider the totality or proportionality of a sentence if the offender is sentenced for more than one offence.

Ideally, this process would result in unbiased and consistent sentencing. However, the picture of sentencing painted by the official statistics, the disparities in sentencing, and the changes in sentencing patterns across recent years suggest that something may be awry. In 2009, for adults sentenced for indictable offences in the Crown Court, immediate custody and community sentences have declined since 1999 (Ministry of Justice, 2010). For indictable offences in the magistrates' courts, community sentences have increased and fines have mostly declined since 1999. These changes across time cannot be fully explained by changes in the severity of offences committed over the same period.

There is variation in the proportion of offenders given specific sentences across criminal justice (police and prosecution) areas (Ministry of Justice, 2010). For example, for indictable offences, in 2009, in magistrates' courts, the proportion of offenders given immediate custody ranged from 5% (in Wiltshire) to 18% (in the West Midlands). The proportion given community sentences ranged from 30% (in Dorset) to 48% (in West Yorkshire), and the proportion given fines ranged from 20% (in Avon and Somerset) to 48% (in West Yorkshire). Similarly, for indictable offences in 2009, in the Crown Court, the proportion of offenders given immediate custody ranged from 44% (in Durham) to 65% (in Northamptonshire), the proportion given community sentences ranged from 9% (in Warwickshire) to 24% (in Durham), and the proportion of those fined ranged from 1% to 4%.

There are also differences in sentences given out by the two different types of criminal court (Ministry of Justice, 2010). For indictable offences, from June 2011 to June 2012, offenders were more likely to be given immediate custody in the Crown Court than the magistrates' courts (58% vs. 13%). Fines were more likely to be imposed in the magistrates' courts than Crown Court (24% vs. 1%). Finally, there appear to be differences in the sentences meted out to different types of offenders. For indictable offences, in 2009, males were more likely to be given immediate custody and fines, but females were more likely to be given a community sentence and a suspended sentence (Ministry of Justice, 2010). In terms of race and ethnicity, for indictable offences, in 2012, the most common sentence for white offenders was a community sentence, whereas the most common sentence for black and Asian offenders was immediate custody (Ministry of Justice, 2013).

Methodological approaches to conducting sentencing research

Therefore, given the changing trends in sentencing patterns over time and the apparent variation in sentencing across areas, courts and offenders, researchers have attempted to identify the factors that may influence sentencing decisions. The primary interest has been in identifying the biasing effect of 'extra-legal' (legally irrelevant) factors.

To this end, researchers have employed a variety of methodological approaches such as analysing published sentencing statistics (e.g., Mason, de Silva, Sharma, Brown, and Harper, 2007), analysing court records (e.g., Flood-Page and Mackie, 1998), observing sentencing hearings (e.g., Hedderman, 1990; Ipsos MORI, 2011), surveying sentencers (e.g., Ipsos MORI, 2011; Hough, Jacobson, and Millie, 2003), and presenting sentencers with simulated cases in controlled experiments (e.g., Raine and Dunstan, 2009). Each of these approaches has strengths and weaknesses with regard to their ability to explore the influence of a broad range of legal and extra-legal factors on sentencing decisions.

Interview and questionnaire surveys of sentencers can be criticized because sentencers may not accurately report the factors that influenced their decisions. Introspection, recall and articulation of cognitive processes are notoriously difficult (Nisbett and Wilson, 1977). Beyond this, efforts to avoid criticism may encourage sentencers to provide socially desirable responses (Paulhus, 1991). Although controlled experiments measuring sentencing behaviour can overcome the problems associated with self-reports, they typically involve simulated cases where only one or few variables are manipulated. This can lead to the creation of artificial or rare cases and unrepresentative conditions that may produce atypical sentencing behaviour (see Dhami, Hertwig, and Hoffrage, 2004 regarding the design of experiments that are more representative of the environment).

Conversely, the major strength of studies involving courtroom observations and analysis of published sentencing statistics is that they are based on real cases. However, these two approaches are typically limited by the inability to observe or analyse all information available to a sentencer. Conducting observations requires reliable and valid recording of all the information presented to the sentencer in real time: no mean feat in the absence of video or audio recording technology. By contrast, published sentencing statistics are severely limited as they generally only include information on an offender's age (adult vs. youth), gender, ethnicity, offence type, number of previous convictions, court type and criminal justice area (Merrall, Dhami, and Bird, 2010). In fact, for those offenders who are sentenced for more than one offence, the published sentencing statistics only pertain to the sentence given to the principal offence (i.e., that with the highest maximum penalty).

We argue that although the findings of studies based on an analysis of court records can be criticized for omitting variables that may have been presented in the courtroom, typically, this is the most comprehensive source of data available for research on sentencing. Court records refer to the official documents held on file at court on each case handled by that court. Analysis of court records can yield a highly detailed, representative and accurate picture of the sentencing process.

Studying sentencing using court records

What information do court records contain?

Each record comprises a variety of documents containing a range of information about the case as it has tracked through the justice system to the final point of sentence. The records therefore not only contain legal factors that ought to influence the sentencing decision, but also a host of extra-legal ones that may have a potentially biasing effect on sentencing; the impact of many of these remains to be studied.

A variety of documents may be available in the record of a sentenced court case. Some are common across magistrates' courts (both youth and adult) and Crown Court centres, and some are specific to one type of court only. In a study assessing the feasibility of collecting data from court records, Dhami and Souza (2009b) suggested that the most useful documents are the file cover/jacket/folder, court list, court orders, pre-sentence report (PSR), NIL report, bail after charge – police, bail form (court), file front sheet, charge sheet, record sheet trial (Crown), referral order report (YOS), medical and psychiatric reports, and police national computer record (PNC), judge's remarks/magistrates' reasons for sentence, and the case log. Dhami and Souza (2009b) found that many of these documents were available in close to or more than 50% of records in the different types of court. (The appendix to this chapter contains a non-exhaustive list of the legal and extra-legal information typically available in the court records.) However, some information was more likely to be unavailable (i.e., mitigating circumstances, offender's nationality, educational level, and risk of self-harm, date of last period in custody and type of court previously convicted in).

Findings of sentencing research using court records

Despite the broad range of information available in court records, few researchers have chosen this methodological approach to studying sentencing decisions. Below, we provide a brief review of the findings of the small body of literature. Farrington and Morris (1983) investigated the effect of gender on sentencing in the magistrates' courts, using a sample of 287 court records of male offenders and 108 females in a single court. There was no main effect of gender on sentence severity (any punishment greater than a fine of £75). However, the availability of various socioeconomic data in the court files enabled the authors to identify a number of interaction effects. For example, unemployed men were more likely to receive a severe sentence, while women who were married or had children were less likely to receive a severe sentence.

Moxon (1988) published the first large-scale study of sentencing practice in the Crown Court. He examined 2,077 cases randomly selected from 18 court centres (supplemented by courtroom observational data). Differences in the characteristics of the offence and the offender's previous convictions accounted for the majority of variation in sentencing between male and female offenders. When these factors were controlled for, men with no prior convictions were nearly twice as likely as women to receive a custodial sentence. Using cases from Moxon's (1988) dataset, Hedderman (1991) demonstrated that for theft offences, women were also less likely than men to receive custody.

In the classic study of race and sentencing, Hood (1992) sampled the court records of approximately 2,800 male and 400 female offenders in five Crown Court centres. It was found that the difference in custody rates for black and white female offenders could be explained by differences in legal factors such as offence seriousness and previous convictions. However, for male offenders, only around 80% of the difference was attributable to relevant legal factors. Without access to court records, Hood could not have controlled for as many legal factors, so he would have been less able to assess the true extent of any unexplained racial disparity in custody rates. Even so, Hood was criticised for failing to take account of extra-legal factors other than race (e.g., offenders' employment and marital status, family background and any drug/alcohol abuse; see Halevy, 1995).

Moxon and Hedderman (1994) compared sentencing practices in the magistrates' courts and the Crown Court for specific triable either-way offences (i.e., theft, burglary in a non-dwelling, assault occasioning actual bodily harm, and wounding, which can all be tried either in magistrates' court or the Crown Court; see also Hedderman and Moxon, 1992). Data on mode of trial (and who chose it), offender, offence and sentence were collected from court records for approximately 240 cases in 7 magistrates' courts and for 400 cases in 5 Crown Court centres. Importantly, the researchers were able to make more reasonable comparisons between the two court types than would be possible from an analysis of sentencing statistics alone. First, since the records indicated if the defendant had elected to be tried (and sentenced) in the Crown Court, or if the magistrates had declined to either hear the case or to sentence it, the researchers could compare like with like – that is, cases sentenced in the magistrates' courts were compared with those that the magistrates agreed to hear but where the defendant elected to be tried and sentenced in the Crown Court instead. Second, since the records contained information on other factors that could potentially influence sentencing decisions (such as the financial value involved in an offence), the offender's criminal history, plea, and whether he/she was remanded in custody, the researchers could match the cases in the two court types on these variables.

Moxon and Hedderman (1994) found that comparable offences received three times as many and two-and-a-half times longer custodial sentences in the Crown Court than in magistrates' courts. Furthermore, 62% of Crown Court cases that were declined by magistrates resulted in a sentence less severe than six months' immediate custody (and thus could have been dealt with in the magistrates' courts). Finally, Moxon and Hedderman (1994) also examined sentencing variations across the individual courts, and found, for example, that the rate at which magistrates declined jurisdiction in either-way offences varied between 5% and 18%. The rate at which the Crown Court centres imposed immediate custody for actual bodily harm ranged from 28% to 41%. This level of analysis could not have been possible using published sentencing statistics.

Flood-Page and Mackie's (1998) relatively large-scale study involved an examination of the records of 3,000 cases from 25 magistrates' courts and 1,800 from 18 Crown Court centres. Across both types of court, custody was shown to be more likely for offenders with previous convictions, whereas fines were imposed most often for first-time offenders who were in employment. Women were less likely than men to receive custodial sentences in the Crown Court and more likely to receive a discharge than a fine in the magistrates' courts. The researchers, however, had to supplement data from the court records with that from courtroom observations because aggravating and mitigating factors were often unavailable in the court records. Statistical models showed that offender race, gender and other case factors correctly predicted between 65% and 70% of custodial sentences. Finally, it was also shown that stipendiary magistrates (District Judges) imposed custody more often than lay magistrates, even after controlling for other potentially relevant factors such as offence type and number of previous convictions.

Aside from providing a rich source of data for sentencing research, court records have also served as a useful supplement to data gathered from other sources or using other methods. Brown and Hullin (1992) supplemented data from a survey of court clerks with that from court records. The records were used to gather details on an offender's previous offences (including number of previous sentenced offences, number of previous convictions for the same offence, three most serious sentences for the same offence, and most severe previous sentence imposed). This enabled the researchers to demonstrate that differences in criminal history between black and white offenders in the sample largely accounted for the observed difference in custody rates for the two groups.

In a study aimed at assessing the cost-effectiveness and practical feasibility of rolling out electronic monitoring of curfew orders across England and Wales, Mortimer and May (1997) conducted a survey of magistrates and electronic tagging contractors. This was supplemented with data from approximately 500 magistrates' courts records. The court record data enabled the researchers to identify the types of offences where electronic tagging was proving to be particularly common (e.g., theft and burglary) or infrequent (e.g., criminal damage and public order offences). Finally, in Speed and Burrows' (2006) study of the factors that influence sentencing in cases of theft from shops, data was gathered from the Crown Prosecution Service (CPS) files, but court records were used to ensure that the CPS data were complete in terms of the offender's criminal history, the sentence imposed, and the type of sentencer (i.e. magistrate or district judge).[1] One interesting finding to emerge from this study was that District Judges were twice as likely as magistrates to impose custodial sentences.

Unfortunately, several of the studies that have used court records as a data source are now out of date because they were conducted prior to legislative changes to the sentencing framework in England and Wales that came into force from 2004 onwards.[2] In addition, although most studies involved relatively large samples of court records, the procedures used to sample them were not always random or representative. Finally, not all studies took account of the potentially confounding effects of other factors contained in the court records. Nevertheless, the above research does illustrate the kind of information that can be amassed about sentencing using court records as well as the advantage that an analysis of court records may have over other approaches.

Pitfalls and possibilities of using court records

The dearth of research on sentencing employing court records is not easy to explain. Difficulty accessing largely closed settings such as courts and highly sensitive and confidential data is one potential explanation. Another may be the considerable time and effort involved in extracting data from court records. Below, we discuss these two major challenges and some possible solutions. Later, we identify the range of research opportunities that are afforded by an analysis of court records.

Accessing court records

Perhaps the greatest obstacle to all applied research is that of gaining access to data sources, in this case, records of cases that have been sentenced in a court. Courts are closed settings, and access to court documents is controlled by individuals or gatekeepers at various levels, from the Ministry of Justice to individual court staff, each of whom can restrict access for a variety of reasons. As Dhami and Souza (2009a) report, obtaining access to court records can be a complex, lengthy and costly process, even when the research is financially sponsored by government bodies with some oversight of the courts.

Dhami and Souza (2009a) encountered these access issues:

- **Security clearance procedures** lead to delays and financial obligations in order to research court records.
- **A Catch-22 situation to obtain an access agreement** from the department that oversees research in the courts, which required researchers to first identify the sample of records they wanted to study – yet without the access agreement, they were not authorized to view any courts or records and so were unable to select these records.
- **Restrictive access agreements** regarding the dates and duration of access to courts.
- **Informal gatekeepers**, such as the court managers and court staff, inhibited researchers' access to court records in practice, though they were authorized in theory.
- **The court records' attrition rate** was, Dhami and Souza (2009b) calculated, on average 39% of the records sampled that could not actually be found in the court. This may be partly explained by the official policy on the length of time court records should be retained, which limits the scope of studying historical patterns of sentencing.

Dhami and Souza were able to complete their pilot study despite the hurdles they encountered. Their experience shows that government approval to access court records can be obtained successfully, but additional time and money must be included in any research plan to allow for negotiating an access agreement and arranging security clearance for research staff. The 'Catch-22' situation described above was resolved, in the end, by the government providing sampling data from a different source, namely the statistics office. The time-restrictive nature of access agreements can be managed through rigorous scheduling of the data collection process and having a comprehensive risk management strategy to cope with possible delays.[3] Issues caused by informal gatekeepers at individual courts can be minimised by contacting courts well in advance and by identifying a staff member at each court to act as liaison. Finally, the relatively high attrition rate of court records can be dealt with by appropriate oversampling. Dhami and Souza (2009b) recommend oversampling by 20% and limiting the sample to cases sentenced within the last three years.

How can data be extracted from court records?

Given that it is not feasible to study the court records of all cases sentenced in one year, it is important to sample records so that they are representative of the population to which the findings need to be generalized. In addition, the sample size should be large enough to obtain statistically robust estimates.[4] Once court records have been sampled, researchers must extract data from them in a reliable and efficient manner. Dhami and Souza (2009b) developed an instrument that can be used to do this.[5] The instrument lists the most useful documents available in the court records together with the information that they may contain. The fact that some information may be available from multiple documents within a record also means that handwritten documents, which may be illegible, can be avoided. Using a fairly comprehensive version of the instrument, Dhami and Souza (2009b) found that this approach facilitated efficient data collection, with the daily data collection rate being 4.5 records from the magistrates' courts (youth and adult) and 2.5 in the Crown Court. This rate would increase if the number of variables being coded was reduced.

Reliability is an important consideration in extracting data from court records. This ensures that the same variables are being coded in the same way across cases and across coders (researchers). If there is one researcher, then intracoder reliability ought to be assessed (i.e., by the researcher coding a subset of the same records twice), and if there is more than one researcher, intercoder reliability should also be assessed (i.e., by both researchers coding the same records).[6] Dhami and Souza (2009b) found that trained fieldworkers demonstrated very high levels of reliability in collecting data from court records. The average test-retest reliability across fieldworkers was from 81.8% to 100%. Some variables (e.g., number of offences taken into consideration and police bail decision) nevertheless showed a wide range of reliabilities, indicating that fieldworkers may require additional training.

Future research based on court record data

To date, the small body of past research on sentencing in England and Wales based on court records has examined a limited set of issues. The studies have explored disparities in the sentences meted out to male and female offenders (Farrington and Morris, 1983; Flood-Page and Mackie, 1998; Moxon, 1988), as well as offenders from different racial or ethnic backgrounds (Brown and Hullin, 1992; Hood, 1992). Studies have also explored disparities in the sentencing practices of different types of sentencers (Flood-Page and Mackie, 1998; Speed and Burrows, 2006) as well as different courts (Flood-Page and Mackie, 1998; Moxon and Hedderman, 1994). Although their findings have been valuable, there are still considerable gaps in our understanding of how different legal- and extra-legal factors may influence sentencing as well as changes in sentencing trends. Below, we offer a few suggestions for future research that could be conducted using data from court records.

First, research could use court records to systematically examine the effects of a host of other extra-legal factors beyond gender and race such as educational level, employment status, family history and alcohol, drug and/or mental health problems and treatment. These variables have largely gone unstudied using other methods, and hence their potential biasing influence on sentencing may have gone undetected. Similarly, court records could be used to assess if sentencers are using legal factors such as aggravating and mitigating factors, previous convictions and initial plea in the manner that is expected of them according to their training and the sentencing guidelines.

Second, future studies could use court records to explore the interplay that may exist between legal factors as well as between legal- and extra-legal variables. Here, both moderator and mediator effects are worth exploring. Moderating variables are those that can increase or reduce the effect of another variable on sentencing. For example, Mueller-Johnson and Dhami (2010) point out that the effect of an offender's old age on sentencing may be moderated by the effect of his/her health. In the case of mediation, the effect of one variable may occur either wholly or partially via the effect of another. For example, the effect of offence seriousness on sentencing may be mediated by the effect of previous convictions.

Third, beyond attempting to reveal the effects of a host of new case-level factors and their interplay on sentencing decisions, future research based on court records could explore the utility of multilevel models of sentencing. These suggest that sentencing might be predicted by case-, court- and area-level factors. Indeed, case-level factors cannot fully explain the variation in sentences across areas in England and Wales (Mason et al., 2007), and some researchers have suggested that sentencing may be affected by sociological features of courts, such as their structure/organisation, workloads and culture or norms (Mason et al., 2007; Rumgay, 1995). However, to date, only one study (Pina-Sanchez and Linacre, 2013) has used multilevel modelling techniques to examine sentencing decisions in England and Wales. Pina-Sanchez and Linacre used the Crown Court sentencing survey (CCSS) data to perform a multilevel analysis of 5,527 assault cases across all 77 Crown Court centres. They found that case-level factors accounted for almost all (98.2%) of the variation in custodial sentence length between courts. However, the variety of data available from the CCSS is much more limited than that which can be obtained from court records, so there may be other higher-level factors such as sentencer characteristics (e.g. magistrate versus District Judge and sentencer gender) that could be influential in a multilevel analysis.

Fourth, given that the sentencing decision is the final one in a long succession of decisions made as the case progresses through the criminal justice process, some researchers have suggested that sentences may partly be determined by a culmination of the previous decisions made on the case. For instance, Flood-Page and Mackie (1998) found that in the Crown Court, offenders remanded in custody were more likely to receive a custodial sentence than those on bail. Mode of trial decisions also influence sentencing, as shown by Moxon and Hedderman's (1994) finding that offenders guilty of either-way offences were more likely to receive custody (and longer terms) in the Crown Court than in magistrates' courts. However, these studies have usually only investigated the independent effects of pre-sentence decisions. Therefore, researchers could use court records to examine the independent and interactive effects of pre-sentence decisions such as alteration of the initial charge, plea, bail/remand and mode of trial (allocation and sending) on sentencing.

Fifth, court records (via the Crown Court judges' sentencing remarks and the magistrates' reasons for sentencing form) can be used to explore the ways in which sentencers communicate their sentences to offenders, their victims and the public. The transparency of sentencing, which taps into notions of procedural justice, is probably as important as the consistency of sentencing when it comes to perceptions of fairness, and confidence in the criminal justice system (Hough, Bradford, Jackson and Roberts, 2013). Indeed, one of the aims of the Sentencing Council is to increase the transparency of the sentencing process and the public's confidence in sentencing.

Finally, court records could be used to establish the reliability and validity of the data contained in the CCSS, which is fast becoming a new source of data for researchers interested in sentencing in England and Wales (Pina-Sanchez and Linacre, 2013; Sentencing Council, 2013). Since 2010, the CCSS has been gathering information from sentencers in the Crown Court on each sentence they pass. The survey covers different types of offences grouped into ten categories where there are similar aggravating and mitigating factors. It asks sentencers to record (using primarily a tick-box exercise) details of the factors they think they relied on when deciding the sentence, and which will have been stated in court.

Although this offers a cost-effective alternative source of Crown Court sentencing data, it is not a substitute for the court records themselves, particularly because it excludes a host of extra-legal factors that could potentially also influence (bias) sentencing decisions. The fact that the CCSS is only completed for the principal offence in cases where an offender is sentenced for more than one offence means that not all sentencing data is captured. The CCSS currently also suffers from a relatively high non-response rate of 39%, so the data may not be representative (Pina-Sanchez and Linacre, 2013). Most importantly, the vast majority of criminal sentences (92% in the 12 months to June 2012; Ministry of Justice, 2012) were imposed by the magistrates' courts, for which no equivalent survey exists, so court records for them remain the only source of detailed sentencing data, beyond the limited published sentencing statistics that were critiqued earlier.

Conclusion

Researchers studying sentencing in England and Wales have used a variety of methods to identify the factors that influence sentencing decisions. However, although all of these methods have their strengths and limitations, some offer greater potential for providing a comprehensive picture of sentencing. In this chapter, we have highlighted the value of studying sentencing using court records. All of the data on sentencing (except observations of sentencing hearings), including sentencers' self-reported experiences such as the CCSS and the published sentencing statistics, either should or do derive from these records. It is therefore surprising that so few researchers have used these as a source of data. And, although there are a number of difficulties involved in accessing court records and extracting data from them, these are not insurmountable. In this chapter, we have provided solutions to the challenges of studying sentencing using court records. With sufficient foresight, planning and determination, researchers can avoid the potential pitfalls and seize the many opportunities to be gleaned from studying sentencing using court records. The wealth of data contained in these court records can help illuminate the dynamics of sentencing.

Appendix: Examples of Information Available in Court Records

Sentencing decision

- sentences passed, including details of duration and amounts
- ancillary orders
- if multiple sentences, whether concurrent or consecutive
- whether longer than commensurate sentence given to protect public

Case-related information

- type of principal charge/offence (incl. law broken) and date of initial charge
- other offences charged
- brief description of principal and other offences
- whether charge and/or plea was altered and when
- number of co-defendants
- plea and date
- appearance at court and preliminary hearing dates
- bail/custody status (police and court) and any conditions imposed
- mode of trial (allocation and sending)
- breach of court orders and warrants for arrest
- number of witnesses

- evidence available
- aggravating factors
- mitigating factors
- whether offender was handcuffed in court
- probation recommendation
- offences taken into consideration

Offender information

- date of birth
- ethnicity
- gender
- nationality
- occupation
- mental health
- previous convictions
- previous sentences
- offender assessment (e.g., alcohol/drug problems and treatment)
- assessment of risk to the public and the likelihood of reoffending
- assessment of risk of self-harm
- access to legal aid
- family history (incl. whether abused)
- education level
- marital status
- accommodation status

Information on victim

- number of victims
- age
- gender
- whether vulnerable
- whether public official
- victim-offender relationship (if any)

Court- and sentencer-related information

- prosecutor
- defence
- sentencers
- type of court
- court location
- charging police station

Notes

1. District judges are full-time, professional members of the judiciary who hear cases in the magistrates' courts. Magistrates are trained (but not necessarily legally qualified), unpaid members of the local community.
2. For example, the Criminal Justice Act 2003 and the Coroners and Justice Act 2009, as well as the sentencing guidelines.
3. See Dhami and Souza (2009b) for details of a risk management strategy dealing with conducting sentencing research using court records.
4. For discussions of sampling court records for sentencing research, see Dhami and Souza (2009b) and Merrall, Dhami and Bird (2010).
5. A copy can be obtained from the first author.
6. Both measures of reliability can be calculated using appropriate statistical tests: Pearson's correlation coefficient can be used for variables that are measured on a continuous/interval scale, Spearman's correlation or Kendall's tau-b correlation for ordinal variables, and Chi-square or Cohen's Kappa for nominal variables (see Dhami, 2006).

References

Brown, I. and Hullin, R. (1992) A Study of Sentencing in the Leeds Magistrates' Courts. *British Journal of Criminology,* 32: 41–53. http://bjc.oxfordjournals.org/content/32/1/41.full.pdf+html.

Cammiss, S. and Stride, C. (2008) Modelling Mode of Trial. *British Journal of Criminology,* 48: 482–501. DOI: 10.1093/bjc/azn029.

Dhami, M.K., Hertwig, R. and Hoffrage, U. (2004) The Role of Representative Design in an Ecological Approach to Cognition. *Psychological Bulletin,* 130: 959–988. DOI: 10.1037/0033-2909.130.6.959.

Dhami, M.K. and Souza, K.A. (2009a) Breaking into court. In: D.L. Streiner and S. Sidani (eds) *When Research Goes off the Rails: Why It Happens and What You Can Do about It.* New York: Guildford Press.

—— (2009b) *Study of Sentencing and its Outcomes: Pilot Report* (Ministry of Justice Research Series 2/09). London: Ministry of Justice.

Farrington. D. and Morris, A. (1983) Sex, Sentencing and Reconviction, *British Journal of Criminology,* 23: 229–248. http://bjc.oxfordjournals.org/content/23/3/229.full.pdf+html.

Flood-Page, C. and Mackie, A. (1998) *Sentencing Practice: An Examination of Decisions in Magistrates' Courts and the Crown Court in the Mid-1990's.* (Home Office research study no. 180). http://www.nationalarchives.gov.uk/ERORecords/HO/421/2/P2/RDS/PDFS/HORS180.PDF.

Halevy, T. (1995) Racial Discrimination in Sentencing: A Study with Dubious Conclusions. *Criminal Law Review,* 267–271. http://www.sweetandmaxwell.co.uk/catalogue/productdetails.aspx?recordid=478&productid=7139.

Hedderman, C. (1990) *The Effect of Defendants' Demeanour on Sentencing in Magistrates' courts.* (Home Office Research Study no. 170). London: Home Office.

——(1991) Custody Decisions for Property Offenders in the Crown Court. *Howard Journal of Criminal Justice, 30,* 207–217. DOI: 10.1111/j.1468-2311.1991.tb00709.x.

Hedderman, C. and Moxon, D. (1992) *Magistrates' court or Crown Court? Mode of Trial Decision and Sentencing* (Home Office Research Study no. 125). London: Home Office.

Hood, R. (1992) *Race and Sentencing: A Study in the Crown Court.* Oxford: Clarendon Press.

Hough, M., Bradford, B., Jackson, J. and Roberts, J.V. (2013) Attitudes to Sentencing and Trust in Justice: Exploring Trends from the Crime Survey for England and Wales. https://www.gov.uk/government/uploads/system/uploads/attachment_data/file/230186/Attitudes_to_Sentencing_and_Trust_in_Justice__web_.pdf.

Hough, M., Jacobson, J. and Millie, A. (2003). The Decision to Imprison: Sentencing and the Prison Population. http://www.icpr.org.uk/media/10309/DECISIONTOIMPRISONBOOK.pdf.

Ipsos MORI (2011) The Strengths and Skills of the Judiciary in the Magistrates' Courts. Ministry of Justice Research Series 9/11. https://www.gov.uk/government/uploads/system/uploads/attachment_data/file/217366/strengths-skills-judiciary.pdf.

Mason, T., de Silva, N., Sharma, N., Brown, D. and Harper, G. (2007) 'Local Variation in Sentencing in England and Wales'. https://www.gov.uk/government/uploads/system/uploads/attachment_data/file/217971/local-variation-sentencing-1207.pdf.

Merrall, E.L.C., Dhami, M.K. and Bird, S.M. (2010) Exploring Methods to Investigate Sentencing Decisions, *Evaluation Review*, 34: 185–219. DOI: 10.1177/0193841X10369624.

Ministry of Justice (2010) *Sentencing Statistics: England and Wales 2009 Statistics Bulletin.* https://www.gov.uk/government/uploads/system/uploads/attachment_data/file/218034/sentencing-stats2009.pdf.

—— (2012) *Criminal Justice Statistics Quarterly Update to June 2012: Ministry of Justice Statistics Bulletin.* https://www.gov.uk/government/uploads/system/uploads/attachment_data/file/220090/criminal-justice-stats-sept-2012.pdf.

—— (2013) *Statistics on Race and the Criminal Justice System 2012.* https://www.gov.uk/government/uploads/system/uploads/attachment_data/file/269399/Race-and-cjs-2012.pdf.

Mortimer, E. and May, C. (1997) *Electronic Monitoring in Practice: The Second Year of the Trials of Curfew Orders* (Home Office research study no. 177). http://www.nationalarchives.gov.uk/ERORecords/HO/421/2/P2/RDS/PDFS/HORS177.PDF.

Moxon, D. (1988) *Sentencing Practice in the Crown Court* (Home Office research study no. 103). London: Home Office.

Moxon, D. and Hedderman, C. (1994) Mode of Trial Decisions and Sentencing Differences between Courts. *Howard Journal of Criminal Justice,* 33: 97–108. DOI: 10.1111/j.1468–2311.1994.tb00798.x.

Mueller-Johnson, K., and Dhami, M.K. (2010) Effects of Offenders' Age and Health on Sentencing Decisions. *Journal of Social Psychology,* 150: 77–97. DOI: 10.1080/00224540903365315.

Nisbett, R.E. and Wilson, T.D. (1977) Telling More Than We Can Know: Verbal Reports on Mental Processes. *Psychological Review,* 84: 231–259. DOI: 10.1037/0033–295X.84.3.231.

Paulhus, D.L. (1991) Measurement and control of response bias. In: J.P. Robinson, P.R. Shaver and L.S. Wrightsman (eds) *Measures of Personality and*

Social Psychological Attitudes. Measures of Social Psychological Attitudes, Vol. 1. San Diego, CA: Academic Press.
Pina-Sánchez, J. and Linacre, R. (2013) Sentence Consistency in England and Wales: Evidence from the Crown Court Sentencing Survey. *British Journal of Criminology,* 53: 1118–1138. DOI: 10.1093/bjc/azt040.
Raine, J.W. and Dunstan, E. (2009) How Well Do Sentencing Guidelines Work? Equity, Proportionality and Consistency in the Determination of Fine Levels in the Magistrates' Courts of England and Wales. *Howard Journal of Criminal Justice,* 48: 13–36. DOI: 10.1111/j.1468-2311.2008.00546.x.
Rumgay, J. (1995) Custodial Decision Making in a Magistrates' Court. *British Journal of Criminology,* 35: 201–217. http://bjc.oxfordjournals.org/.
Sentencing Council (2013) *Crown Court Sentencing Survey.* http://sentencing-council.judiciary.gov.uk/facts/sentencing-survey.htm.
Speed, M. and Burrows, J. (2006) *Sentencing in Cases of Theft from Shops* (Sentencing Advisory Panel Research Report 3). London: Sentencing Advisory Panel.

3
Sentencing Practices and Trends, 1999–2013

Julian V. Roberts and Keir Irwin-Rogers

Sentencing statistics

This chapter explores trends from the Ministry of Justice sentencing statistics (available at www.gov.uk/government/collections/criminal-justice-statistics-quarterly). Understanding sentencing patterns is complicated by the fact that offenders often appear for sentencing having been convicted of several offences. Sometimes the offender has been charged with multiple crimes arising from the same incident; sometimes the offender will be charged with a single offence but will ask the court to take a number of others into consideration. Offenders may ask a court to impose punishment for crimes for which they have not been charged in order to clear their account as it were, perhaps because they are aware that at some point charges will be laid. The other reason for asking for other offences to be taken into account is that although additional punishment will be imposed, the offender is likely to benefit from some reduction for having freely conceded the crimes.

When an offender is to be sentenced on multiple charges, the court must impose a sentence for each conviction. Yet only one sentence is recorded in the database. Common practice in most jurisdictions is to record the sentence imposed for the principal offence – usually the most serious – which is the one resulting in the most severe sentence.[1] For example, consider an offender convicted of domestic burglary and three less serious crimes. He receives a one-year term of immediate custody for the burglary and less severe, non-custodial sanctions for the lesser offences. This case will enter the statistical database as a one-year sentence for domestic burglary. The data reported in this chapter and found on the Ministry's website follow the principal offence rule.

The consequence of this practice is that the statistics will underreport the true volume of less severe penalties. The less serious offences are likely to attract less severe penalties. Finally, although we do not explore the issue any further here, it is worth noting that approximately 60% of offenders appearing for sentence receive more than a single disposal. This arises either from a court imposing multiple sentences for the same conviction, or multiple sentences for multiple convictions.

Volume of cases sentenced

Perhaps the most basic question to address concerns changes in the sentencing caseloads in the magistrates' courts (MC) and the Crown Courts (CC). As can be seen in Table 3.1, in 2013 just over one million cases were sentenced in the former and 86,129 in the latter. Thus, fully 93% of sentences were imposed in the MC, mostly by magistrates. The distribution of cases across the levels of court has remained generally stable over the 15-year period: in 1999, 95% of sentences were imposed in the summary conviction courts. In terms of numbers of cases sentenced, the lay magistracy remains the most significant element of sentencing in England and Wales: district judges sitting in the MC will account for only a small percentage of the total cases sentenced. The trends in volume of cases in both court levels combined are presented graphically in Figure 3.1.

The combined caseload of the courts has been declining in recent years. A total of 1,169,727 cases were sentenced in 2013, down from the peak of 1,547,352 cases in 2004. This constitutes a decrease of 24% over the period 2004–2013, representing almost 400,000 fewer cases. The drop in caseload reflects the fall in crime rates over this period, and to a lesser degree an increase in the use of out of court disposals. It is interesting to note, however, that the volume of sentenced cases does not perfectly track the volume of crimes reported and prosecuted, which have steadily declined over this period.

Moreover, the significant recent drop in the overall volume of cases masks a different pattern in the two levels of court. Over the period from 2004 to 2013, there was a 26% decline in the number sentenced in the MC (Figure 3.2), yet a 13% increase in cases sentenced in the Crown Court (Figure 3.3). Most recently, the volume of cases has continued to decline in the MC and has now begun dropping in the Crown Court, where the number of cases sentenced fell by 16% from 2011 to 2013.[2]

Table 3.1 Cases sentenced in the magistrates' courts and the Crown Court, 1999–2013

	1999	2000	2001	2002	2003	2004	2005	2006	2007	2008	2009	2010	2011	2012	2013
Magistrates' courts	1,330,828	1,350,008	1,276,426	1,343,417	1,413,764	1,471,098	1,406,712	1,343,985	1,333,236	1,273,236	1,312,315	1,263,396	1,210,575	1,139,263	1,083,598
Crown Court	77,170	74,341	72,068	76,191	76,063	76,254	75,741	76,586	81,506	88,828	94,590	101,951	102,164	90,564	86,129

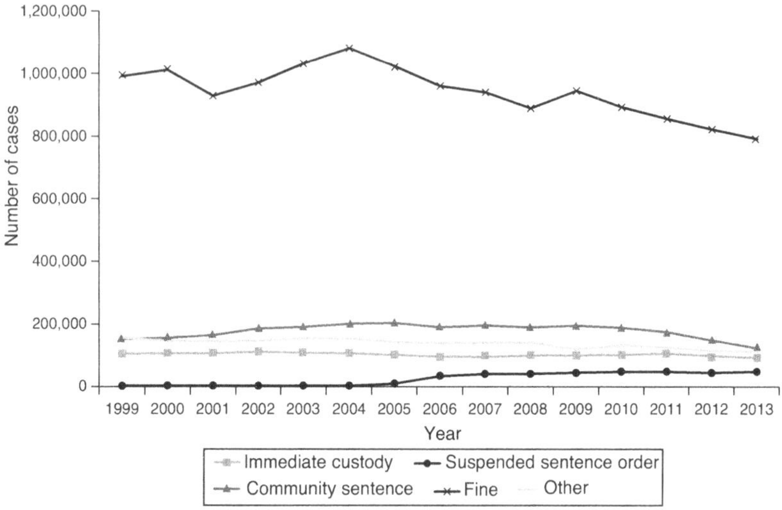

Figure 3.1 Trends in all disposals, all courts, 1999–2013

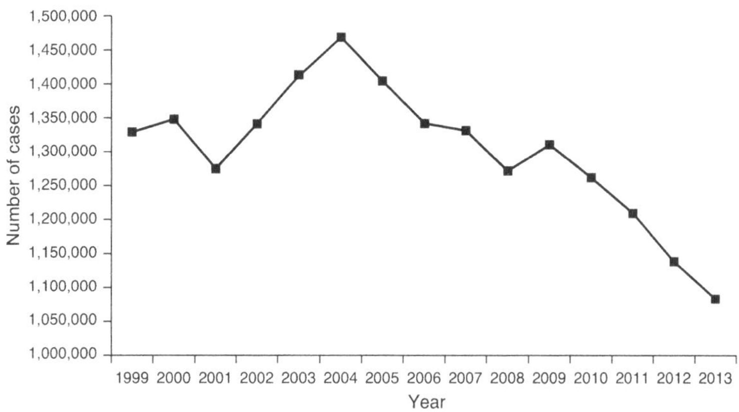

Figure 3.2 Trends in cases sentenced, magistrates' courts, 1999–2013

Relative use of disposals

Figure 3.4 illustrates the use of the principal disposals in both courts combined in 2013. Table 3.2 summarises the relative use of the principal disposals, both levels of court combined for the period from 1999 to 2013. Consistent with sentencing trends in other Western

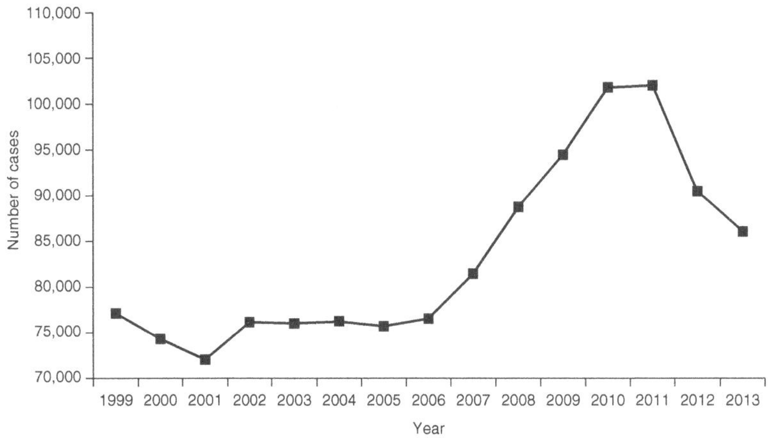

Figure 3.3 Trends in cases sentenced, Crown Court, 1999–2013

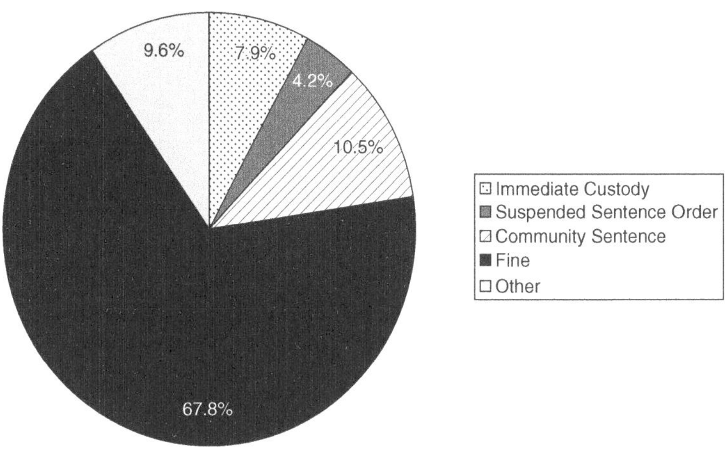

Figure 3.4 Rates of all disposals, all courts, 2013

nations, a fine was the most frequently imposed sentence in 2013 (as well as every preceding year), accounting for slightly more than two-thirds (68%[3]) of all cases (Table 3.2). Community orders (CO) were the next most frequent disposal, accounting for 11% of all cases. Other disposals (including absolute and conditional discharges) accounted for approximately the same proportion of cases (10%). Taken together,

Table 3.2 Volumes and rates of all disposals, all courts, 1999–2013

	1999	2000	2001	2002	2003	2004	2005	2006	2007	2008	2009	2010	2011	2012	2013
Immediate Custody	105,323	106,187	106,273	111,607	107,670	106,322	101,236	96,017	95,206	99,525	100,231	101,513	106,170	98,047	92,799
Rate	8	8	8	8	7	7	7	7	7	7	7	7	8	8	8
Suspended Sentence	3,161	3,072	2,755	2,519	2,717	2,855	9,666	33,509	40,688	41,151	45,157	48,118	48,153	44,642	48,628
Rate	0.2	0.2	0.2	0.2	0.2	0.2	1	2	3	3	3	4	4	4	4
Community Sentence	151,633	155,538	164,997	186,520	191,422	201,503	204,247	190,837	196,424	190,171	195,903	189,321	175,525	149,327	123,087
Rate	11	11	12	13	13	13	14	13	14	14	14	14	13	12	11
Fine	992,420	1,013,347	930,121	972,737	1,033,617	1,082,690	1,025,064	961,535	941,534	890,296	946,146	893,931	856,808	823,298	792,942
Rate	71	71	69	69	69	70	69	68	67	65	67	66	65	67	68
Other[5]	155,461	146,205	144,348	146,225	154,401	153,982	142,240	138,673	140,890	140,921	119,468	132,464	126,083	114,513	112,271
Rate	11	10	11	10	10	10	10	10	10	10	9	10	10	9	10
Total Offenders Sentenced	1,407,998	1,424,349	1,348,494	1,419,608	1,489,827	1,547,352	1,482,453	1,420,571	1,414,742	1,362,064	1,406,905	1,365,347	1,312,739	1,229,827	1,169,727

immediate and suspended sentence orders (SSO) of imprisonment accounted for 12% of cases. Of these, immediate custody accounted for twice the percentage of suspended sentences.[4] We shall examine the SSO in more detail later in this chapter, as use of this disposal represents one of most dramatic recent changes in sentencing practices. Table 3.3 provides the volume and rates of all disposals in all courts, for indictable offences only.

Figures 3.5 and 3.6 reveal the relative use of the principal disposals in, respectively, the Crown Court and the magistrates' courts in 2013. The corresponding data are found in Tables 3.4 and 3.5, respectively. As can be seen, fines are heavily used in the MC – accounting for approximately three-quarters of all cases. Community sentences and other disposals (including conditional and absolute discharges) each account for a further 10%, while only 4% of cases attracted a sentence of immediate custody. Unsurprisingly, the trend is very different in the Crown Court, where fines account for only 2% of all cases. Custody on the other hand is common: Over four-fifths of cases in the Crown Court involved immediate or suspended sentences of custody.

Overall shifts in the use of different disposals

The proportionate use of different disposals has changed little over the 15-year period. Although the volume of almost all disposals[7] has declined (to reflect the drop in cases sentenced), the courts appear to be using the principal disposals in consistent proportions over the years. Fines, for example, were imposed in 68% of cases in 2013 and approximately the same percentage a decade earlier. Similarly, community orders accounted for a comparable percentage of cases in 2013 (11%) and 1999 (11%). The proportionate use of immediate custody was also invariable, accounting for 7% or 8% of all cases over the 15 years. Figure 3.7 illustrates the use of the principal disposals in all courts over the period 1999–2013. Figure 3.8 plots the use of immediate custody over the same period for both levels of court.

Decline in Cases

The costs of sentencing to the criminal justice system will have declined in recent years by virtue of the fall in cases sentenced: 2013 recorded almost 7,000 fewer custodial sentences than in 2008. It is hard to make accurate estimates of the savings involved. Comparison of the two court levels reveals similar patterns of custody rates. In the Crown Court, just

Table 3.3 Volumes and rates of all disposals, indictable offences, all courts, 2003–2013

Sentence	2003	2004	2005	2006	2007	2008	2009	2010	2011	2012	2013
Immediate Custody	80,794	79,938	76,291	73,532	74,037	79,058	80,265	82,939	87,558	81,082	77,843
Rate	24	25	25	24	24	25	25	24	26	26	27
Suspended Sentence	2,055	2,143	5,610	20,799	27,254	28,455	31,131	34,176	34,422	31,883	35,429
Rate	1	1	2	7	9	9	10	10	10	10	12
Community Sentences	109,549	111,013	111,724	102,971	105,142	102,782	107,924	108,495	100,286	82,815	66,487
Rate	33	35	37	34	34	33	33	31	29	27	23
Fine	77,097	63,999	57,382	50,665	48,452	48,736	55,351	59,437	58,288	53,667	53,159
Rate	23	20	19	17	16	15	17	17	17	18	18
Other[6]	62,971	58,713	54,495	53,521	56,306	55,910	51,921	62,375	61,304	56,669	57,981
Rate	19	19	18	18	18	18	16	18	18	19	20
Total Offenders Sentenced	332,466	315,806	305,502	301,488	311,191	314,941	326,592	347,422	341,858	306,116	290,899

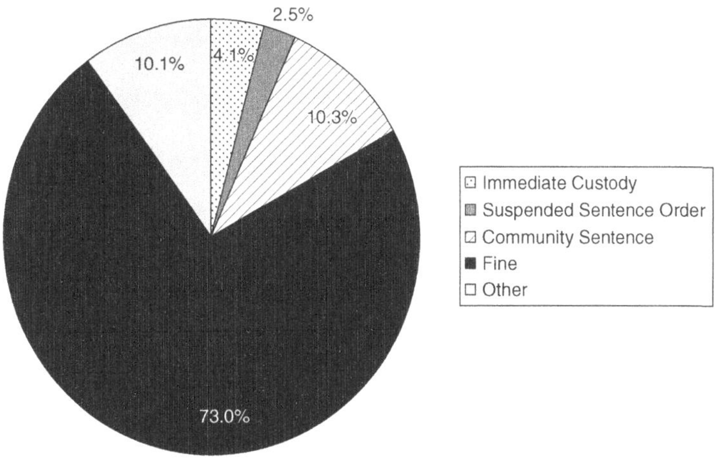

Figure 3.5 Rates of all disposals, magistrates' courts, 2013

over half of the cases sentenced in 2013 received immediate custody,

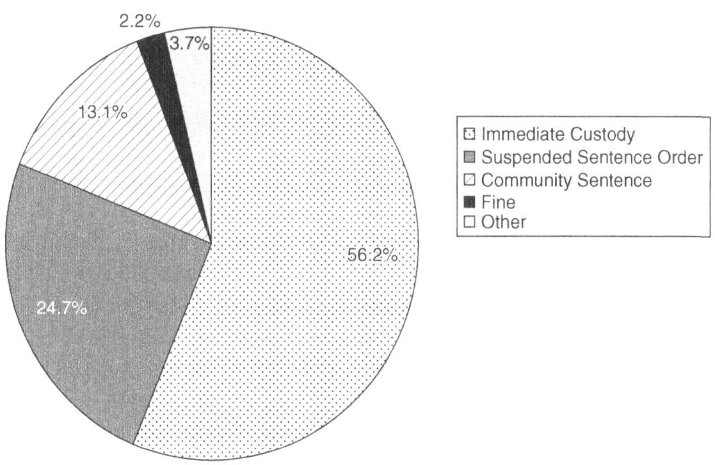

Figure 3.6 Rates of all disposals, Crown Court, 2013

and as can be seen in Table 3.4, there has been little fluctuation in this rate in recent years, although the current Crown Court custody rate is slightly lower than the first year of the 15-year cycle, when it was 61%. As can be seen in Table 3.5, the imprisonment rate in the MC has

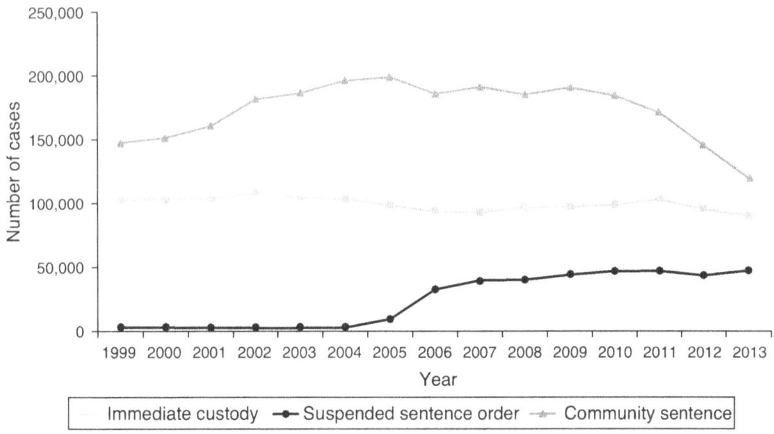

Figure 3.7 Trends in custody, suspended sentence orders and community sentences, all courts, 1999–2013

also been stable, being 4% or 5% over the entire period. The decline in volume of cases means that 2013 saw significantly fewer admissions to custody. The number of cases receiving immediate custody in 2013 is 13% lower than just two years earlier; this converts to over 13,000 fewer admissions to custody during the recent year.

Community orders and suspended sentence orders

In the magistrates' courts, the proportion of community orders imposed has declined modestly in recent years, from a high of 14% (2007–2010) to 10% of cases in 2013. This represents a 38% decrease in the absolute number of community orders imposed by the magistrates' courts over these years, from 181,607 in 2007 to 111,820 in 2013. Changes in the volume of community orders and fines are presented in Figure 3.9 and Figure 3.10 respectively. There was a significant increase in the use of SSOs in the magistrates' courts between 2004 and 2006; since 2006 their use has been relatively stable.

The Crown Court has also experienced a steady and significant decline in the number of community orders. As can be seen in Table 3.4, as recently as 2005 this disposal accounted for almost one third of all Crown Court cases; by 2013 this had declined to 13%. The rate of immediate custody was relatively stable over this period – an average rate of 57% in the period from 2005 to 2007, and the use of fines was also stable. In order to understand the decline of the community order in

Table 3.4 Volumes and rates of all disposals, Crown Court, 1999–2013

	1999	2000	2001	2002	2003	2004	2005	2006	2007	2008	2009	2010	2011	2012	2013
Immediate Custody	47,349	46,212	44,405	46,694	44,274	44,938	43,986	42,586	44,034	49,177	51,802	52,609	56,663	50,683	48,424
Rate	61	62	62	61	58	59	59	56	56	58	57	54	55	52	57
Suspended Sentence	2,002	1,901	1,633	1,506	1,558	1,555	2,585	10,235	15,217	17,446	19,749	21,927	21,569	19,976	21,310
Rate	3	3	2	2	2	2	3	13	20	20	22	23	21	20	25
Community Sentences	20,656	19,606	19,528	21,656	23,094	22,807	22,403	17,232	14,817	15,339	16,174	19,238	17,090	14,579	11,267
Rate	27	26	27	28	30	30	30	23	19	18	18	20	17	15	13
Fine	2,707	2,512	2,550	2,353	2,699	2,454	2,354	2,141	2,488	2,320	2,302	2,511	2,032	1,672	1,925
Rate	4	3	4	3	4	3	3	3	3	3	3	3	2	2	2
Other Disposals	4,456	4,110	3,952	3,982	4,438	4,500	4,413	4,392	4,950	4,546	4,563	5,666	4,810	3,654	3,203
Rate	6	6	6	5	6	6	6	6	6	5	5	6	4	4	4
Total Offenders Sentenced	77,170	74,341	72,068	76,191	76,063	76,254	75,741	76,586	81,506	88,828	94,590	101,951	102,164	90,564	86,129

Table 3.5 Volumes and rates of all disposals, magistrates' courts, 1999–2013

	1999	2000	2001	2002	2003	2004	2005	2006	2007	2008	2009	2010	2011	2012	2013
Immediate Custody	57,974	59,975	61,868	64,913	63,396	61,384	57,250	53,431	51,172	50,348	48,429	48,904	49,507	47,364	44,375
Rate	4	4	5	5	5	4	4	4	4	4	4	4	4	4	4
Suspended Sentence	1,159	1,171	1,122	1,013	1,159	1,300	7,081	23,274	25,471	23,705	25,408	26,191	26,584	24,666	27,318
Rate	0.1	0.1	0.1	0.1	0.1	0.1	1	2	2	2	2	2	2	2	3
Community Sentence	130,977	135,932	145,469	186,864	168,328	178,696	181,844	173,605	181,607	174,832	179,729	170,083	158,435	134,748	111,820
Rate	10	10	11	14	12	12	13	13	14	14	14	14	13	12	10
Fine	989,713	1,010,835	927,571	970,384	1,030,918	1,080,236	1,022,710	959,394	939,046	887,976	943,844	891,420	854,776	821,626	791,017
Rate	74	75	73	72	73	73	73	71	70	60	72	71	71	72	73
Other Disposal	151,005	142,095	140,396	142,243	149,963	149,482	137,827	134,281	135,940	136,375	114,905	126,798	121,273	110,859	109,068
Rate	11	11	11	11	11	10	10	10	10	11	9	10	10	10	10
Total Offenders Sentenced	1,330,828	1,350,008	1,276,426	1,343,417	1,413,764	1,471,098	1,406,712	1,343,985	1,333,236	1,273,236	1,312,315	1,263,396	1,210,575	1,139,263	1,083,598

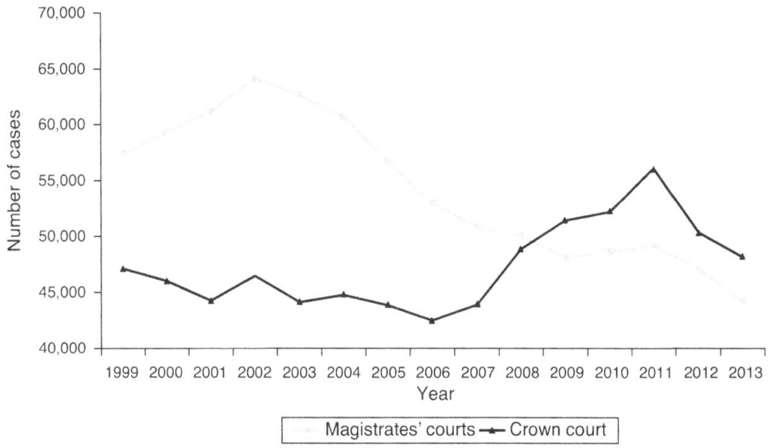

Figure 3.8 Trends in immediate custody, all offences, magistrates' courts and Crown Court, 1999–2013

the Crown Court, we must review the status of the only disposal to have changed significantly in terms of its relevant usage in recent years: the Suspended Sentence Order (SSO).

Although the suspended sentence of imprisonment has been available to courts since 1967 (see Ashworth, 2010 for discussion), the disposal was given fresh life in 2003 when the Criminal Justice Act abolished the restriction that this form of custody could be imposed only in exceptional circumstances. The anticipated consequence of the reform was an increase in the use of SSOs, and so it has proved, although the impact of the reform was not apparent until the relevant provisions came into effect in 2005.

Suspended sentence orders accounted for only 3% of Crown Court cases in 2005, but (as noted), 25% in 2013. In fact, the SSO rate rose dramatically from 2005 to 2007 (from 3% to 20%), was then relatively stable, and has increased by an additional 5% over the last year (2012–2013). It would appear then that the SSO has been imposed in cases which previously would have attracted a community penalty. The rise of the SSO and the concomitant declining use of the community order represents the most dramatic shift in sentencing patterns in recent years, and is worthy of additional commentary. In terms of numbers of cases, in 2004 fewer than 3,000 offenders received a suspended sentence; by 2013, across all courts, almost 50,000 offenders were serving a suspended sentence.

In light of the fact that an SSO has the status of a term of custody, it is surprising that the courts appear to be imposing it in cases which formerly attracted a community order. A number of scholars have drawn attention to this issue of 'up-tariffing' (e.g., Ashworth, 2010; Hedderman and Barnes, this volume). This refers to the process in which a sanction that was designed to replace a more severe sanction instead replaces a less severe sanction in practice. There is, of course, a danger that a certain percentage of SSO cases will ultimately be committed to custody following breach of their conditions. Given the potential for this to

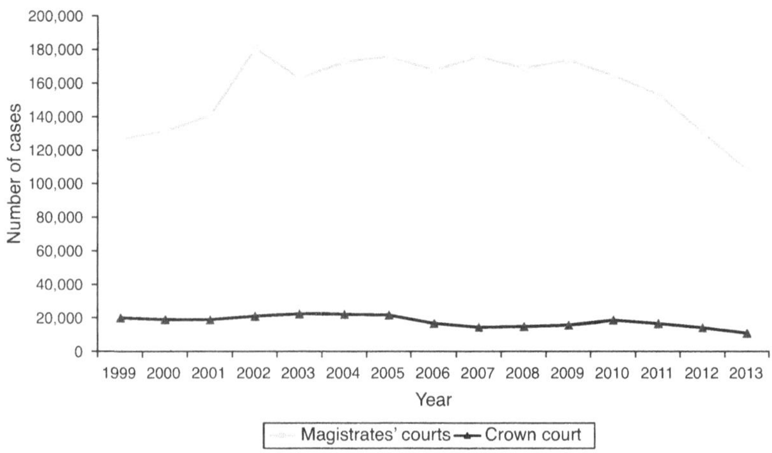

Figure 3.9 Trends in community sentence orders, magistrates' courts and Crown Court, 1999–2013

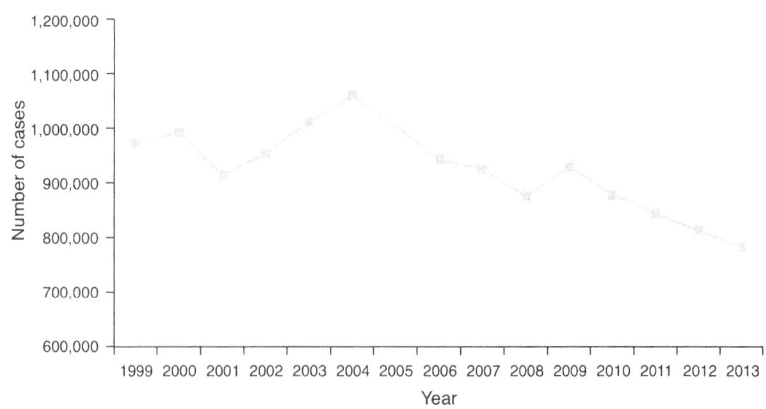

Figure 3.10 Trends in fines, magistrates' courts, 1999–2013

happen, it is unclear why the courts are not restricting the imposition of SSOs to cases in which only custody is appropriate.

Trends in the use of custody by offence category

Tables 3.6 and 3.7 summarise trends in the use of custody for various offence categories sentenced in the magistrates' courts and the Crown Court respectively. A number of conclusions may be drawn from these tables. First, public order offences and theft offences attracted custody rates approximately equivalent to crimes of violence: respectively 23%; 19% and 23% in the MC. In the Crown Court, theft offences attracted a higher custody rate than violence (67% compared to 58%).

The comparable degree of severity may at first be puzzling; one explanation involves the criminal records of offenders in these categories. Theft is a 'high frequency', 'high recidivism' crime, and many offenders convicted of theft have very lengthy criminal records. Offenders convicted of crimes of violence are less likely to have multiple prior convictions relevant to sentencing. The independent effects of previous convictions and current offence seriousness cannot be disentangled in these statistics. (The issue is developed further in Chapter 9 of this volume.)

For most offences, the use of custody is fairly consistent over the 15-year period. Offences and offence categories with relatively high custody rates in 2003 retained high rates in 2013. One of the few exceptions to this observation would appear to be robbery in the magistrates' courts. In 2003, 22% of robbery cases attracted an immediate custodial term. The percentage of immediate custody cases declined steadily thereafter, accounting for only 13% in 2013. No such decline in the use of custody occurred in the Crown Court, where approximately four-fifths of cases received an immediate sentence of custody over the entire 15 years.

Trends in community orders

Tables 3.8 and 3.9 summarise rates in the use of community sentences in the MC and the CC, respectively. In the MC, rates of community sentences are variable across offence categories, yet relatively consistent over time. If the rate was high in 2003, it generally remained high a decade later, although there are some important exceptions to this observation. For one thing, the use of community orders for crimes of violence appears to have declined steadily, from a high of 61% in 2005 to 41% in 2012, and 2013 records a new low of 24%. Public order offences

Table 3.6 Trends in immediate custody rates by principal offence group, magistrates' courts, 2003–2013

	Offence Group												
	Violence	Sexual Offences	Robbery	Theft Offences	Criminal Damage and Arson	Drug Offences	Possession of Weapons	Public Order Offences	Miscellaneous Crimes Against Society	Fraud Offences	Total Indictable	Total Summary	Total All Offences
2003	17	19	22	20	6	3	12	16	11	12	14	2	5
2004	18	18	21	19	5	3	12	18	13	12	15	2	4
2005	18	14	19	19	6	3	13	17	13	11	14	2	4
2006	16	14	19	19	6	4	13	14	13	8	14	2	4
2007	15	13	14	17	6	4	14	15	13	7	13	2	4
2008	16	15	17	18	6	3	15	15	14	7	14	2	4
2009	15	13	14	16	5	2	15	24	11	8	13	2	4
2010	15	11	13	17	6	3	15	22	11	7	13	2	4
2011	18	12	14	17	6	2	17	23	11	8	13	2	4
2012	22	16	12	19	6	2	17	24	11	9	14	2	4
2013	22	15	13	19	5	2	17	23	11	8	15	2	4

Table 3.7 Trends in immediate custody rates by principal offence group, Crown Court, 2003–2013

	Offence Group												
	Violence	Sexual Offences	Robbery	Theft Offences	Criminal Damage and Arson	Drug Offences	Possession of Weapons	Public Order Offences	Miscellaneous Crimes Against Society	Fraud Offences	Total Indictable	Total Summary	Total All Offences
2003	56	74	85	64	37	67	47	40	53	45	60	24	58
2004	58	76	85	63	37	69	49	42	54	47	61	25	59
2005	58	74	82	62	40	66	47	42	57	48	60	26	58
2006	53	72	82	61	40	64	47	36	56	43	57	24	56
2007	52	71	79	58	42	62	46	35	57	37	56	24	54
2008	54	71	82	60	40	62	50	36	57	37	57	27	56
2009	54	72	82	61	41	61	43	41	54	41	57	27	55
2010	51	71	81	60	42	57	41	38	49	37	54	25	52
2011	55	71	83	65	50	57	46	43	51	42	57	30	56
2012	58	73	82	66	55	53	47	45	50	42	58	27	56
2013	58	75	83	67	57	52	46	45	51	43	58	29	56

Table 3.8 Trends in community sentence rates by principal offence group, magistrates' courts, 2003–2013

	Offence Group												
	Violence	Sexual Offences	Robbery	Theft Offences	Criminal Damage and Arson	Drug Offences	Possession of Weapons	Public Order Offences	Miscellaneous Crimes Against Society	Fraud Offences	Total Indictable	Total Summary	Total All Offences
2003	60	45	75	38	46	18	41	59	20	47	34	7	12
2004	61	54	77	40	49	23	46	58	22	49	37	7	12
2005	61	59	80	42	52	25	50	59	23	49	39	8	13
2006	54	54	79	40	52	25	51	59	23	45	38	8	13
2007	54	58	83	41	49	26	52	59	26	45	39	8	14
2008	55	61	81	40	48	26	53	58	27	43	38	8	14
2009	57	64	84	41	51	28	54	42	27	47	39	8	14
2010	54	65	79	38	47	24	53	39	24	47	36	8	14
2011	48	63	80	37	47	23	51	20	25	47	35	8	13
2012	41	60	84	34	43	21	48	18	23	45	32	7	12
2013	24	57	85	29	42	18	45	16	22	44	27	6	10

Table 3.9 Trends in community sentence rates by principal offence group, Crown Court, 2003–2013

	Offence Group												
	Violence	Sexual Offences	Robbery	Theft Offences	Criminal Damage and Arson	Drug Offences	Possession of Weapons	Public Order Offences	Miscellaneous Crimes Against Society	Fraud Offences	Total Indictable	Total Summary	Total All Offences
2003	33	20	13	31	42	22	32	48	33	40	30	36	30
2004	31	19	13	31	41	22	31	47	33	38	30	36	30
2005	30	19	15	31	40	24	32	46	29	37	29	36	30
2006	22	18	12	23	31	17	23	39	22	30	22	30	23
2007	16	17	12	20	24	14	22	30	16	22	18	27	18
2008	15	17	9	18	27	14	19	29	15	20	17	27	17
2009	15	17	9	17	28	14	23	25	16	18	17	27	17
2010	17	17	9	18	25	16	25	26	18	23	18	29	19
2011	16	17	7	15	20	15	21	23	17	19	16	28	17
2012	13	16	7	14	18	17	21	21	18	16	15	30	16
2013	10	13	5	11	13	13	17	17	15	14	12	27	13

reveal a similar decline, and these two offence categories contribute to the decline in community orders imposed for indictable offences from 34% in 2003 to 27% in 2013.

The pattern is more striking in the Crown Court (Table 3.9). The use of community orders for indictable offences reveals a smooth and significant downward pattern: from 30% in 2003 to 12% a decade later. Unlike the MC, community sentence rates declined for most offence categories in the Crown Court. With the exception of summary offences, community sentence rates declined for all categories of offending, and across all cases declined from 30% in 2003 to 13% in the most recent year (2013). This represents a very significant shift in sentencing practices in the Crown Court. The declining use of community orders is represented graphically in Figure 3.9.

Trends in suspended sentences

Tables 3.10 and 3.11 provide the SSO rates for the MC and the CC. As noted earlier, the use of this disposal has grown dramatically in recent years in the Crown Court. The increase can be seen in almost all offence categories but is particularly striking in motoring offences, fraud and forgery and crimes of violence. SSO accounted for 1% of cases sentenced in the CC in 2004, rising to one-third of all cases sentenced in 2013. Similarly striking increases were recorded for fraud (6% to 34%) and violence (3% to 27% in 2013). An increased use of this disposal was also seen in the MC, but to a lesser degree. The use of SSO rose from 2% in

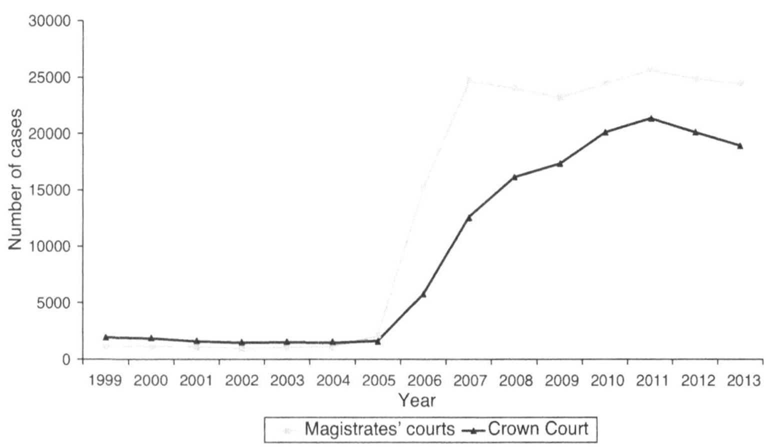

Figure 3.11 Trends in suspended sentence orders, magistrates' courts and Crown Court, 1999–2013

Table 3.10 Trends in suspended sentence order rates by offence group, magistrates' courts, 1999–2012

	Offence Group														
	Violence against the Person	Sexual Offences	Burglary	Robbery	Theft and Handling Stolen Goods	Fraud and Forgery	Criminal Damage	Drug Offences	Other (Excluding Motoring)	Motoring Offences	Total Indictable Offences	Summary Non-Motoring Offences	Summary Motoring Offences	Total Summary Offences	Total All Offences
1999	0.4	0.4	0.2	0.0	0.2	1	0.1	0.1	0.1	0.4	0.2	0.0	0.1	0.1	0.1
2000	1	0.2	0.2	0.0	0.2	1	0.1	0.1	0.2	1	0.2	0.0	0.1	0.1	0.1
2001	0.4	1	0.1	0.0	0.2	1	0.1	0.1	0.2	1	0.2	0.1	0.1	0.1	0.1
2002	0.4	1	0.1	0.0	0.1	1	0.1	0.1	0.1	1	0.2	0.0	0.1	0.1	0.1
2003	0.4	0.4	0.3	0.0	0.2	1	0.1	0.1	0.1	0.3	0.2	0.1	0.1	0.1	0.1
2004	1	1	0.2	0.0	0.2	1	0.1	0.1	0.2	1	0.2	0.1	0.1	0.1	0.1
2005	3	2	2	0.0	1	2	1	1	1	4	1	0.3	0.4	0.3	1
2006	10	6	7	0.1	5	6	2	2	3	15	5	1	1	1	2
2007	12	8	7	0.1	5	7	3	2	3	16	5	1	1	1	2
2008	12	7	7	0.1	5	7	2	2	3	14	5	2	1	1	2
2009	14	8	7	0.0	5	8	2	1	4	13	5	2	1	1	2
2010	13	8	8	0.1	5	9	3	2	4	14	5	2	1	1	2
2011	13	9	9	0.0	5	10	3	2	4	19	6	2	1	1	2
2012	14	9	10	0.0	6	12	3	1	4	19	6	2	1	1	2

Table 3.11 Trends in suspended sentence order rates by offence group, Crown Court, 1999–2012

	Offence Group													
	Violence against the person	Sexual offences	Burglary	Robbery	Theft and Handling Stolen Goods	Fraud and Forgery	Criminal Damage	Drug Offences	Other (Excluding Motoring)	Motoring Offences	Total Indictable Offences	Summary Non-Motoring Offences	Summary Motoring Offences	Total Summary Offences	Total All Offences
1999	3	3	1	1	3	8	2	3	3	2	3	1	1	1	3
2000	3	3	1	1	2	9	2	3	4	2	3	1	0.1	1	3
2001	3	2	1	1	2	8	2	2	3	2	2	1	1	1	2
2002	3	2	1	0.4	2	6	1	2	2	2	2	1	0.2	1	2
2003	3	2	1	1	2	6	2	2	2	2	2	0.4	1	1	2
2004	3	2	1	1	2	7	2	2	3	1	2	1	0.3	1	2
2005	4	3	2	1	3	7	3	4	4	3	4	1	2	1	3
2006	18	6	10	5	15	15	12	13	15	18	14	8	8	8	13
2007	24	9	15	8	21	21	16	18	24	24	19	10	9	9	19
2008	25	8	15	8	22	23	16	18	25	27	20	11	10	11	20
2009	27	8	14	8	22	27	16	19	25	31	21	17	12	16	21
2010	27	8	14	9	23	28	16	21	25	32	22	16	19	17	22
2011	26	9	13	9	22	31	17	22	25	31	22	16	16	16	21
2012	27	8	14	10	25	34	17	24	25	33	22	18	20	18	22

2004 to 12% in 2013; violence rose from <1% to 14%. Overall, the SSO remained, like immediate custody, a relatively rare sanction in the MC, accounting for only 2% of all sentenced cases. The dramatic increase in the use of SSO is represented graphically in Figure 3.11.

Average custodial sentence length (ACSL)

Table 3.12 provides overall average custodial sentence lengths (ACSL) for both levels of court combined, over a slightly longer period for which data are available: 1996–2013. As can be seen, for all offences there has been an increase in ACSL from 11.8 months at the beginning of the decade to 15.5 in the most recent year. This has come about largely as a result of an increase in ACSL for indictable offences. The consequence is that sentencing in England and Wales has become harsher in recent years, at least when the measure of severity is the average sentence of imprisonment.

Further insight into the sentence length trends emerges from Tables 3.13 and 3.14, ACSL in the Crown Court and the magistrates' courts for summary and indictable offences. Average sentence length in the Crown Court was higher in 2013 than in any previous year, and this arises from the increase in ACSL for indictable offences. ACSL in the magistrates' courts shows no such increase; in fact it was marginally lower in 2013 (2.5 months) than a decade earlier (3.0 months in 2004). Finally, Table 3.15 provides more detail on ACSLs in the Crown Court for specific offence categories over time.

Summary of principal findings

- There has been a significant decline in the sentencing caseload in recent years, principally as a result of the fall in crime rates.
- The use of custody has been relatively constant over the past decade, accounting for 7% of all disposals in 2003 and 8% in 2013.
- The most frequently imposed disposal in 2013 was a fine.
- The principal changes in disposal patterns involve an increase in the use of suspended sentence orders.
- The average custodial sentence length has increased by 31%, from 11.8 months in 2001 to 15.5 months in 2013.

Table 3.12 Average custodial sentence lengths (in months), all courts, all persons, 1996–2013

	1996	1997	1998	1999	2000	2001	2002	2003	2004	2005	2006	2007	2008	2009	2010	2011	2012	2013
Indictable offences	15.8	15.7	14.5	14.2	14	14.7	15.5	15.7	16.1	15.8	15.3	15.2	16.0	16.5	16.2	16.8	17.0	18.0
Summary offences	3.1	3.1	3.1	3.1	3.1	3.2	3.2	3.2	3.2	3.1	3.0	3.0	2.8	2.8	2.7	2.6	2.7	2.7
All offences	12.6	12.7	11.8	11.5	11.4	11.8	12.6	12.6	12.9	12.6	12.4	12.4	13.3	13.7	13.7	14.3	14.5	15.5

Table 3.13 Average custodial sentence lengths (in months), Crown Court, all persons, 1999–2013

	1999	2000	2001	2002	2003	2004	2005	2006	2007	2008	2009	2010	2011	2012	2013
Indictable Offences	22.5	22.8	24.5	26.3	26.8	27.0	25.9	25.2	24.6	25.1	25.0	25.0	25.5	26.5	28.3
Summary Offences	3.7	3.6	3.5	3.5	3.6	3.6	3.7	3.9	3.5	3.3	3.2	3.3	3.0	3.1	3.3
All Offences	22.1	22.4	24.2	25.9	26.3	26.5	25.5	24.7	24.0	24.5	24.3	24.3	24.7	25.9	27.6

Table 3.14 Average custodial sentence lengths (in months), magistrates' courts, all persons, 1999–2013

	1999	2000	2001	2002	2003	2004	2005	2006	2007	2008	2009	2010	2011	2012	2013
Indictable Offences	2.7	2.9	3.0	3.0	3.0	3.0	2.9	2.9	2.8	2.7	2.6	2.5	2.6	2.5	2.4
Summary Offences	3.0	3.1	3.2	3.2	3.2	3.2	3.1	3.0	2.9	2.8	2.7	2.6	2.6	2.6	2.7
All Offences	2.8	3.0	3.1	3.1	3.1	3.0	3.0	3.0	2.9	2.7	2.7	2.5	2.6	2.5	2.5

Table 3.15 Average custodial sentence length (in months) by offence group, Crown Court

	Offence Group												
Year	Violence	Sexual Offences	Robbery	Theft Offences	Criminal Damage and Arson	Drug Offences	Possession of Weapons	Public Order Offences	Miscellaneous Crimes Against Society	Fraud Offences	Total Indictable	Total Summary	Total All Offences
2003	26.8	43.8	41.7	20.3	29.2	40.0	23.8	12.6	11.0	17.1	26.8	3.6	26.3
2004	26.7	43.6	41.1	20.6	28.4	41.3	24.3	12.1	11.0	17.2	27.0	3.6	26.5
2005	25.9	44.5	38.0	20.8	27.7	40.4	25.0	12.5	11.4	16.3	25.9	3.7	25.5
2006	24.2	44.2	35.7	20.6	25.6	38.8	25.2	12.1	11.8	16.7	25.2	3.9	24.7
2007	24.1	46.2	34.3	20.0	24.2	36.9	26.5	12.4	11.1	16.1	24.6	3.5	24.0
2008	24.9	47.4	35.3	19.9	24.9	37.5	24.6	13.1	11.2	17.6	25.1	3.3	24.5
2009	24.8	52.0	35.8	20.2	28.4	35.9	21.4	11.3	11.3	15.9	25.0	3.2	24.3
2010	24.7	51.5	36.6	20.0	26.5	34.6	21.9	11.1	11.5	17.5	25.0	3.3	24.3
2011	26.3	56.4	37.7	19.5	27.1	34.2	21.1	11.6	12.1	18.9	25.5	3.0	24.7
2012	28.7	58.2	37.7	20.7	32.7	32.1	21.4	12.5	12.5	19.2	26.5	3.1	25.9
2013	30.9	62.8	41.4	21.4	34.0	34.8	21.2	13.0	12.8	19.0	28.3	3.3	27.6

Notes

1. In some countries, this is referred to as the 'most serious offence' or 'most severe sentence' rule.
2. The Crown Court statistics for 2012 were higher as a result of the cases being sentenced for offences committed in the 2011 riots. As of August 2012, 2,138 persons had been sentenced for offences during the period of social disorder, and fully two-thirds of these were sentenced in the Crown Court (Ministry of Justice, 2012).
3. Most statistics in this chapter and the accompanying tables have been rounded to the nearest percentage for readability.
4. A suspended sentence order is a sentence of imprisonment, and as such, before imposing an SSO, a court must have satisfied the test for the imposition of custody, namely that the custody threshold has been passed.
5. Includes absolute discharge, conditional discharge, and otherwise dealt with.
6. Includes absolute discharge, conditional discharge, and otherwise dealt with.
7. Suspended sentence orders being the exception: there were only 3,161 in 1999, but almost 50,000 imposed in 2013 (Table 3.2).

References

Bottomley, K. and Pease, K. (1986) *Crime and Punishment. Interpreting the Data.* Milton Keynes: Open University Press.

Ministry of Justice (2007) *Statistical Bulletin, Sentencing Statistics, England and Wales 2006.* London: Ministry of Justice.

——— (2010) *Sentencing Statistics, England and Wales 2009, Main Bulletin Tables and Supplementary Tables* London: Ministry of Justice.

——— (2012) *Statistical Bulletin on the Public Disorder of 6th to 9th August 2011. September 2012 Update.* London: Ministry of Justice.

——— (2014) *Criminal Justice Statistics Quarterly: December 2013, Sentencing Tables.* London: Ministry of Justice.

Roberts, J.V. (2004) *The Virtual Prison. Community Custody and the Evolution of Imprisonment.* Cambridge: Cambridge University Press.

Sentencing Guidelines Council (2004) *New Sentences: Criminal Justice Act 2003.* Guideline. London: Sentencing Guidelines Council.

4
Exploring Public Knowledge of Sentencing Practices

Martina Feilzer

There has been a significant growth in research on public knowledge of sentencing over the past 20 years, often in relation to how this affects public attitudes to sentencers and sentencing. This chapter reviews the evidence on public knowledge of sentencing. This includes a critical discussion of the current ways of thinking about the relationship between public knowledge, public opinion, and sentencing practices. The chapter concludes by discussing the link between levels of public knowledge and public punitiveness, and the role and importance of communicating sentencing statistics and sentencing research in promoting greater public understanding of sentencing.

Public knowledge of crime and sentencing practices is poor

Concern about levels of public knowledge of crime, justice and sentencing is neither new nor confined to England and Wales. As long ago as 1966, a survey of public attitudes towards crime and the penal system was carried out as part of the Royal Commission on the Penal System. This investigation included items measuring public knowledge of crime trends, as well as prisons and prison life (Banks et al., 1975, p. 238). As in many surveys since, that research found that a majority of respondents overestimated crime rates and that knowledge of the judicial system was poor. The survey tested respondents' knowledge of prison life and found people to be 'generally misinformed' (ibid., pp. 229–235). As early as 1955, researchers in the United States pointed to the discrepancy between the sentences imposed by the judiciary and public views as to the appropriate punishments for a list of specified crimes (Rose and Prell, 1955, p. 248) . This has since been termed the 'punitiveness gap' between sentencers and the public (de Keijser et al., 2007, p. 132).

By the late 1970s public opinion research on crime and criminal justice was more prevalent across Europe and the United States, and in 1978, the 13th Criminological Research Conference in Strasbourg was devoted to public opinion in relation to crime and criminal justice. In line with earlier findings, researchers at the time felt that the public's knowledge of the criminal justice system was poor (Robert, 1978, p. 63) and that exposure to crime stories in the mass media could lead to a perception (whether accurate or not) of an increase in crime and, in turn, to calls for more repressive crime control policies (Van Dijk, 1978, p. 34).

Nearly 40 years later, after extensive research has documented public knowledge and opinion of crime and criminal justice, many of the above observations are still pertinent and confirmed across a number of different cultural and social contexts. Crime rates in England and Wales have been decreasing since the mid-1990s, as measured by police statistics and the British Crime Survey/Crime Survey for England and Wales (CSEW). Regardless of the statistics, a significant majority of the public (fairly consistently around 80%) believe that crime is rising, at least nationally. The misperception of crime trends has been associated with declining confidence in the criminal justice system. Knowledge of sentencing is also poor, and members of the public perceive the criminal justice system (or more specifically the courts) as being lenient towards offenders, and sentencers to be out of touch with the views of 'ordinary' people (Hutton, 2005, p. 248; Roberts and Hough, 2005, 13–15; Hough et al., 2013; Roberts et al., 2012). Hough and Roberts (2012, p. 286) report similar findings of perceived judicial leniency in South Africa, Scotland, Belgium, Germany, Barbados, and the United States. This perception of judicial leniency is considered a problem as it is thought to undermine the legitimacy of the sentencing system (de Keijser 2009, p. 48).

Why does public knowledge of sentencing matter?

Research on public knowledge and public opinion has in part been driven by the belief that a punitive public is driving sentencers to impose increasingly punitive sentences (Roberts and Hough, 2005, pp. 17–19). Thus, a perceived punitive public pushes sentencers to contribute to an ever-increasing prison population, with the prison system in England and Wales in the midst of an almost permanent prison crisis. Similarly, policymakers and legislators respond to the punitive public – whether imagined or real – by introducing more repressive crime control policies including mandatory minimum sentences for certain types of crime; and indeterminate prison sentences for certain types of offenders. Matthews (2005) provides an excellent discussion of the complexity of the concept of punitiveness and how loosely it has been used in describing the British public.

Public opinion matters, then, however poorly conceptualised or measured. Whilst it is trite to assert the importance of the public to the functioning of the criminal justice system through reporting crime, being willing to attend court as witnesses and jurors, and volunteering as magistrates and special constables, recent years have seen an expansion of the already significant involvement of the public in the criminal justice system. The past 20 years have seen the introduction of volunteer members of Youth Offending Panels, community reinvestment schemes, the introduction of locally elected police and crime commissioners, the requirement on the Sentencing Council to consider public views, and other shifts of central responsibilities from criminal justice to the local community. Thus, public views are an important consideration not only as a communication to government and as a concern for the legitimacy of sentencing practices but also as the public influence criminal justice practices directly.

The link between (the lack of) public knowledge of sentencing and public opinion, in particular the effect of a lack of public knowledge on levels of punitiveness, has been described as arising from a cognitive deficit model. This model suggests that members of the public know little about crime, criminal justice, and sentencing and this explains their perception of rising crime and their dissatisfaction with lenient sentences (Loader 2011, pp. 348–351). Proponents of the cognitive deficit model see public education campaigns as a means to gain public support for a more progressive, liberal, and rational criminal justice system. In many respects the debates around the deficit model of criminal justice are similar to those relating to public understanding of science (see Bauer et al., 2007).

In relation to public knowledge of sentencing, evidence to support the cognitive deficit model comes from three sources: the link between survey respondents' levels of education and attitudes to sentencing; methodological advances in measuring public knowledge and attitudes; and experimental research testing the impact of providing information and improving knowledge on public opinion. In some studies, the level of education of survey respondents has been shown to correlate with attitudes to crime, criminal justice and sentencing. Survey respondents with a university education are considered to be more supportive of community sentences (Maruna and King, 2004, p. 98), and years spent in education are a predictor of levels of punitiveness, with a university education carrying the most explanatory power in this regard (Maruna and King, 2009, p. 18; for a discussion of the problematic concept of punitiveness, see Hutton, 2005; Matthews, 2005).

A further source of evidence is the improved way of measuring attitudes towards sentencing by asking for specific attitudes in relation to sentencing rather than global or categorical attitudes. Providing survey respondents with vignettes of a particular offender, offence, or sentencing scenario changes responses in such a way that respondents' perceptions of appropriate sentences and/or sentencing choices fall into line with judicial practice. Finally, a variety of experimental interventions of differing scale and quality testing the hypothesis that information affects opinion show that the provision of factual information about sentencing, crime and criminal justice leads to improved attitudes and perceptions of judicial leniency, thus closing the punitiveness gap between sentencers and the public. These experiments include deliberative polls, the provision of leaflets or videos, newspaper jury experiments, and many other quasi-experimental interventions.

Measuring public knowledge of sentencing

Public knowledge of sentencing has been measured in different ways over time and across jurisdictions. Over a period of over 30 years, the British Crime Survey (now the Crime Survey for England and Wales, CSEW) included a variety of questions on public knowledge of sentencing patterns, as well as perceptions of local and national levels of crime. Establishing long-term trends on public knowledge is difficult, as different sweeps of the crime survey in England and Wales have asked differing knowledge questions. Nevertheless, previous research has shown consistently that public knowledge of sentencing practices is poor (Hutton, 2005, p. 247). Recent research by Roberts et al. (2012, pp. 1078–1079) indicates that fewer than half of those surveyed (44%) were aware that lay magistrates as well as professional judges imposed sentences. In addition, only 14% of respondents reported having heard of the Sentencing Council.

More detailed exploration of public knowledge of sentencing patterns confirms the familiar story of low levels of public knowledge. Hough et al. (2013, pp. 19–22) discuss public knowledge of sentencing patterns with reference to questions in the crime survey for England and Wales asking respondents to estimate the average custody rate for domestic burglary and rape and the average custodial sentence length for rape.

Table 4.1 summarises the findings: respondents clearly tend to underestimate sentence severity to a significant extent – ranging from 48% who largely underestimated the proportion of rapists sentenced to imprisonment to 86% of respondents who largely underestimated the custody rate for domestic burglary. In 2010–2011, the custody rate for men aged 21 or over convicted of rape was 99%; the proportion of men aged 21 or over convicted of domestic burglary was 71% (ibid., pp. 20–22).

Research carried out by the author (see Feilzer, 2007 and 2009) confirmed that not only did survey respondents know little about the sentencing trends queried but that answers were influenced by popular misconceptions about sentencing. In the local survey undertaken for the research, 84% of respondents indicated that they were guessing when responding to the question about the custody rate for adult men convicted of robbery. If respondents had indeed randomly guessed at an answer, at least 20% of the sample should have guessed correctly. However, in this survey less than 2% of those identifying themselves as 'guessers' chose the right answer – 81–100% – while nearly three-quarters (73%) 'guessed' that the rate of imprisonment for convicted robbers was between 1% and 40%, with 44% assuming that the rate of imprisonment was less than 20%. This would imply that survey respondents when forced to make a choice, despite being aware of their lack of knowledge, subscribe to certain perceptions of what the trends are (i.e., the rate of imprisonment for convicted robbers is low). (See Hough et al., 2013 for a similar conclusion.)

Table 4.1 Public estimates of the average custody rate for domestic burglary/rape, 2011

	Domestic Burglary	Rape
Overestimate of Custody Rate Burglary: > 90% Rape: N/A	2%	0
Roughly Accurate Estimate of Custody Rate *Burglary: 60% – 90%* *Rape: 80% – 100%*	*9%*	*29%*
Small Underestimate of Burglary Rate: > 50% to < 60% Rape: > 60% < 80%	<1%	23%
Large Underestimate of Burglary Rate: < 50% Rape: 60% or less	88%	48%
	100%	*100%*

Question: Out of every 100 men aged 21 or over who are tried and found guilty of house burglary / rape, how many are sent to prison?

Source: Hough et al. (2013).

Measures of public knowledge of sentencing are not sufficiently systematic to track knowledge changes over time; however, there is a clear consensus amongst academics on levels of public knowledge and there is little reason to believe aggregate knowledge levels about sentencing would have changed significantly over time. Research findings based on a significant amount of research studies from across the globe leave no doubt that the public knows little about sentencing. So, what then does this mean?

Methodological advances in measuring public knowledge and public opinion

Over the past 50–60 years, measures of public knowledge and opinion have improved considerably. Research has established that general or global questions about sentencing levels, such as the CSEW question on perceptions of sentencing, trigger scenarios of the worst offender committing the worst offences in survey respondents' minds (Roberts and Stalans, 2000, p. 223). General questions may lead to categorical responses to sentencing preferences whereas decision-making in the criminal justice process and sentencing in particular is based on an individual, case-by-case, assessment. Thus, global survey questions have been criticised for being simplistic, too general, and inadequate for assessing public attitudes to sentencing (Hough and Roberts, 1998; Roberts et al., 2011) as they are bound to elicit people's spontaneous and emotive responses, their 'gut feelings' rather than their more considered views (Stalans, 2002).

As a result of these criticisms, researchers have adopted a more nuanced approach to measuring public sentencing preferences by anchoring individual survey responses to a particular scenario, a vignette. Once members of the public are presented with detailed vignettes of offences and offenders to be sentenced, the sentences proposed fall broadly into line with the sentences imposed by the judiciary (see, for example, Hough, 1996, pp. 191–192; Hough and Moxon, 1985, p. 171; but for a slightly more complex finding using a sophisticated mixed methods study, see De Kejser et al., 2007). This is confirmed in the largest 'vignette' experiment, which compares public sentencing preferences with real-life judgments to date, the Youth Be the Judge website (see Cuthbertson 2013; ybtj.justice.gov.uk.). The site contains video clips of real-life offences, offenders, and subsequent court processes and sentencing. It allows viewers to answer a number of questions about the sentencing process and ultimately to choose a sentence. Cuthbertson (2013) analysed 74,000 user experiences collected over three years, comparing the judges' original sentence and user sentences and found that users chose the same sentence as the judge in 39% of cases; a more lenient sentence in 45% of cases, and a more severe sentence in only 16% of cases.

There were significant differences amongst You Be the Judge website users and the general public in terms of perceived leniency as measured by the CSEW; in the CSEW for 2012–2013, 69% of respondents felt that sentences were too lenient, in contrast to 41% of You Be the Judge users. Nevertheless, the analysis of the You Be the Judge website experiences indicate that going 'through the sentencing process' had an effect on users. By the end of the process, users were asked to indicate their perception of sentencer leniency again, and 28% of users who had initially indicated that they felt sentencing was too lenient, subsequently indicated that they thought sentencing was about right. These findings are very likely to be, at least in part, a result of the Hawthorne effect, discussed below, as the expectation of a change is obvious from the website interface.

Another important finding contributing evidence to the cognitive deficit model is that when members of the public are given information about both custodial and non-custodial sentences (rather than just custodial), alternatives to prison attract considerable support (Hough and Park, 2002; Maruna and King, 2004, pp. 91; Roberts et al., 2011). A feature of survey research, however, is that survey respondents and interview participants, once they have agreed to take part in research, 'accept the framework of questions and try earnestly to work within [the] framework' (Schumann and Presser, 1996, pp. 299) of the response options provided. This is similar to the finding above that survey respondents despite their awareness of their own ignorance will respond to questions about sentencing trends. It should be noted in this context that some survey respondents do so reluctantly and will note comments and criticisms of survey research on the forms. However, most survey research will ignore such comments. To regard survey results as accurate reflections of survey respondents' attitudes and beliefs ignores a considerable body of social psychological research and scholarship but also survey respondents' explicit concerns about the limitations of tick-box questionnaires (for discussion, see Feilzer 2010).

Improving knowledge through the provision of information

Social scientists have turned to a wide range of methods to test the hypothesis that improving levels of knowledge will improve public opinion. Focus groups, deliberative polls, convenience samples, and experiments have gained prominence amongst researchers. In 1994, the first deliberative poll on crime took place in Britain over a period of two days. The aim was to address the lack of knowledge on a particular issue, and elicit respondents' views after they have been given relevant information and had the chance to deliberate; thus, the deliberative poll sought to construct 'informed public opinion' (Luskin et al., 2002, pp. 458). Deliberative polling showed that the provision of information produced substantial changes in opinions and increases in levels of knowledge and that opinion changes were associated with increases in knowledge as well as, to a somewhat lesser degree, with group mechanisms (ibid., pp. 481).

The impact of the deliberative poll on participants' level of knowledge and their attitudes was measured again 10 months later. It was found that changes towards a more liberal view of sentencing had persisted, although to a lesser extent than the short-term change observed immediately after the experiment. What remained unclear, however, was whether it was the information provided that had caused the change or other aspects of the weekend, such as particularly charismatic presenters, or the small group discussions (Hough and Park, 2002, pp. 176–180). In 2001, the Home Office commissioned research exploring public views of sentencing. This study found that information improved levels of knowledge regardless of the medium used; additionally, information reduced respondents' worry about victimisation and the perception that sentencing was too lenient (Chapman, et al., 2002, pp. ix-xi).

This Home Office study was replicated in 2002–2003, when British Crime Survey respondents received a copy of the booklet used in the original research. The information was less successful in this instance: of those who had received the booklet, less than 20% of respondents had read it in full, whereas 63% had looked at some sections or flicked through it. The level of knowledge of those respondents who had looked at the book improved on some questions but not on others (Salisbury, 2004, pp. 7–9). As regards an improvement in levels of confidence in the criminal justice system, the study found that, on a number of items, the level of confidence increased for those who had looked at the booklet just as it did for a control group of British Crime Survey respondents who had *not* received the booklet (Salisbury, 2004, pp. 9–12). Thus, participation in the survey itself, or the repeat interview seemed to have increased levels of confidence in the criminal justice system (ibid., 12). This could be interpreted as a Hawthorne effect – respondents felt special by taking part (Cook and

Campbell, 1979, p. 60) – or a result of participants' greater engagement with the issues they were questioned about, and consequently, a more thoughtful response to the questions posed. This is a problem which affects many experimental research projects where the desired outcome of the research is obvious to participants (see also Maruna and King, 2004, p. 101).

A more recent experimental study on the impact of knowledge on sentencing preferences in particular was carried out by Roberts et al. (2012) on knowledge of lay magistrates and sentencing guidelines. The research used three different methods to assess the impact of information on public opinion: an experimental online survey; a laboratory-based replication; and focus groups. The authors found that providing information about the process of sentencing had a moderating impact on levels of punitiveness. It confirmed the notion that an 'information effect' can be found in experimental settings.

Experimental research on attitude change related to crime and criminal justice shows that the impact of information on levels of knowledge appears robust (at least in the short-term) whereas evidence on the impact of information on attitude and confidence is less consistent. Thus, a clear distinction has to be made between educating the public about crime and criminal justice as an end in itself, as opposed to being a means to achieving a change in public opinion, such as an improvement in confidence.

Following the research above, a number of researchers designed projects which tested the impact of factual information in a more naturalistic setting to exploit the notion that the media has a significant role in informing the public on issues of crime, criminal justice and sentencing. Researchers in the Netherlands carried out experimental research on the 'effect of media information on people's attitudes towards the justice system' (Elffers et al., 2007, p. 163). Over a year, a local Dutch newspaper reported on readers' experiences and perceptions of regularly attending criminal proceedings in court (the group of readers attending court was dubbed a 'newspaper jury'). Readers of the newspaper were surveyed (using a postal questionnaire) on their attitudes towards crime and justice. The main finding was that the change in media reporting style had no significant impact on the attitudes of the readers of the local newspaper (Elffers et al., 2007). Similarly, Feilzer (2007 and 2009) found that a weekly column about crime and criminal justice in a local newspaper did not have any significant effect on those who reported reading the columns, both in terms of changes in levels of knowledge or attitudes.

There is mixed evidence then on how much impact the provision of information has on levels of public knowledge and public opinion of crime and sentencing. The lack of effect of the provision of information in more naturalistic experiments raises some questions about the feasibility of effecting changes to public knowledge on a larger scale. These are practical considerations, however, and the section below addresses some of the more fundamental questions about the impact of public knowledge on public opinion of sentencing.

Public knowledge and a punitive public: beyond the cognitive-deficit model?

The discussion above focused on the evidence available to support the hypothesis that public knowledge and public opinion are linked. This section will review some of the assumptions at the heart of the links made between public knowledge and public opinion. It will ask the question whether it is necessary to move on from the cognitive-deficit model much in the way that the 'public understanding of science' debate has moved on. It is clear from the debate above, and the long-running debates in the political sciences and the public understanding of science, that information matters for the formation and expression of attitudes (Bauer et al., 2007, p. 87). However, in the context of sentencing it is important to explore in more detail how information is linked to particular attitudes, and most significantly, to punitiveness.

Information is important in anchoring survey respondents' attitudes to sentencing. The vignette approach has done much to improve our understanding of what members of the public think when asked questions about sentencing preferences for specific crimes and specific offenders. Additionally, providing a realistic and comprehensive range of sentencing options is necessary to measure public attitudes to sentencing more accurately. These methodological advances clearly indicate that the public is not as punitive as global and limiting questions on sentencing may suggest.

Information is also important when asking what could be termed evaluative questions. The CSEW question[1] asks respondents to express views about whether current sentencing levels are too harsh or too lenient. This is clearly a problematic global question in its breadth – respondents are asked to express their views on sentencing as a whole – from the sentencing of vandalism to murder. It is also an evaluative question based on the empirical reality of sentencing trends at a particular point in time and the answer depends on respondents' knowledge of these sentencing trends. Equally, the British Social Attitudes Survey (BSAS) has asked an evaluative question about 'stiffer sentences' routinely for more than 60 years.[2] The answers people give derive from their level of knowledge. Despite the various advances in survey methodology, these are still the main measures used when assessing the link between knowledge and public opinion.

Regardless of the validity of these measures as indicators of punitiveness, the trend data presented has some interesting implications. Figure 4.1 demonstrates that levels of punitiveness (as measured by these two questions) have remained relatively stable over the past 30 years with few upward *or* downward outliers. This is the case despite significant changes in penal policy over the past 30 years, as well as changes in public debate and governmental rhetoric in relation to crime, criminal justice, and sentencing. Given that the questions assessing perceptions of judicial leniency discussed above are methodologically problematic, it may be time to remove them from survey research and replace them with the more accurate vignette questions assessing sentencing preferences.

Finally, headline rates as used above hide important group mechanisms and variations in views. Comparative research, for example, has noted significant national differences in levels of punitive attitudes, and

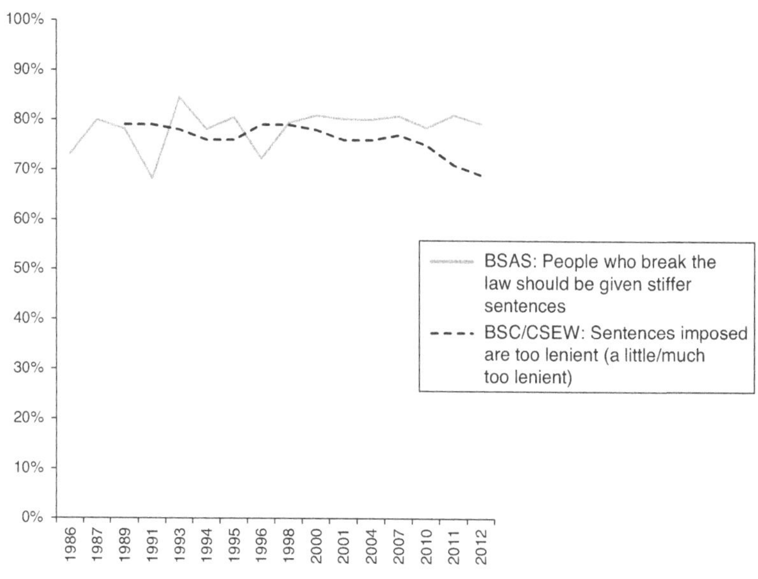

Figure 4.1 Trends in Levels of punitiveness

individual-level as well as group differences are obvious within national opinion polls (Brown, 2006; Hough and Roberts, 1998; Maruna et al., 2004, p. 278). It is difficult to reconcile these national and group differences with the interpretation that public knowledge is a primary factor in punitiveness. Existing evidence suggests that public knowledge is equally poor across different demographic groups, different countries, and time periods, so other influences must explain the dramatic cultural differences in punitiveness (for the role of culture, see Green, 2009).

Discussion

Our understanding of public knowledge of and attitudes toward sentencing has come a long way in the past 50–60 years. Empirical research supports the conclusion that public knowledge of many aspects of sentencing is poor, and we can now say with confidence that the public is not as punitive as simplistic survey methods would have us believe; in fact, public sentencing preferences in many countries are in line with judicial sentencing practices. Information clearly matters in coming to the above conclusions, as it allowed us to measure public attitudes more accurately. There is less certainty concerning the impact of providing sentencing 'facts' on public knowledge and public opinion. Public opinion in relation to crime and sentencing has an expressive or symbolic function, and it is important to acknowledge that this may limit the effect of information-based approaches to improving public knowledge and public opinion. Individual value systems, the affective dimension of narratives of crime, criminal justice, and sentencing, as well as the disputed notion of the existence of facts in criminal justice and sentencing have been neglected in the debates on how best to communicate 'facts' about criminal justice and sentencing. It may be time to move on from the idea of simply providing information to the public with the aim of making it more liberal.

Nevertheless, for those convinced that the provision of information is key to producing a more liberal, tolerant public, accepting and confident of sentencing practices and outcomes, a number of important questions remain. How much information needs to be provided until the public can be assessed as sufficiently informed? How is manipulation of the public avoided in an arena where the provision of some information about criminal justice – for example, detection and conviction rates – may not provide the desired reassurance or increase confidence? How do you define 'facts' in a pluralist criminology where agreement may be difficult to come by? How could any provision of factual information (where it may exist) compete with media narratives about sentencing and individualised stories about sentencing 'scandals'?

Public debate and the provision of relevant and interesting information about crime, criminal justice, and sentencing are important in their own right and a hallmark of mature democracies without the expectation of instrumental, consequentialist outcomes. Offering a wider range of narratives about what sentences can achieve is an important feature of this debate. Whilst there may be some suspicion of the extent to which restorative justice has been adopted as the new paradigm in sentencing, the availability of an alternative narrative to retribution and rehabilitation should be welcomed, as it allows a public debate and political rhetoric which is less constrained by notions of the toughest sentence and the most repressive criminal justice policy. The research driven by the cognitive deficit model has led to great advances in methodology and understanding of what the public knows and thinks about sentencing practices, but it may now be time to explore public opinion from a different position.

Notes

1. BCS/CSEW question: Sentences imposed by the courts are... [too harsh, too lenient or about right].
2. BSAS question: People who break the law should be given stiffer sentences.

References

Banks, C., Maloney, E., and Willcock, H.D. (1975) Public Attitudes to Crime and the Penal System. *British Journal of Criminology*, 15: 228–240.

Bauer, M.W., Allum, N., and Miller, S. (2007) What Can We Learn from 25 Years of PUS Survey Research? Liberating and Expanding the Agenda. *Public Understanding of Science*, 16: 79–95.

Brown, E. (2006) The Dog That Did Not Bark. *Punishment and Society*, 8: 287–312.

Chapman, B., Mirrlees-Black, C., and Brawn, C. (2002) *Improving Public Attitudes to the Criminal Justice System: The Impact of Information*. London: Home Office.

Cook, T., and Campbell, D. (1979) *Quasi Experimentation – Design and Analysis Issues for Field Settings*. Boston: Houghton Mifflin Company.

Cuthbertson, S. (2013) *Analysis of 'You Be the Judge' Website Experiences*. Ministry of Justice Analytical Summary. London: Crown Copyright. Accessed 7 April 2014. https://www.gov.uk/government/uploads/system/uploads/attachment_data/file/203006/Analysis_of_complete_You_be_the_Judge_website_Experiences__web_.pdf.

De Keijser, J.W., Van Koppen, P J., and Elffers, H. (2007) Bridging the Gap between Judges and the Public? A Multi-Method Study. *Journal of Experimental Criminology*, 3: 131–161.

Elffers, H., De Keijser, J.W.., Van Koppen, P.J., and Van Haeringen, L. (2007) Newspaper Juries: A Field Experiment Concerning the Effect of Information on Attitudes towards the Criminal Justice System. *Journal of Experimental Criminology,* 3: 163–182.

Feilzer, M. (2007) Criminologists Making News? Providing Factual Information on Crime and Criminal Justice through a Weekly Newspaper Column. *Crime, Media, Culture,* 3: 285–304.

Feilzer, M. Y. (2009) The Importance of Telling a Good Story – An Experiment in Public Criminology. *Howard Journal of Criminal Justice,* 48: 472–484.

Feilzer, M.Y. (2010) Doing Mixed Methods Research Pragmatically – Implications for the Rediscovery of Pragmatism as a Research Paradigm. *Journal of Mixed Methods Research,* 4: 6–16.

Green, D.A. (2009) Feeding Wolves, Punitiveness and Culture. *European Journal of Criminology,* 69: 517–536.

Hough, M. (1996) People Talking about Punishment. *The Howard Journal,* 35: 191–214.

Hough, M., Bradford, B. Jackson, J., and Roberts, J.V. (2013) *Attitudes to Sentencing and Trust in Justice.* Ministry of Justice Analytical Series. London: Crown Copyright. Accessed 7 April 2014. https://www.gov.uk/government/uploads/system/uploads/attachment_data/file/230186/Attitudes_to_Sentencing_and_Trust_in_Justice__web_.pdf.

Hough, M., and Moxon, D. (1985) Dealing with Offenders: Popular Opinion and the Views of Victims. *Howard Journal of Criminal Justice,* 24: 160–175.

Hough, M., and Park, A. (2002) How malleable are attitudes to crime and punishment? In: J.V. Roberts and M. Hough (eds) *Changing Attitudes to Punishment.* Cullompton: Willan Publishing.

Hough, M., and Roberts, J.V. (1998) *Attitudes to Punishment: Findings from the British Crime Survey.* London: Home Office.

——— (2012) Public opinion, crime and criminal justice. In: M. Maguire, R. Morgan, and R. Reiner (eds) *The Oxford Handbook of Criminology.* 5th ed. Oxford: Oxford University Press.

Hutton, N. (2005) Beyond Populist Punitiveness? *Punishment and Society,* 7: 243–258.

Loader, I. (2011) Playing with Fire? Democracy and the emotions of crime and punishment. In: S. Karstedt, I. Loader and H. Strang (eds) *Emotions and Crime.* Oxford: Hart.

Luskin, R. C., Fishkin, J.S., and Jowell, R. (2002) Considered Opinions: Deliberative Polling in Britain. *British Journal of Political Sciences,* 32: 455–487.

Maruna, S. and King, A. (2004) Public opinion and community penalties. In: A. Bottoms, S. Rex and G. Robinson (eds) *Alternatives to Prison: Options for an Insecure Society.* Cullompton: Willan.

Maruna, S. and King, A. (2009) Once a Criminal, Always a Criminal?: 'Redeemability' and the Psychology of Punitive Public Attitudes. *European Journal on Criminal Policy and Research,* 15: 7–24.

Maruna, S., Matravers, A., & King, A. (2004) Disowning Our Shadow: A Psychoanalytic Approach to Understanding Punitive Public Attitudes. *Deviant Behaviour,* 25: 277–299.

Matthews, R. (2005) The Myth of Punitiveness. *Theoretical Criminology,* 9: 175–201.

Robert, P. (1978) *Public Opinion in Relation to Crime and Criminal Justice.* Paper presented at the Thirteenth Criminological Conference, Strasbourg.

Roberts, J.V., Feilzer, M. and Hough, M. (2011) Measuring public attitudes to criminal justice. In: D. Gadd, S. Karstedt, and S. Messner (eds) *The Sage Handbook of Criminological Research Methods*. Sage: London.

Roberts, J. V., and Hough, M. (2005) *Understanding Public Attitudes to Criminal Justice*. Maidenhead: Open University Press.

Roberts, J.V., Hough, M., Jackson, J. and Gerber, M.M. (2012) Public Opinion towards the Lay Magistracy and the Sentencing Council Guidelines. *British Journal of Criminology*, 52: 1072–1091.

Roberts, J.V., and Stalans, L.J. (2000) *Public Opinion, Crime, and Criminal Justice*. Colorado: Westview Press.

Rose, A.M., and Prell, A.E. (1955) Does the Punishment Fit the Crime? A Study in Social Valuation. *The American Journal of Sociology*, 61: 247–259.

Salisbury, H. (2004) *Public Attitudes to the Criminal Justice System: The Impact of Providing Information to British Crime Survey Respondents*. Home Office Online Report 64/04). Accessed: 7 April 2014. http://217.35.77.12/CB/england/papers/pdfs/2004/rdsolr6404.pdf

Schumann, H., and Presser, S. (1996) *Questions and Answers in Attitude Surveys: Experiments in Question Form, Wording and Context*. London: Sage.

Stalans, L.J. (2002) Measuring attitudes to sentencing. In: J.V. Roberts and M. Hough (eds) *Changing Attitudes to Punishment*. Cullompton: Willan Publishing.

Sturgis, P., Roberts, C., and Allum, N. (2005) A Different Take on the Deliberative Poll. *Public Opinion Quarterly*, 69: 30–65.

Van Dijk, J. (1978) 'Public Opinion in Relation to Crime and Criminal Justice'. Paper presented at the Thirteenth Criminological Research Conference, Strasbourg.

5
Defining and Measuring Consistency in Sentencing

Jose Pina-Sánchez

Sentencing consistency, or the extent to which like cases are treated alike, is a fundamental principle of justice. It generates transparency and predictability in sentencing practices, enhances public confidence in sentencing (Council of Europe, 1993) and helps promote the legitimacy of the criminal justice system (Roberts and Plesnicar, 2015). However, the means by which this consistency in sentencing may be achieved is far from clear-cut and highly controversial.

Over the years, critics of the sentencing process have contended that unstructured discretion results in sentencing disparity. In the influential publication 'Lawlessness in Sentencing' (Frankel, 1972), Judge Marvin Frankel claimed that unstructured discretion had led to discrimination and disparity in the United States. In response, many states introduced greater structure in the sentencing process through the implementation of sentencing guidelines. These guidelines vary in structure but all share the goal of establishing objective standards so that the degree of punishment an offender receives does not depend on the values, attitudes, and beliefs of the judge (Walker, Spohn and Delone, 2007).

This move towards structuring discretion at sentencing has been adopted by other common law jurisdictions outside the United States, including England and Wales. Sentencers in England and Wales used to enjoy a substantial degree of discretion with the only restrictions on sentencers arising from statutory limits and the guidance offered by appellate review (Ashworth and Roberts, 2013, p. 1). The Criminal Justice Act 2003 tightened this flexible and highly discretionary framework, created the Sentencing Guidelines Council – an independent body responsible for generating definitive guidelines, and established a duty on courts to have regard to any guidelines produced by the council.

The Sentencing Guidelines Council produced guidelines for specific offence categories (such as assault) as well as generic guidelines applicable across all offences.[1] This development was further reinforced with the Coroners and Justice Act 2009, which created the Sentencing Council for England and Wales, endowed it with new analytical responsibilities, and made the guidelines more binding on courts.[2] The guidelines process reached a state of maturity when in June 2011, a new guideline for the assault offences came into force.[3] This new format guideline replaced the assault offences guideline issued by the former Sentencing Guidelines Council in 2007.[4] Specifically, the new guideline sought to correct some problems of applicability and to introduce a clearer and more structured stepwise process to the sentencing exercise. In the words of the first chair of the Sentencing Council, this new structure aimed to 'increase the consistency of approach to sentencing so that offenders receive the same approach whether they're being sentenced in Bristol, Birmingham, Bolton or Basildon' (Lord Justice Leveson, 2011).[5]

In spite of the interest in the new sentencing guidelines, little is known about the degree of variability in sentencing, or the effectiveness of the sentencing guidelines in promoting greater consistency. This may be explained by the elusiveness of the concept, which makes it hard to be operationalised under a quantitative approach, and also by an absence (to date at least) of adequate data. As a result of the publication of the Crown Court Sentencing Survey (CCSS), a new wave of studies on the topic has emerged.[6] These studies have employed different empirical methods and have examined different aspects of sentencing. The Sentencing Council (2012) analysed departures from the guideline ranges for some offences of assault; Roberts (2013) and Roberts and Bradford (2015) explored guilty plea reductions, while Pina-Sánchez and Linacre (2013; 2014) focused on analyses of custodial sentence length.

Overview

This chapter provides more generalizable results on the topic of consistency in sentencing by replicating most of the methods that have been implemented in earlier studies and by considering the study of custodial types. In particular, the analysis considers the use of custody versus other disposals for cases of assault. Compared to the study of consistency in sentence length, the study of disposal types is more comprehensive since it makes use of all cases, not just those that were sentenced to custody. In addition, where possible, analyses aiming to assess changes in consistency after the new assault guideline came into force have also been carried out. The next section, 'Measuring consistency in sentencing', reviews the scope and limitations of the methods used for the measurement of consistency. 'Analysis using the Crown Court's sentencing survey (CCSS)' presents results from the analysis. Finally, I conclude with a summary of the main findings.

Measuring consistency in sentencing

The simplest way to document consistency in sentencing is through the study of guidelines compliance statistics. This method involves calculating the percentage of offences that receive sentences within the ranges prescribed by the sentencing guidelines. In its most basic form, the study of compliance can be implemented in any jurisdiction structured by sentencing guidelines where individual-level data on the type of offence and the sentence outcome are available. Accordingly, it has been widely used to assess the effectiveness of the sentencing guidelines in the United States (Frase, 2005; Kramer and Ulmer, 2002; Minnesota Sentencing Guidelines Commission, 2010; Oregon Criminal Sentencing Commission, 2003; Scott, 2010; Tonry, 1987; Ulmer et al., 2011). The CCSS has permitted a comparable approach in England and Wales (Sentencing Council, 2012; Roberts, 2013).

The Sentencing Council (2012) reported the percentage of sentences imposed for actual bodily harm (ABH), grievous bodily harm (GBH), grievous bodily harm with intent (GBH with intent) and common assault that fell within the guideline ranges after the new guideline came into force. The percentages for those four offences were 97%, 97%, 92% and 99%, respectively. These results demonstrate high levels of compliance. However, since the Sentencing Council did not include analyses of trends prior to the new guideline coming into force, we cannot attribute the observed findings to the change in guidelines. These high rates of compliance may be due to the more binding nature of guidelines after the Coroners and Justice Act (2009) or simply to the very wide range of disposals available to courts within the assault guidelines. For example, for ABH, the total offence guideline range runs from a fine up to three years of custody. It may be argued that almost all sentences would have fallen within this range, even in the absence of a guideline.

In addition, although guidelines-based compliance statistics can be used to shed light on consistency, they can only be approximations of the actual measures of consistency that we are seeking. By revealing levels of departure from the guidelines, compliance statistics reflect a normative view of consistency. This is the view used in some US jurisdictions such as Minnesota or Oregon, where the guidelines aim to achieve uniformity through the implementation of a grid-based system that places offences into a limited number of categories linked to specific ranges of sentence outcomes.

Grid-based sentencing guidelines were rejected by the Sentencing Commission Working Group (2008) as being too restrictive and contrary to the traditions of English sentencing. In contrast, the system of guidelines developed in England and Wales seeks to promote consistency of approach. This is achieved by assisting sentencers in determining the most appropriate sentence outcome using a structured decision-making process that incorporates the legal factors relevant in each case. The logic of the guidelines is that if all sentencers follow the same methodical approach, sentencing outcomes will become more consistent. In this way, consistency can be promoted without undermining the judicial discretion necessary to differentiate between cases.

To obtain estimates that better differentiate consistency from uniformity, we need to use methods that overcome the simple measures of compliance rates (i.e. whether sentences fall within or without the guidelines range). One such method is 'exact matching' (Hofer et al., 1999, and Pina-Sánchez and Linacre, 2014). This method involves combining offences into groups that are as homogenous as possible and exploring the variability of sentence outcomes observed within each of these groups.[7] This procedure reflects a direct operationalization of the concept of consistency as it is commonly understood: the extent to which like cases are treated alike. By the use of matched groups, we can ensure that offences are as 'alike' as possible, and by the study of the within group variability we assess how 'alike' they are being treated. Pina-Sánchez and Linacre (2014) used this approach to assess changes in the variability of sentence lengths for assault after the new guideline came into force. They found that more than half (57%) of the groups of offences showed less variability after the new guideline came into force, while the overall variability decreased by 7%.

Other methods used in the literature have complemented the study of the variability within types of offences by examining whether that variability is a result of differences in sentencing between courts. In this way, different measures can be obtained that respond to a broader definition of consistency: the extent to which similar offences attract similar sentences regardless of where they are sentenced. Tarling (2006) and Mason et al. (2007) used descriptive statistics to explore the degree of variability between courts in England and Wales. Tarling (2006) compared custody rates for burglary in 30 magistrates' courts in 1974 and 2000, while Mason et al. (2007) explored variability in custody rates, sentence lengths, and other disposal types across the 42 criminal justice areas from 2003 to 2006. Both studies found substantial differences among courts or criminal justice areas, although such variability remained relatively constant during the periods studied.

Tarling (2006) found that differences among magistrates' courts with the highest and lowest uses of custodial sentences and fines in 1975 ranged by 17.7% and 30.1%, respectively, and those differences remained relatively unchanged after replicating the analysis using data from the year 2000. Interestingly, Tarling found even greater variation in the use of various disposal types between courts after replicating the analysis for offences of burglary only. For example, the use of fines ranged by 22 percentage points, while that of custodial sentences reached 32.

Mason et al. (2007) explored disparities across magistrates' and Crown Courts in the use of custodial rates, custodial sentence length, and indeterminate sentences for public protection. Similar results demonstrating high variability were found for the three sentence outcomes and the two sentencing courts. For example, from 2003 to 2006, the range in the use of custodial rates between Crown Courts remained stable at an average of 24 percentage points. Specifically, in 2006, the use of custody rate ranged from 45% to 68%. The authors also pointed out that the majority of courts were close to the average of 56% and that just a few courts showing more extreme results created the wider range. Furthermore, disparities appeared to be systematic over time for certain courts. Of those with custody rates in the top five for 2006, two (Northamptonshire and Bedfordshire) were consistently in the top five for 2003, 2004 and 2005, whereas from those in the bottom five for 2006, one (Northumbria) was consistently in the bottom five for 2003, 2004 and 2005.

Interpreting variability

As noted earlier, the problem with using these descriptive measures of between court variability is that one cannot tell whether the observed differences are due to a genuine lack of consistency or to differences in the composition of offences sentenced in each court. For example, in the study of variability of custodial rates using offences of assault, we would expect that courts where serious cases (e.g., GBH with intent) are more prevalent will have higher custody rates than those where common assaults are the most frequent offence.

This problem could be partially addressed by restricting the analysis to specific offences. However, we would still expect a substantial level of legitimate variability in sentencing within relatively diverse offences such as ABH or common assault. In order to overcome this problem of unexplained heterogeneity within types of offences, we can use a statistical technique known as 'multilevel modelling'. This technique allows us to control simultaneously for the multiple legal factors defining an offence while reporting different estimates of variability among courts.

The majority of examples of multilevel models applied to the study of consistency stem from the United States (Anderson, Kling and Stith, 1999; Anderson and Spohn, 2010; Ulmer, Light and Kramer, 2011). One exception is Pina-Sánchez and Linacre (2013) who applied these techniques to study consistency in sentence lengths for offences of assault, robbery and burglary in England and Wales. The authors reported substantial levels of consistency. Specifically, one of their models for assault estimated that only 1.8% of the variation in sentence length was attributable to sentencing differences across courts (Pina-Sánchez and Linacre, 2013, p. 1119). However, substantial disparities were found with regards to the way specific aggravating factors are taken into account. The most serious case related to disparities in the weight of the aggravating factor of 'sustained assault on the same victim'. For example, for an offence of ABH where this aggravating factor was present, but with no other aggravating or mitigating factors, the average custodial length was 8.1 months, ranging from 6.4 to 9.8 months depending on the court being sentenced (Pina-Sánchez and Linacre, 2013, p.1120).

Analysis using the Crown Court Sentencing Survey (CCSS)

Compliance and exact matching

The first measure of consistency to be explored is the guideline compliance rates. The analysis compares the 'before' and 'after' scenarios for GBH with intent. Both the old and new guidelines recommended a minimum of three years custody, which makes this offence an ideal case to be studied using compliance rates since only one disposal type is covered. In 2011, 95% of GBH with intent offences were sentenced to custody, and a comparison between the same offences sentenced from January to May with those between July and December shows an increase of compliance rates from 94% to 97%.[8] This change is relatively modest, but it is statistically significant, which demonstrates a positive effect of the new guideline.[9] Simply put, for the case of GBH with intent, sentencers were more likely to comply with the prescribed outcome after the new guideline came into force.

This preliminary analysis using compliance rates can be complemented with the implementation of exact matching. In particular, the analysis of GBH with intent offences presented above is explored through the use of matched groups using the seven most prevalent sentencing factors found in offences of assault:

- the number of previous convictions
- whether the offender:
  - showed remorse
  - pleaded guilty at first opportunity
  - was a member of a gang
  - acted under the influence of alcohol or drugs
  - targeted a vulnerable victim
  - perpetrated a repeated or sustained assault against the same victim

This approach permits estimation of consistency in sentencing for specific types of offences with a remarkable degree of accuracy.[10] We can explore the high levels of compliance across GBH with intent offences, and determine how the proportion of cases attracting a custodial sentence varies according to the legal factors that define the offence. For example, in cases of GBH with intent with no previous convictions, guilty plea not entered at first opportunity, and no aggravating and mitigating factors, offenders are sentenced to custody 88.5% of the time. The degree of variability increases even more for offences like the one just described and where the offender also shows remorse. In such cases, the use of custody drops slightly to 85.5%. On the other hand, similar cases where no remorse was shown, and the assault was sustained on the same victim, sentences are remarkably consistent, with 96.2% of offenders being sentenced to custody.

Although very precise, these results are not perfect measures of consistency, since in addition to the type of offence and the seven most prevalent aggravating and mitigating factors, there are other relevant legal factors that were not considered in the generation of matched groups. It would be impossible to account for all the relevant legal factors using this approach, since for every additional factor, the number of groups is duplicated.[11] This fact highlights a trade-off between the precision with which matched groups are created and the number of observations contained in each one of them. Thus, some of the variability reported here might be due to legitimate differences between the cases.

Between court variability and multilevel modelling

If we replicate the study of the between-court variability used in Tarling (2006) and Mason et al. (2007), we can see that the average custodial rate for assault in 2011 across Crown Courts was 47.5%, with a majority of courts reporting a custodial rate close to this average. However, the level of geographical dispersion is much greater if we examine the range between courts with the highest and lowest custody rates, which amounts to 39%. This is shown in Figure 5.1, where the custody rates for each court are plotted, with Winchester (a custodial rate of 28.2%) and Dorchester (67.6%) at the lower and upper limits of that range.

Performing the same analysis for offences imposed before and after the new guideline came into force reveals a reduction in variability. The average custody rates amongst courts stayed at 47% in both periods, but their standard deviations and ranges decreased from 10.7 to 9.3 and from 53.7 to 42.7 percentage points, respectively, which suggests an improvement in consistency. The next analysis replicates those reported by Pina-Sánchez and Linacre (2013) while shifting the focus from custodial sentence length to the use of custodial sentences (as opposed to other disposals). This increases the sample from 5,527 to 12,508 cases and thus enhances the generalizability and precision of the analysis.

The models employed distinguish between the ten most common assault offences.[12] In addition, to address differences between cases, these models also control for the ten most prevalent aggravating and mitigating factors. Ideally, the analysis should incorporate all of the legal factors considered in the guidelines and recorded by the CCSS. However, the change in assault guidelines was followed by a change in the survey forms, resulting in substantial differences in structure and wording. In order to avoid inconsistencies, the analysis is restricted to factors presented similarly in both CCSS forms.

- Whether a guilty plea was entered
- Whether the plea was entered at the first reasonable opportunity
- The number of previous convictions taken into account
- Whether the offender
  - showed remorse
  - was the main carer of a dependent person, and/or perpetrated on a vulnerable person
  - was a member of a gang

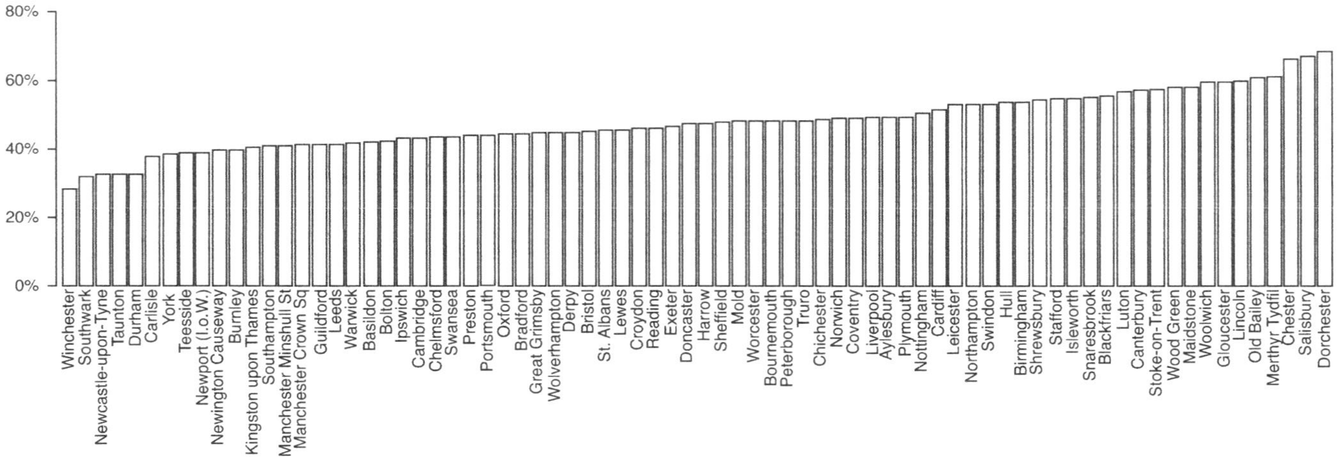

Figure 5.1 Custody rates for assault offences by court

- committed an offence against a public worker
- was under the effect of drugs
- committed a sustained or repeated on the same victim

Results reveal levels of dispersion amongst courts that are relatively low although statistically significant.[13] For example, the custodial rate before the new guideline came into force for a reference case of an offence of common assault with no aggravating and mitigating factor ranged from 10% to 29%.[14] It is striking to compare this range of 19 percentage points with that of 39.4 percentage points found for all offences of assault shown in Figure 5.1. The two figures are not entirely comparable, as the former represents variability for a very specific type of common assault. However, this difference in ranges larger than 20 percentage points illustrates very clearly how biased measures of between court variability using descriptive statistics can be.

In addition, it is interesting to note that after the new guideline came into force, the range for common assault narrowed to an interval running from 13% to 29%. This was due to a slight increase in sentence severity for common assault and a small reduction in 'between courts' variability. Furthermore, although there are some differences in the use of custodial sentences between courts, those differences are not systematic. This is shown in Figure 5.2, which presents the different probabilities of being sentenced to custody for the reference case of common assault in the ten most extreme courts before and after the guideline came into force.

Specifically, none of the courts that were amongst the ten with the lowest or highest probabilities of sentencing to custody in the pre-guideline period can be found amongst the same bottom or top positions after the new guideline came into force. As can be seen in Figure 5.2,

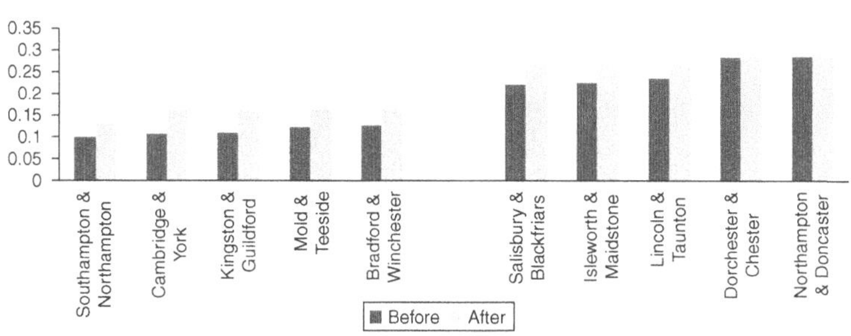

Figure 5.2 Top ten courts with highest and lowest probabilities of custody for common assault before and after the new guideline came into force

Southampton, Cambridge, Kingston, Mold and Bradford led the ranking of 'most lenient' courts before the guideline came into force. Salisbury, Isleworth, Lincoln, Dorchester and Northampton were amongst the harshest. However, after the arrival of the new guideline, none of these courts could be found amongst the same extreme positions. This finding is interesting for two reasons. First, it challenges the results of Mason et al. (2007) that suggested systematic differences existed in the use of custody between courts over time. Second, it illustrates the greater accuracy in the measurement of consistency using multilevel models, which suggest lower levels of variability than previously reported in the literature.

In order to explore the extent to which these positive findings can be generalised beyond cases of common assault, the analysis was replicated to other offences of assault such as affray, ABH, GBH, and GBH with intent, where no aggravating or mitigating factors were present in each of them. The results are presented in Figure 5.3, in which circles denote the average probability of custody for each reference case, and vertical lines around those circles reflect their between court variability.

Figure 5.3 reveals that the level of between court variability differs substantially across the cases studied. There are some cases that attract a higher consensual response than others. For offences where the probability to be sentenced to custody is either very high or very low (such as GBH with intent or common assault) the levels of consistency are

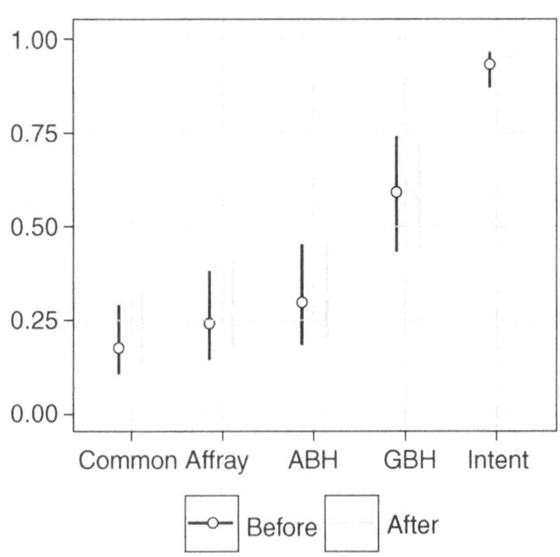

Figure 5.3 Between courts variability in the probability of custody before and after the new guideline came into force[15]

remarkably high, whereas offences that have a probability of being sentenced to custody close to .5 (such as affray, ABH, and GBH) show lower levels of consistency. A second important finding to note is that consistency improved in all the offences studied after the new guideline came into force. That improvement was less noticeable for the reference cases of common assault and affray than for GBH with intent, which became almost perfectly consistent.

As can be seen, consistency improved in all the offences studied after the new guidelines came into effect. In addition, it is important to note that in spite of the accuracy achieved by the measures of variability plotted in Figure 5.3, they are not perfect measures since some of the between court variability will be due to legitimate legal factors considered by sentencers that could not be included in the models. Hence, the actual levels of between court variability will be lower than those reported here, which makes us more confident about the overall level of consistency amongst offences of assault sentenced in the Crown Courts.

To conclude the analysis, I present results obtained using multilevel models capable of estimating the between court variability in the application of specific aggravating and mitigating factors.[16] This approach can also explore the degree of consistency in the sentencing process, as opposed to the measures of consistency in the sentence outcome seen so far. In particular, I studied the effect of remorse and the aggravating factor 'sustained assault': two legal factors that were found to exercise a significant influence over custody rates under the exact matching approach. To observe the between court variability in the application of those factors amongst different reference cases before and after the new guideline came into force, results from their respective multilevel models were plotted in Figure 5.4.

Figure 5.4 reveals that the degree of between court variability in the application of the aggravating factor, sustained assault, is significant, which corroborates Pina-Sánchez and Linacre's findings (2013) where the degree of inconsistency was measured in custodial sentence length. On the other hand, for the application of remorse, we can see a more common approach across courts. These results could be due to the greater importance assigned to sustained assault than to remorse in the new assault guidelines: the former is a step one factor whilst the latter is a step two factor. However, given the high levels of disparity observed, we should consider the possibility that there are significant differences in the way this factor is interpreted by sentencers. In addition, as was observed in Figure 5.3, it is offences where the probability of being sentenced to custody is not close to 0 or 1 where variability

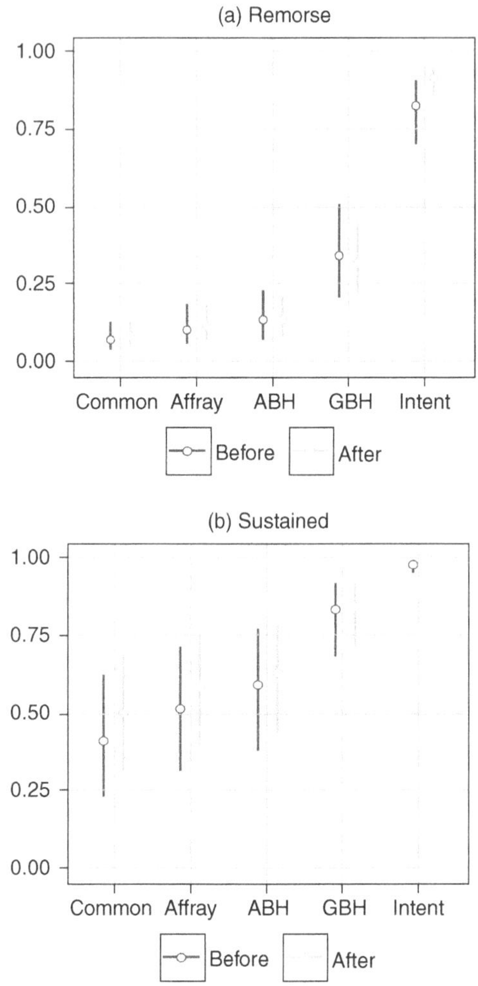

Figure 5.4 Variability in the probability of custody, considering aggravating and mitigating factors, before and after the new guideline came into force[17]

between courts is more noticeable. Finally, it is reassuring to observe that after the new guideline came into force, the level of variation between courts shrunk in all the cases studied, although that reduction was more striking in the application of the mitigating factor of remorse than the aggravating factor of a sustained assault.

Conclusions

Until recently, studies on sentencing consistency in England and Wales were rare and methodologically limited. The arrival of the CCSS has radically changed matters. Thanks to its level of detail with regards to the factors taken into account by courts, new and more accurate analyses have become possible (Sentencing Council, 2012; Pina-Sánchez and Linacre, 2013 and 2014; Roberts, 2013). However, our understanding of the subject remains partial since each of these studies has explored consistency using different samples of offences and different methodologies.

The analysis presented here can be summarised in two main conclusions:

1) The level of consistency in sentencing is higher than found in previous studies using simple descriptive statistics (e.g., Tarling, 2006; Mason et al., 2007). Whether the level of consistency is acceptable or not is a matter of opinion. My conclusion would be that the level of consistency for the Crown Courts of England and Wales in 2011 seems adequate, although some variation remains in the application of certain aggravating factors, such as sustained assault, that might need to be reviewed in future guidelines.
2) Consistency in sentencing improved after the new guidelines, regardless of the method used to assess that change. The majority of measures suggest modest but detectable increases in consistency after the new assault guideline came into force. More generally, results from the multilevel models showed decreases in between-court variability for all the most frequent offences of assault. In particular, considering a reference case of common assault with no aggravating or mitigating factors, the range in the use of custodial sentences between the most severe and the most lenient courts decreased from 19 to 16 percentage points. Moreover, none of the courts among the ten harshest and ten most lenient before the new guideline came into force could be found in the same bottom or top positions after the arrival of the guideline, which suggests an absence of systematic inconsistencies between courts in 2011.

Finally, more research into consistency is necessary. It could be argued that the changes we have observed over a period of six months are only temporary, or that the higher consistency observed responds to the effect of a different process, such as the more binding nature of the guidelines brought about by the Coroners and Justice Act 2009. Additional releases of data from the CCSS will allow us to increase both the statistical power and the timespan covered by the analysis, enabling us to explore such issues in the future.

Notes

I would like to thank Robin Linacre for his willingness to engage in methodological discussions on the measurement of consistency and for contributing to the analyses presented here.

1. For example, the definitive guideline on sentence reductions for a guilty plea (see Sentencing Guidelines Council, 2007).
2. The act provides that *'Every court must, in sentencing an offender, follow any sentencing guidelines which are relevant to the offender's case...unless the court is satisfied that it would be contrary to the interests of justice to do so'* (s.128 (1) (a) Coroners and Justice Act, 2009), whilst under previous legislation, courts were only required to 'have regard to' sentencing guidelines (s.172, Criminal Justice Act, 2003).
3. The new assault guideline can be downloaded at http://sentencingcouncil.judiciary.gov.uk/docs/Assault_definitive_guideline_-_Crown_Court.pdf.
4. The old assault guideline can be downloaded at http://webarchive.nationalarchives.gov.uk/20100305172947/http://www.sentencing-guidelines.gov.uk/guidelines/council/final.html.
5. This excerpt is part of an interview with the BBC, which can be downloaded at http://www.bbc.co.uk/news/uk-12681250.
6. See Chapter 1 of this volume for a description of the CCSS.
7. For example, the United States Sentencing Commission (1991) matched offences of cocaine/heroine distribution into groups using factors such as the amount of drugs, injury caused to any victims, the defendant's role in the offence, criminal record, and whether the defendant pleaded guilty.
8. The number of offences of GBH with intent sentenced in the before and after period as defined here are 449 and 546, respectively.
9. The difference in proportions was tested using the value of Pearson's chi-squared test statistic, which was equal to 4.24, with p-value .04.
10. In order to obtain robust estimates, I only considered matched groups that comprise at least 50 cases.
11. This problem is known as the curse of dimensionality (Bellman, 1961).
12. These are ABH, GBH, GBH with intent, common assault, affray, assault with the intent to resist an arrest, assault on a police constable, fear or provocation of violence, harassment, and violent disorder.
13. These findings are based on the statistically significant variance of the random intercepts both before and after the guideline came into force.
14. Results from the random intercepts multilevel logit models used here should be interpreted in terms of probabilities; however, for the sake of facilitating the comparability of results with previous, they are often reported here as percentages.

15. The vertical lines around each circle represent the 95% confidence intervals calculated using the standard deviations of the random intercept term.
16. Specifically, this analysis is carried out using random slopes models, which could be considered to offer more robust measures of between court variability. See Pina-Sánchez and Linacre (2013) for a discussion on how random slopes estimates offer more robust measures of consistency in the presence of omitted relevant variables than random intercept estimates.
17. The vertical lines around each circle represent the 95% confidence intervals calculated using the standard deviations of the random slopes term for remorse (left) and sustained assault (right).

References

Anderson, J., Kling, J. and Stith, K. (1999) Measuring Inter-Judge Sentencing Disparity: Before and After the Federal Sentencing Guidelines. *Journal of Law & Economics*, 42: 271–307.

Anderson, A. and Spohn, C. (2010) Lawlessness in the Federal Sentencing Process: A Test for Uniformity and Consistency in Sentence Outcomes, *Justice Quarterly*, 27: 362–393.

Ashworth, A., and Roberts, J. (2013) The origins and nature of the sentencing guidelines in England and Wales. In: A. Ashworth and J.V. Roberts (eds) *Sentencing Guidelines. Exploring the English Model*. Oxford: Oxford University Press.

Bellman, R. E. (1961) *Adaptive Control Processes: A Guided Tour*. Princeton: Princeton University Press.

Council of Europe (1993) Consistency in Sentencing. *Legal Issues*, 92. http://book.coe.int/EN/ficheouvrage.php?PAGEID=36&=EN&produit_aliasid=809.

Frankel, M. (1972) Lawlessness in Sentencing. *University of Cincinnati Law Review*, 41(1):1.

Frase, R.S. (2005) Sentencing Guidelines in Minnesota, 1978–2003. *Crime and Justice*, 32: 131–219.

Kramer, J. and Ulmer, J. (2002) Downward Departures for Serious Violent Offenders: Local Court 'Corrections' to Pennsylvania's Sentencing Guidelines. *Criminology*, 40: 807–932.

Mason, T., de Silva, N., Sharma, N., Brown, D. and Harper, G. (2007) *Local Variation in Sentencing in England and Wales*. London: Ministry of Justice.

Minnesota Sentencing Guidelines Commission (2012) *Sentencing Practices: Controlled Substance Offenses Sentenced in 2010*. http://www.leg.state.mn.us/docs/2013/other/130860.pdf.

Oregon Criminal Sentencing Commission (2003) *Sentencing Practices: Summary Statistics for Felony Offenders Sentenced in 2001*. http://www.oregon.gov/CJC/docs/SG01v2.pdf.

Pina-Sanchez, J, and Linacre, R. (2013) Sentence Consistency in England and Wales: Evidence from the Crown Court Sentencing Survey. *British Journal of Criminology*, 53: 1118–1138.

——(2014) *Impact of the 2011 England and Wales Assault Guidelines*. Available from authors.

Roberts, J. (2013) Complying with sentencing guidelines: latest findings from the Crown Court Sentencing Survey. In: A. Ashworth and J.V. Roberts, (eds) *Sentencing Guidelines*. Oxford: Oxford University Press.

Roberts, J.V. and Bradford, B. (2015) Sentence Reductions for a Guilty Plea: New Empirical Evidence from England and Wales. *Journal of Empirical Legal Studies*, in press.

Roberts, J. and Plesnicar, M. (2015) Legitimacy and the Sentencing Process. In: G. Meszko and J. Tankebe (eds) *Legitimacy and Criminal Justice in Europe*. Amsterdam: Springer.

Sentencing Commission Working Group (2008) *Sentencing Guidelines in England and Wales: An Evolutionary Approach*. London: SCWG.

Sentencing Council (2012) *Crown Court Sentencing Survey: Annual Publication, 2011*. http://sentencingcouncil.judiciary.gov.uk/docs/CCSS_Annual_2011.pdf.

Sentencing Guidelines Council (2007) *Sentence Reductions for a Guilty Plea. Definitive Guideline*. London: Sentencing Guidelines Council.

Scott, R. (2010) Inter-Judge Sentencing Disparity After Booker: A First Look, *Express*. http://works.bepress.com/ryan_scott/2/.

Tarling, R. (2006) Sentencing Practice in Magistrates' Courts Revisited. *The Howard Journal*, 45: 29–41.

Tonry, M. H. (1987) *Sentencing Reform Impacts*. Rockville: National Institute of Justice.

Ulmer, J., Light, M. and Kramer, J. (2011) The 'Liberation' of Federal Judges' Discretion in the Wake of the Booker/Fanfan Decision: Is There Increased Disparity and Divergence between Courts? *Justice Quarterly*, 28: 799–837.

von Hirsch, A., Ashworth, A., Roberts, J. (2009) *Principled Sentencing: Readings on Theory and Policy*. Portland: Hart Publishing.

Walker, S., Spohn, C. and Delone, M. (2007) *The Color of Justice: Race, Ethnicity, and Crime in America*. Belmont: Wadsworth.

6
Sentencing Women: An Analysis of Recent Trends

Carol Hedderman and Rebecca Barnes

This chapter analyses changes in the sentencing of women between 2000 and 2012. We update an earlier analysis conducted by Hedderman (2004) which explored why the number of women going to prison increased so steeply between 1992 and 2000. Since 2000, there have been important changes in sentencing policies and government responses to women offenders. Media portrayals have also shifted to emphasise a 'ladette' culture of female drinking, anti-social behaviour and violence. This chapter reflects on the consequences of these changes and considers how the sentencing of women has changed since 2000, including the use of custody and new sentences such as suspended sentence orders. It examines how far Labour's policy of diverting women from custody during its second term of office fed through into court practice, and it assesses what has happened since the Conservative-Liberal Democrat coalition took power.

Drawing on analyses of official statistics and on a recent interview study with a small sample of magistrates and judges, the findings indicate that whilst overall the use of custody appears to have remained fairly static, there are interesting differences between the sentencing practices of magistrates and Crown Court sentencers. Moreover, rather than witnessing significant shifts between immediate custody and noncustodial options for women, a key finding of this analysis concerns the shifting landscape within noncustodial sentencing, particularly the increasing use of suspended sentence orders, introduced in the Criminal Justice Act (2003) as an alternative to custody, which seem instead to be used in place of other lower-tariff community orders (Stanley, 2009).

The chapter concludes by raising concerns about how this shift, combined with the restriction of judicial discretion when orders are breached, may lead noncustodial sentences to become precursors, rather than alternatives, to custody. Community-based options for women who offend have been developed in the light of evidence concerning differences in their offending-related needs and responses to punishment, especially prison (for example, the Together Women project, discussed later in this chapter). It is important that sentencers, particularly magistrates, are informed of the value of such facilities and understand that using them in place of custody constitutes an appropriate rather than an unduly favourable response to most women who offend.

Understanding the context

In the eight years leading up to the new millennium, the number of women in prison more than doubled to reach 3,350 (Home Office, 2001a). Previous research concluded that this was because of changing criminal justice responses to female offenders rather than changes in underlying offending (Hedderman, 2004). Hedderman's analysis found that there had been a move away from cautioning and towards sending women to court, together with a generally harsher sentencing climate. Thus, when women reached court and were convicted, even those dealt with for minor offences were much more likely to receive a custodial sentence. Most strikingly, a third of the additional women being sentenced to prison over this period were convicted of theft and handling, and the proportionate use of custody for this group rose more than for any other offence (Hedderman, 2004).

There are at least three reasons to think that the sentencing of women is likely to have changed since 2000. First, there have been a number of legislative changes that could be expected to have implications for the treatment of women in the criminal justice system. Second, for at least part of this period, diverting women from custody was an explicit government policy objective. This included devoting funds to develop local community-based support services for women offenders. Third, official statistics suggest that the female prison population has changed over this period. While this could be related to recall and release decisions, it may also indicate a change in sentencing behaviour. More speculatively, some media reports suggest that women's offending behaviour has also changed and that women in particular have become more violent. If this is true, or simply perceived to be true by sentencers, this may also affect the sentences women receive.

Legislative changes to the sentencing environment

Between 1997 and 2008, the Labour government put forward more than 50 criminal justice bills and created more than 3000 new criminal offences (Travis, 2007; Open University, 2008–2009). Some of these changes have had significant implications for the sentencing of women, not least through the Criminal Justice Act (2003) (henceforth CJA 2003) and the Equality Acts of 2006 and 2010.

The CJA 2003 substantially revised the range of noncustodial sentences available to the courts. In particular, it introduced suspended sentence orders (SSOs), which were expected to reduce the use of purely custodial sentences. The Act also combined most other forms of community orders, which had previously all held different places on the sentencing tariff, into options which could be imposed as part of a single generic community order (CO) (Mair, Cross and Taylor, 2008). The CJA 2003 also created the Sentencing Guidelines Council, the precursor to the current Sentencing Council, whose guidance was expected to discourage sentencers from imposing too many conditions as part of a CO or using SSOs instead of noncustodial options.[1] This is important, as sentencers had sometimes previously been found to skip lower steps on the tariff when sentencing women (Dowds and Hedderman, 1997); reducing the number of steps might be expected to exacerbate this tendency. Unfortunately, as Stanley (2009) has shown, the SSO has replaced other community sentences more often than it has replaced custody for women. This then leads to women entering custody if they fail to comply, especially as the CJA 2003 also decreased magistrates' discretion to use noncustodial measures when dealing with breach.

The expansion of equality legislation has also influenced the sentencing of women. While Section 95 of the Criminal Justice Act 1991 required the government to publish information intended to help in combating discrimination on the grounds of gender, race or other 'improper grounds', the Equality Act 2006 placed a legal duty on public bodies to actively promote gender equality and eliminate discrimination. The Equality Act 2010 goes even further in that it requires public bodies to demonstrate compliance with that duty and to set equality objectives. This can include the use of special measures, as the 2010 Act recognises that gender inequality is 'persistent, durable and institutionalised' (Fawcett Society, 2013, p.11). Its decision to review the equality duty suggests that the coalition government is resiling from this position, as do the cuts it has made to the funding of bodies responsible for ensuring that the duty is upheld, and its statements characterising the duty as 'red tape' (ibid, p. 7.). However, as discussed below, divergent understandings of gender equality mean that, for some, this requires different responses to women in recognition of their different needs. For others, achieving equality involves subjecting men and women to the same response regardless of any preexisting differences between them.

Recent policy changes in relation to the sentencing of women

The Labour government (1997–2010) eventually responded to the increased use of custody for women by publishing a strategy which was aimed at reducing women's involvement in crime and diverting them from prosecution and prison (Home Office, 2004a). Arguably, this policy was not very effectively implemented, except insofar as it, and the subsequent Corston Review (2007), led to the government funding the development of community-based services for women (Hedderman, 2010). These services were aimed at securing women's access to the help they needed in relation to problems such as substance misuse, mental health, social isolation, poverty and housing.[2] It was assumed that increasing the availability of such services would, in itself, lead the police and courts to eschew the use of custody for women, though there are indications that this has not happened (Jolliffe et al., 2011; Hedderman and Gunby, 2013).

Early announcements by the coalition government's first Secretary of State for Justice, Ken Clarke, about the general ineffectiveness of prison and his decision to ring-fence the funding of women's centres, indicated that he would continue to support the policy of diverting women from the criminal justice system (Hedderman and Gunby, 2013). However, the consequences of other criminal justice policy developments, such as the decision to adopt a 'payment by results' approach, seemed likely to undo some of the progress made in securing good quality services for women in the community (Gelsthorpe and Hedderman, 2012). Under his replacement, Chris Grayling, the ring-fenced budget for women's services has disappeared, and a much more mixed message on women is emerging. On the one hand, Grayling's 'transforming rehabilitation' strategy (Ministry of Justice, 2013a) acknowledges that women's offending differs from men's, and that different responses may therefore be desirable. On the other, this acknowledgement appears not to have affected the government's commissioning and implementation plans in any material respect. A weakening in the government's commitment to diverting women is also signalled by its rejection of the Justice

Select Committee's recommendation to strengthen its advisory board on female offenders, and its statement that, 'Whilst women have some different needs to men, the Government believes that there should be one justice system for all offenders who commit crimes. It does not agree that prison is ineffective.' (Ministry of Justice, 2013b, p. 5)

Given these shifting policy messages about the needs of women offenders, the use and value of custody, and the support for – and then retreating from – diversion for women, it is timely to update Hedderman's (2004) analysis of the sentencing of women between 1992–2000 by examining sentencing trends post-2000.

Data sources for this analysis

The analysis in this chapter examines changes in the sentencing of adult women (i.e., aged 21 and over) between 2000 and 2012, drawing mainly on official statistics in England and Wales. Younger women and girls have been excluded from the analysis because of differences in the sentencing options available for them. Annual statistics are used because these smooth out short-term volatility and enable changes over time to be monitored. These statistics are usually published 12 to 18 months after the period to which they relate, so the chapter covers the period to 2012, the latest available at the time of writing (March 2014). Where figures are taken from several sources, this is noted, as are changes or omission in annual series.

This fresh statistical analysis is complemented by the findings of a recent small-scale interview study with twenty sentencers. The latter was conducted as part of a Home Office evaluation of the Together Women project (TWP), a government-funded, community-based initiative run at five centres in the North of England between 2007 and 2010 (see Hedderman and Gunby, 2013; Hedderman, Palmer and Hollin, 2008). Five semi-structured group interviews took place involving fourteen magistrates from four courts and six sentencers (five judges and one recorder) were interviewed at four Crown Court centres. Interviews lasted from forty minutes to just under an hour and a half, and all but two were recorded and transcribed.[3] The interviews explored sentencers' perceptions of women's offending, how they make decisions about the use of custody, and their views on the value of TWP and whether it offers a viable alternative to custody.

The interview sample comprised experienced sentencers: all had at least five years' experience, with judges having on average twelve years, and magistrates fifteen years. Equal numbers of men and women were interviewed, and all but one were white. Given the small size of the sample, no claims can be made to its representativeness; nonetheless, the interview data help to contextualise some of the statistical findings and provide valuable insights into sentencers' priorities and practices.

Changes to the sentenced prison population

The annual prison population statistics show that the sentenced male prison population rose by 43% between 2000 and 2012, and the female population rose by 34% (Ministry of Justice, 2013c). The year-on-year changes for both men and women show that the largest increase was greatest in the early part of this period, preceding policy changes aimed at reducing the number of women going into custody and the more widespread availability of women's community-based support services (Table 6.1).

The size of the sentenced prison population is also determined by the length of sentences being imposed currently and in previous years, and by decisions to release and recall offenders from and to prison. Moreover, even if the number of women sent to prison over this period increased, this is not in itself a sign that sentencing has become more severe, as this could be related to changes in the number and types of women coming before the courts for sentence. These possibilities will be explored in the next section.

Has the profile of women coming before the courts changed?

Increases in the number of girls and women arrested for violence were, initially at least, treated by the media as a sign that women are becoming more violent (for example, Ford, 2009; McVeigh, 2009; Whitehead, 2009). However, this seems to have had at least as much to do with changes in the police response to such behaviour as changes in the behaviour itself (Hedderman, 2010). What is important in terms of current sentencing is whether the profile of women coming before the courts has changed and whether sentencers think it has changed, even if it has not .

Interviews with sentencers revealed that some believed that women's offending had become more prevalent and more serious. Magistrates who sat in courts devoted to dealing with drug offences and traffic courts were particularly likely to think that the number of women had increased so much that they now dealt with equal numbers of men and women. Moreover, whilst sentencers generally agreed that most female

Table 6.1 The prison population under sentence 2000–2012

	2000	2001	2002	2003	2004	2005	2006	2007	2008	2009	2010	2011	2012
Men	42,822	43,545	46,128	48,458	50,189	51,327	52,368	54,007	56,270	56,882	57,088	59,951	61,394
% change		2%	6%	5%	4%	2%	2%	3%	4%	1%	<1%	5%	2%
Women	2,336	2,524	2,877	3,112	3,091	3,153	3,185	3,009	3,164	3,088	3,098	3,112	3,136
% change		8%	14%	8%	–1%	2%	1%	–6%	5%	–2%	0	0	1%

Home Office (2004b) Table 8.6 and Ministry of Justice (2013c) Table A1.6.

offending comprised nonviolent offences such as theft, benefit fraud and drug possession, many felt that women's violence, particularly under the influence of alcohol, was increasing:

> **J4M**[4] I think one of the biggest areas of growth is drink-related violence by women ... Um, the norms of behaviour ... seems to permit violence being used as a means of reprisal and control. And whereas 10 years ago, this was almost entirely, I think, male-related. Now, very, very substantial numbers of women, er, fall into this category as well.
>
> **M4F** You only have to put the TV on and watch one of these programmes ... and you see them tottering around the city centres. They are so drunk they can hardly stand up, and then they get themselves into trouble.

However, as the second quote shows, sentencers' perceptions did not necessarily derive from their experiences in court, but rather from watching reality television programmes, or for one female magistrate, her experience of walking through the city centre at night. These external influences on perceptions of women's offending are important because they help to shape the '*interpretive behaviour of sentencers* who draw on their own knowledge, experience and values' (Player, 2005, p. 434; original emphasis). In this case, they may lead sentencers to respond more severely to women offenders either because they are seen as a greater threat to public safety or because alcohol-fuelled female violence is seen as a growing menace which merits a deterrent response.

The figures in Table 6.2 suggest that sentencers who believed that the number of women coming to court for drug or driving offences had risen were mistaken. Indeed, both have actually fallen slightly. At first sight, sentencers' perceptions that women's offending is on the increase seems justified, as the number of women they dealt with for violent offences increased by 1,000 between 2000 and 2012, and some courts may have seen greater increases in violent women offenders than others. However, this seems to have been driven by a change in government policy regarding the use of pre-court disposals rather than an increase in offending. As the Ministry of Justice explains, the proportion of cases ending in pre-court disposals fell because it 'coincided with the replacement, in April 2008, of a target to increase offences brought to justice, with one placing more emphasis on bringing serious crime to justice. The latter target was subsequently removed in May 2010' (2012, p. 51). The result in the case of violence was that in 2007, the courts dealt with

Table 6.2 Number and percentage of women convicted of indictable offences

Offence	2000		2012	
Violence	**Thousands**	**Per cent**	**Thousands**	**Per cent**
Sexual Offences	2.1	6.3	3.1	8.6
Burglary	0.0	0.0	0.1	0.3
Robbery	0.5	1.5	0.7	1.9
Theft and Handling	0.2	0.6	0.3	0.8
Fraud and Forgery	17.8	53.1	19.8	55.2
Criminal damage	4.5	13.4	4.1	11.4
Drugs	0.5	1.5	0.5	1.4
Other	3.7	11.0	3.6	10.0
(Non-motoring)	3.9	11.6	3.7	10.3
Motoring	0.4	1.2	0.2	0.6
Total	33.5		35.9	

Home Office (2001b) Table 5.6 and Ministry of Justice (2013d) Table Q5b. Percentages may not add up to 100 due to rounding.

27% of women found guilty or cautioned for violence, whereas by 2012, this had risen to 53.5%.[5]

While the intention behind the revised target may have been to bring more serious cases to justice, Table 6.2 suggests that both targets may have inadvertently brought a greater number of less serious cases to court. For example, the biggest numeric change was that an additional 2,000 theft and handling cases were brought to court in 2012, and these made up two-thirds of the overall increase in convictions. Further support for this contention lies in the fact that the proportion of women offenders with no previous record who were brought to court and convicted, rather than being cautioned, has been rising since 2006, reaching 48% in 2012, bringing it close to the male rate of 50.5%.[6]

Table 6.3 shows that the overall number of women being formally dealt with in the criminal justice system declined by 48,660 between 2007 and 2011, but an increased proportion were prosecuted, with the result that nearly 6,000 more women appeared in court during 2011 than had appeared in 2007. Meanwhile the overall number of men in the system decreased even more sharply, while the rise in the proportion being prosecuted was less dramatic. The net result was that 238,030 fewer men appeared in court in 2011 than 2007. In other words, what some sentencers perceived as a steep increase in the number of women coming to court might be characterised more accurately as a steep *decline*

Table 6.3 Number of out of court disposals and court proceedings by gender, all ages, 2007–2011

	Females			Males		
	Out of Court	Court Proceedings	Total System	Out of Court	Court Proceedings	Total System
2007	28.8%	71.2%	484,891	23.8%	76.2%	1,807,037
2008	26.7%	73.3%	463,442	23.1%	76.9%	1,644,142
2009	24.0%	76.0%	487,853	21.4%	78.6%	1,610,029
2010	20.7%	79.3%	458,832	19.0%	81.0%	1,518,022
2011	19.5%	80.5%	436,231	19.4%	80.6%	1,413,067

Ministry of Justice (2012) Table 4.01. These were the most up-to-date figures at the time of writing. Breakdowns for 2000–2006 and separate figures for different age groups are not available.

in the number of men doing so, and in both cases, a change in policy (and related performance targets) seem to be the cause.

Unfortunately, it is not possible to say whether the number of women being sentenced who have previous convictions has changed since the start of the new millennium. Although such statistics are still produced,[7] they contain unexplained anomalies. For example, adding up the percentages of women with different numbers of previous convictions in 2002 leads to a total of 106%, whereas in 2012, it is only adds to 92%.

Changes in sentencing to immediate custody: magistrates' courts vs. Crown Courts

Table 6.4 shows the proportion of adult women sentenced to custody for both summary and indictable offences ranged between 2.5% and 3% throughout the period, with no clear directional trend. The proportion sentenced to custody for indictable offences alone was also stable at between 16% and 18%. Of course, the fact that the percentage use of custody remained broadly stable, while the number of women being sentenced rose, means that more women were sentenced to custody.

However, this relatively static overall picture disguises three interesting changes at the Crown Court (Table 6.5). First, the number of women coming to the Crown Court for sentence rose by 60% between 2001 and 2011, to reach over 9,000 in 2011. Second, this seems to have been associated with a fall in the proportion of cases in which a custodial

Table 6.4 The sentencing of adult women to custody, 2000–2012

	2000	2001	2002	2003	2004	2005	2006	2007	2008	2009	2010	2011	2012
Total Custody	6,337	6,546	7,228	7,413	7,491	6,898	6,540	6,522	7,124	6,913	7,199	7,562	7,015
Total Sentenced	225,914	208,111	228,763	230,222	248,043	250,127	245,008	255,231	253,514	278,395	272,775	270,437	270,641
Percent Custody	2.8%	3.1	3.2%	3.2%	3.0%	2.8%	2.7%	2.6%	2.8%	2.5%	2.6%	2.8%	2.6%
Custody – Indictable	5,500	5,700	6,357	6,416	6,423	5,839	5,579	5,629	6,231	6,017	6,275	6,585	6,061
Sentenced Indictable	33,600	33,500	36,387	37,474	35,960	33,580	32,176	33,391	35,198	37,450	40,398	39,640	35,867
Percent Custody	16%	17%	17%	17%	18%	17%	17%	17%	18%	16%	16%	17%	17%
Avg Length Months	N/A	N/A	11.4	11.5	11.6	11.2	10.9	10.6	10.7	11.0	10.3	11.0	10.7

Ministry of Justice (2009) Tables 2f and 2j and Ministry of Justice (2013d) Table 5d. The notation 'N/A' in this and subsequent tables signifies that the particular breakdown was not available, and it could not be calculated accurately or on a comparable basis from the information which was available.

Table 6.5 The use of custody for adult women sentenced for indictable offences by court venue, 2000–2012

	2000	2001	2002	2003	2004	2005	2006	2007	2008	2009	2010	2011	2012
Crown Court													
Use of custody	42%	45%	44%	41%	42%	39%	38%	37%	37%	36%	32%	36%	35%
Sentenced Indictable	5722	5645	5,952	6,209	6,476	6,661	6,677	7,181	7,943	8,449	8,953	9,048	7,852
Average length Months	21	24.2	24.7	25.3	24.4	22.4	21.7	20.6	20.5	20.1	20.3	20.5	21.3
Magistrates' Courts													
Use of custody	11%	12%	12%	12%	13%	12%	12%	11%	12%	10%	11%	11%	12%
Sentenced Indictable	27,946	27,282	30,435	31,265	29,484	26,919	25,499	26,210	27,255	29,001	31,445	30,592	28,015
Av length months	2.3	2.3	2.3	2.3	2.2	2.2	2.1	2.1	2.0	2.0	1.9	2.0	2.0

Home Office (2002) Table 7.13, Home Office (2004b) Table 5.2, Ministry of Justice (2009) Table 2.h and Ministry of Justice (2013d) Table 5a.

sentence was imposed. Third, the average sentence length imposed on women at the Crown Court also fell from 2003 from around 2 years to 20 months. Meanwhile, the number of women being sentenced by magistrates' courts fell between 2003 and 2009, although the use of custody remained stable at around 11% (with fluctuations), as did the average sentence length (2 months).

Magistrates' use of custody for women has also been fairly stable at the individual offence level. However, again, the Crown Court figures show some interesting changes. As Table 6.6 shows, whilst sentencing to immediate custody increased for certain offences (for example, criminal damage and burglary) between 2000 and 2012, for other offences it either remained stable or declined. The starkest change is that 32% of women convicted of drugs offences were sentenced to immediate custody in 2012, compared to 55% in 2000.

The two most likely explanations for this pattern are, first, that judges are responding more actively to the call to divert women from custody, and second, that some of the cases which were previously dealt with by magistrates are now being sentenced in the Crown Court. In the latter situation, because these cases are less serious than those the Crown Court usually deals with, they are not being sentenced to custody.[8] Unfortunately, direct information about whether this has changed over time is not available. However, this may explain why, for example, the Crown Courts' use of custody for theft and handling has fallen.

Table 6.6 Proportion of adult women (over 21) convicted of indictable offences who were sentenced to immediate custody at the Crown Court

Offence	2000	2012
	% Custody	% Custody
Violence	33	33
Sexual Offences	(67)	(73)
Burglary	53	59
Robbery	75	70
Theft and Handling	41	34
Fraud and Forgery	32	28
Criminal Damage	25	43
Drugs	55	31
Other (Non-motoring)	30	32
Motoring	(32)	21
Average all indictable offences	42	35

Home Office (2001b) Table 7.16 and Ministry of Justice (2013d) Table S2.1 (G).
( ) less than 100 cases.

The interview data add further context to these statistics by indicating some differences between magistrates' and Crown Court sentencers' use of custody. When asked how frequently they saw women who were at risk of immediate custody, magistrates tended to regard this as extremely rare, citing sentencing guidelines which encouraged them to avoid custody and favour noncustodial alternatives. Whilst sentencing trends vary among courts, with recently published figures indicating stark geographical disparities in the use of custody (Howard League, 2013), the message conveyed by the (albeit small) sample of magistrates is that in the current policy climate, sentencing anyone to custody is extremely rare, as illustrated by the following dialogue:

> **M5F** Particularly now – ten years ago, we sent more people to prison. Now we send so few people to prison that it really is the end of the road.
>
> **M4F** Yes, we did. When I first came on the bench, we sent some, but it's got gradually less and less. And now it's rare. Now you've really got to think about it.

Yet this message contrasts with the statistics presented above (Table 6.5) which indicate that the use of custodial sentences by magistrates has remained fairly static. Moreover, when magistrates recounted instances where they had sentenced women to custody, this was often as a result of breach of community or suspended sentence orders, as opposed to the original offence. Commonly, magistrates used such phrases as having 'run out of road', or using custody as a 'last resort', or 'if all else fails', as the following quote indicates:

> **M5F** We have a procedure when sentencing, and you work through the procedure, and when you've tried everything else, ad nauseam, there comes a point where there is no alternative. You're not thinking of anything other than, "There is no other road." I don't think you are thinking, "Is it punishment?" "Is it protection of the public?" You're thinking, "I have no choice in this."

Hence, where magistrates impose custody, it appears that this is frequently for offences which would not reach the custody threshold in their own right, but rather as the only perceived option in situations of noncompliance.[9] Unfortunately, published sentencing statistics do not include the level of detail needed to investigate this further.

Although prison reception figures might provide some insight into this, the detailed breakdown is not available for more recent years. It is interesting to note the Ministry of Justice's comment, however, in the last year this breakdown was available, that 'Legislative and policy changes have…increased the likelihood of offenders being imprisoned for breach of noncustodial sentences' (2010, p. 4). They also noted that breaches of a court order accounted for 53% of 'other offences' and that 'the number of sentenced prison receptions for "other offences" increased by 70 per cent from 12,900 in 1999 to 21,900 in 2009' (2010, p. 52).

In contrast to magistrates, judges seemed keener to avoid sentencing women or men to immediate custody, even though they routinely deal with more serious cases than magistrates. Typically, they spoke of custody being reserved for crimes which were so serious that no other punishment would be appropriate and/or where custody served the purpose of public protection. Most noted that while sentencing guidelines had to be adhered to, these left room for discretion, and wherever possible, they used this, particularly to avoid short prison sentences. For example:

> **J2M** I don't like sending people to prison. If there is any way around it, you do it. Prison is punishment. I don't think it rehabilitates. I don't think they've got the resources. And if it's punishment and keeping people out of circulation, there is a reason for that.
>
> **J5M** The chances of it doing any good are so limited that really the custodial sentence is there to protect the public, by putting somebody who is dangerous out of public contact, for as long as possible. Which means that short-term sentences really are a waste of time, for the most part.

Conversely, most of the magistrates interviewed felt overly restricted by what they referred to as 'sentencing guidelines' (although what they actually described were often statutory provisions). A key example of this can be found in the contrasting responses to the question of whether sentencers would use the Together Women Programme (TWP) – a non-mandatory, community-based diversion – as an alternative to custody. Whilst magistrates welcomed TWP as a supplement to community orders, both its non-statutory status and the rigidity of the custody threshold (at that time) were both regarded as barriers to sentencing women to TWP in isolation. In contrast, judges were generally more open to using TWP in this way, as the following response to the question of whether the judge in question had ever used TWP in this way demonstrates:

> **J6M** Many times. Oh yeah, it's often been... I am very loath to send women into custody. Because I believe there is very little positive that comes out of a woman going to prison unless, as I've said already, they're in that category of people where they, frankly, are a danger to themselves or to others.

Similar views were expressed by the small sample of judges in Mair et al.,'s (2008) study of sentencers' views on the newly introduced community sentences. In the final part of this analysis, noncustodial options will be examined more closely to assess how sentencers have used the available options and to critically examine the suitability of existing noncustodial options for women.

The changing landscape of noncustodial sentencing

As noted earlier, one of the changes in the CJA 2003 involved condensing several components of community sentences into a single generic community order (CO). Simultaneously, changes to the suspended sentence order (SSO) were introduced (see Ashworth, 2010); although it is a custodial sentence, it is discussed in this section, as the presumption is that it is served in the community unless the offender fails to comply or reoffends. It is pertinent to consider, first, whether changes to the availability of noncustodial sentences, and growing recognition that short prison sentences are damaging to those who serve them and do not protect the public (Magistrates Association, 2010), have resulted in changes in the use of custody, and second, how sentencers make decisions about appropriate noncustodial sentences.

Table 6.7 shows that while the overall use of custodial sentences has changed very little, there has been a change *within* noncustodial sentencing, with a dramatic reduction in the use of fines for men and women. Sentencers may have been discouraged from imposing fines on women because of the acute levels of economic disadvantage and financial responsibility which many women offenders face. However, whilst avoiding fines is well intended, this practice can push sentencing upwards by skipping that first stage of sentencing (Dowds and Hedderman, 1997; Player, 2005; Malloch and McIvor, 2011). Moreover, where sentencers felt that the woman required active intervention, up-tariffing was

Table 6.7 The sentencing of adult women and men (over 21) for indictable offences, 2000–2012

	Women		Men	
Sentence	2000	2012	2000	2012
	%	%	%	%
Fine	22	15	28	19
Community Orders	33	28	24	22
Suspended Sentence	2	14	1	11
Immediate Custody	16	16	30	31
Other	27	27	17	17
Numbers	33,600	36,108	184,700	205,936

Home Office (2001b) Table 7.10 and Ministry of Justice (2013d) Tables 5c and 5d.

N.B. Hedderman (2004) separated Discharges from 'Other' sentences, but the published statistics no longer provide this breakdown.

sometimes a temptation, though this was elsewhere recognised and resisted, as the following exchange illustrates:

> **M1M** Sometimes you get a shoplifter, and sometimes you look at her, and the guideline is a fine, but you think, "I really would like to do something different for this individual."
>
> **M2F** But you'd need considerably more information to do that, and if it was a normal theft, you wouldn't hear any background. You'd hear, "It's Ms Blogs, and she went to Morrison's and stole a can of beans." You'd think, "Conditional discharge."

However, in another case, the magistrate justified sentencing a shoplifter to a CO by saying, 'She didn't really reach the threshold to make a community order, but somehow we wangled it.' This decision reportedly led to positive outcomes for the woman concerned, who accessed valuable support from TWP while she was on the CO. However, whilst these magistrates' desires to offer more supportive and constructive responses to offenders are well intended, they are problematic for several reasons. First, while the intention may be to help, it comes at the cost of creating, or adding to, a criminal record, which is both stigmatising and likely to add to a woman's disadvantage. Second, such an approach can backfire if offenders' (typically chaotic) lives mean that they are unable to comply with the conditions of the order and may then face custody for breach. Third, skipping out earlier steps in the sentencing tariff means that women have less distance to travel before 'running out of road' if they reoffend and again find themselves at risk of custody (Hedderman and Gelsthorpe, 1997; Player, 2005).

The figures in Table 6.7 also seem to confirm Stanley's (2009) contention that the introduction of SSOs in the CJA 2003 has largely replaced noncustodial sentences rather than custodial ones for women and for men. However, this overall pattern masks differences in sentencing behaviour between the two court levels. In the magistrates' courts (Table 6.8), the overall pattern is one of SSOs rising as fines decline, with custody rates remaining stable (though with some annual fluctuation). Combined with the tougher breach requirements of the CJA 2003 and the attitudes magistrates expressed about those with previous offences running out of road, this challenges the idea that noncustodial sentences are a diversion from, or alternative to, custody in the magistrates' courts.

At the Crown Court (Table 6.9), the increasing use of SSOs seems to be associated with a steep reduction in the use of COs but also, as intended,

Table 6.8 Changes in magistrates' court sentencing of women (over 21) following the CJA, 2003

Sentence (%)	2003	2004	2005	2006	2007	2008	2009	2010	2011	2012
Fines	24	25	22	20	18	17	18	19	19	19
Community Orders	32	30	32	33	31	31	32	32	31	31
SSO	0	0	1	3	7	7	6	7	7	7
Custody	12	13	12	12	12	12	12	10	11	11
Other	32	33	33	32	33	33	32	31	32	32
Numbers	30,713	31,405	28,206	27,067	25,137	26,359	28,025	29,290	31,678	30,218

Ministry of Justice (2013d) Table Q5.d. Differences between base numbers and percentages shown in this table and Table 5 reflect differences in the source figures.

Table 6.9 Changes in Crown Court sentencing of women (over 21) following the CJA, 2003

Sentence (%)	2003	2004	2005	2006	2007	2008	2009	2010	2011	2012
Fines	2	2	2	2	2	1	1	1	1	1
Community Orders	41	41	40	39	28	22	23	23	25	22
SSO	6	6	7	12	25	31	32	34	33	35
Custody	43	41	41	39	37	37	37	35	33	36
Other	9	9	9	9	8	8	7	7	8	6
Numbers	5,988	6,349	6,317	6,921	6,568	7,522	8,050	8,516	9,125	8,882

Ministry of Justice (2013d) Table Q5.d. Differences between base numbers and percentages shown in this table and Table 5 reflect differences in the source figures.

in the use of immediate custody. Some judges, though, clearly had reservations about using SSOs because of the possible repercussions when such orders are breached. For one, this particularly applied to women:

> **J6M** Rare that I would give a woman a suspended sentence order.... I can't really think of the sorts of cases where I would do that ... because if a suspended sentence is linked to something like a drug rehabilitation requirement, I just think that's ... It's almost setting people up to fail, often.

Echoing these concerns, and given that around one in ten COs and SSOs are terminated for breach each year (Ministry of Justice, 2013c), and that breach can lead to a custodial sentence being activated, especially for SSOs, the notion of diversion from custody is highly conditional and often short-lived. Consequently, many offenders will be imprisoned because of breach, even when a custodial sentence was not initially deemed to be proportionate to the offence(s) committed. Whilst this is an issue for men, too, the complex needs profiles of women offenders means that the likelihood of them breaching an order is heightened by the social, economic and psychological vulnerabilities and care responsibilities which are commonplace within this offending population (Malloch and McIvor, 2011). One judge, for example, explained one woman's complete noncompliance with a SSO:

> **J4M** It was because ... as a result of the woman's personality, um, and experiences of being the victim of serious abuse, with drug and, I think, alcohol problems, and a chaotic, um, lifestyle. She simply did not have the resources, er, in terms of her personality, to commit herself to do this. That's not a criticism of the recommendation. It was worth trying. But she, with the benefit of hindsight, simply, um, breached, um, in a wholesale way.

In contrast to multiple accounts of noncompliance with COs and SSOs, alongside the recognition by most that prison is counterproductive for women, all participants were overwhelmingly positive about the availability of the holistic, woman-specific and flexible nature of TWP centres. The informality, availability of childcare and emphasis on the centres being a woman-only safe space were all hailed as being key to the success of TWP. However, whilst recognising that men's and women's different needs are important to the design of effective interventions, there were different stances regarding what constitutes equality in sentencing – namely, treating women *differently* in an attempt to better respond to their needs, or treating women *the same* as men in order to ensure parity (Carlen, 2002a; Hudson, 2002; Easton and Piper, 2008; Player, 2012).

Yet concerns about differences in sentencing decisions can overlook the critical issue of whether a menu of community sentences originally designed to respond to male offenders – as some interview participants themselves noted – affords equality to women. As Corston suggested 'more is needed by way of alternative sanctions and disposals, which are gender specific and in which sentencers can have confidence' (2007, p. 50). Key questions requiring further investigation are first, how suitable existing community sentences are for women; second, how sentencers decide which requirements to impose on women; and third, whether gender shapes these decisions. For example, sentencers' recognition of women's multiple and complex needs and vulnerabilities – as evidenced in the interview study – may lead to well-intended decisions to offer as much help as possible, either by prolonging an order or by including multiple components within the order. Unfortunately, as Carlen noted over a decade ago, when women fail to comply, there is a severe risk of 'carceral clawback' (2002b, p. 202). Thus, an apparently welfarist approach may jeopardise equality and proportionality, particularly where women are not physically or psychologically ready to accept the mandated support, and are subsequently penalised for their noncompliance by an even more onerous order, or a custodial sentence.

A further consideration is that some of the components of COs have been deemed less suitable for women offenders; for example, concerns have been raised about curfews posing risks to women in abusive relationships as well as interfering with their care commitments (Ministry of Justice, 2011).[10] Unpaid work may also be considered unfeasible due to women's care commitments and patchy provision of women-only opportunities, which may become even scarcer under a payment by results regime (Gelsthrope and Hedderman, 2012). Therefore, as with up-tariffing, the perceived unsuitability of certain components of community sentences shortens the road to custody by reducing the options available to sentencers.

Conclusions

The statistical analysis presented in this chapter has identified important changes in the sentencing of women, whilst the qualitative data from interviews with sentencers have offered deeper insights into how they make decisions about sentencing women. The key findings are as follows:

- Whilst the number of women (and men) entering the criminal justice system declined between 2007–2011, policy changes have led to fewer pre-court disposals and increased prosecutions for less serious offences. The combined effect of 6,000 more women appearing in court and 230,000 fewer men is likely to be (mis)perceived by sentencers as a sign that women's offending is on the increase.
- Following an unprecedented rise in the prison population in the 1990s, the overall use of custody has been stable since the advent of the new millennium. This is because most women are sentenced by magistrates for relatively minor offences, and magistrates' use of immediate custody has remained fairly static. However, although judges deal with intrinsically more serious offences, there has been a marked drop in the extent to which they sentence women to immediate custody.
- The above finding contradicts the perceptions of interviewed magistrates, where the use of custody was described as having reduced substantially and being an inevitable last resort after exhausting all other options.
- Greater changes have been witnessed within noncustodial sentencing; the use of SSOs, introduced by the CJA 2003, has increased at both the magistrates' courts and at the Crown Court. However, at the magistrates' courts, the SSO has largely replaced other community orders, whereas at the Crown Court, it has also had the intended effect of reducing the use of custodial sentences.

Replacing community sentences with SSOs is a worrying development, as breach is likely to lead to imprisonment, even when the original offence does not merit such a sentence.

These findings show that the sentencing of women takes place amid shifting and contradictory policy messages, legislation and media representations. On the one hand, sentencers have been alerted to the need to avoid short custodial sentences, both from a resourcing perspective, and through recognition of the accentuated and often disproportionate consequences of imprisonment for women. On the other hand, sentencers' perceptions of women's offending as being on an upward trajectory, with images of young women being 'out of control' and mirroring men in their use of alcohol and violence, potentially justify harsher sentencing as a deterrent. Further still, whilst growing sensitivity to how women's vulnerabilities shape their offending have highlighted the limitations of criminalising women, some sentencers still see treating men and women identically as fulfilling their gender equality duty. Meanwhile, others respond with well-intended yet problematic overuse of the criminal justice system, up-tariffing to give women some help, rather than a discharge or a fine, or overloading women on COs in order to address their complex needs

Alongside these competing messages, the application of new legislation – particularly the CJA 2003 – has seen an overhaul in sentencing, with three principal issues for this discussion being the condensing of various levels of community sentence into one general CO, the introduction and popularity with sentencers of SSOs, and the more stringent and less flexible procedures for managing breaches of COs and SSOs. This latter issue means that while the use of COs and SSOs ostensibly demonstrate a commitment to diversion from immediate custody, these sentences can become a 'back door' into custody for those who fail to comply. Comprehensive recent statistics on how many women enter custody due to breach are not readily available. However, further investigation is needed into the gender-specific barriers which may make women's successful completion of COs and SSOs less likely and consequently raise concerns about equality and proportionality when custody is imposed for breaching the conditions of an order for an offence which does not pass the custody threshold. Differences between how women are sentenced in the magistrates' and Crown Courts are also important, as this and other previous studies have shown. Judges' more critical attitudes towards the use of custody for women suggest that they have been more influenced by campaigns to reduce the use of custody – in particular, short prison sentences – for women, and moreover, through their different case mix, have a different view of what constitutes 'seriousness' compared to magistrates. Whereas judges are more likely to see seriousness as intrinsic to the act committed, for magistrates, persistence in offending and noncompliance with orders tend to signify seriousness.

Sentencers spoke very positively about gender-specific interventions such as TWP, but magistrates did not see this as an alternative to custody. This was partly because, at the time of interview, they did not think attendance could be made mandatory, although some judges described using it in this way on a number of occasions. More generally, magistrates found the concept of alternatives to custody inherently problematic, arguing that they never considered custody unless there was no alternative. This finding replicates that of earlier studies and is a particular point of concern for that reason.

Sentencers also had different understandings of what gender equality means in sentencing. At the heart of these debates is the question of whether equality is achieved by treating all offenders in the same way, or conversely whether preexisting differences justify different sentencing responses. Concerns about discriminating against male offenders by treating women differently ignore the preexisting gender differences in the causes of crime, impacts and effectiveness of different sentences, particularly regarding the ability of those sentences to address the causes of women's offending and the risk of reoffending. What emerges from this analysis is a conundrum: on the one hand, women offenders are recognised as having specific needs and vulnerabilities which current gender-neutral sentencing options cannot adequately address. On the other hand, the commitment to an understanding of equality, which necessitates sameness rather than difference in sentencing, means that women offenders are expected to respond to both custodial and noncustodial sentences which have predominantly not been designed with their particular needs in mind, with only minor adjustments to content. Unfortunately, the latest statement of strategic policy objectives for women issued by the Government (Ministry of Justice, 2013e) reifies, rather than addresses, this fundamental dilemma.

Notes

1. The Sentencing Guidelines Council (2004) guideline on the use of sentences introduced by the CJA (2003) was not prescriptive about the number of requirements which might be imposed but only mentions the idea of imposing 'two or more' when discussing cases on the cusp of custody. More explicit guidance is provided in relation to the use of suspended sentence, requiring 'a court to be satisfied that the custody threshold has been passed' (p. 24). Since April 2010, following the implementation of the Coroners and Justice Act (2009), the courts are required to follow, rather than simply 'have regard to' the guidelines.
2. See Gelsthorpe, Sharpe and Roberts (2007) for a detailed discussion of the key characteristics of effective community-based services for women.
3. One judge declined to be recorded, and the recording equipment failed in one of the interviews with magistrates. In both cases, detailed notes were taken and subsequently typed up.
4. Participant codes indicate J or M for judge or magistrate respectively, the identification number and finally, M or F for male or female.
5. Ministry of Justice (2008) Table 3.3 and Ministry of Justice (2013d) Table Q2.4.
6. Ministry of Justice (2013d) Table Q7.d.
7. Ministry of Justice (2013d) Table A7.2.

8. See Hedderman and Moxon (1992) for a study which (unusually) compared the sentencing of cases at the Crown and magistrates' court having taken into account a number of mitigating and aggravating factors including offence seriousness. This found that the Crown Court often imposed sentences within the limits of magistrates' sentencing powers.
9. Sentencers interviewed by Hough, Jacobson and Millie (2003) also suggested that magistrates were particularly likely to view custody as inevitable because of the offender's previous offending and sentencing history, rather than because of the intrinsic seriousness of the current offence.
10. Despite these concerns, it is worth noting that the coalition's government's *Strategic Objectives for Female Offenders* policy paper suggests that curfews and tagging be used to strengthen noncustodial sentences for women offenders (Ministry of Justice, 2013e).

References

Ashworth, A. (2010) *Sentencing and Criminal Justice* (5th ed.). Cambridge: Cambridge University Press.

Carlen, P. (2002a) Introduction: women and punishment In: P. Carlen (ed.) *Women and Punishment: The Struggle for Justice*. Cullompton: Willan.

——— (2002b) Women's imprisonment: Cross-national lessons, in P. Carlen (ed.) *Women and Punishment: The Struggle for Justice*. Cullompton: Willan.

Corston, J. (2007) *The Corston Report: a Review of Women with Particular Vulnerabilities in the Criminal Justice System*. London: Home Office.

Dowds, L. and Hedderman, C. (1997) 'The sentencing of men and women'. In: C. Hedderman and L. Gelsthorpe (eds) *Understanding the Sentencing of Women*. London: Home Office.

Easton, S. and Piper, C. (2008) *Sentencing and Punishment: The Quest for Justice* (2nd ed.). Oxford: Oxford University Press.

Fawcett Society (2013) *The Fawcett Society's Policy Submission to the Review of the Public Sector Equality Duty*. London: Fawcett Society. http://www.fawcettsociety.org.uk/wp-content/uploads/2013/04/Fawett-submission-to-Review-of-the-Public-Sector-Equality-Duty-April-2013.pdf.

Ford, R. (2009) Ladettes Push Girl Violence to New High: Sharp Rise in Assaults and Public Disorder. *The Times*, 30 January. http://www.timesonline.co.uk/tol/news/uk/crime/article5614844.ece.

Gelsthorpe, L. and Hedderman, C. (2012) Providing for Women Offenders: The Risk of Adopting a Payment by Results Approach. *Probation Journal*, 59: 374–390.

Gelsthorpe, L., Sharpe, G. and Roberts, J. (2007) *Provision for Women Offenders in the Community*. London: Fawcett Commission.

Hedderman, C. (2004) Why are more women being sentenced to custody? In: G. McIvor (ed.) *Women Who Offend*. London: Jessica Kingsley.

——— (2010) Government Policy on Women Offenders: Labour's Legacy and the Coalition's Challenge, *Punishment and Society*, 12: 485–500.

Hedderman, C. and Gelsthorpe, L. (eds) (1997) *Understanding the Sentencing of Women*. London: Home Office.

Hedderman, C. and Gunby, C. (2013) Diverting Women from Custody: The Importance of Understanding Sentencers' Perspectives. *Probation Journal*, 60: 32–45.
Hedderman, C. and Moxon, D. (1992) *Magistrates' Court or Crown Court? Mode of Trial Decisions and Sentencing*. London: HMSO.
Hedderman, C., Palmer, E. and Hollin, C. (2008) *Implementing Services for Women Offenders and Those 'at Risk' of Offending: Action Research with Together Women*. London: Ministry of Justice.
Home Office (2001a) *Statistics on Women and the Criminal Justice System: A Home Office Publication under Section 95 of the Criminal Justice Act 1991*. London: Home Office.
Home Office (2001b) *Criminal Statistics, England and Wales, 2000*. London: Home Office.
Home Office (2002) *Criminal Statistics, England and Wales, 2001*. London: Home Office.
Home Office (2004a) *Women's Offending Reduction Programme (WORP) Action Plan*. London: Home Office.
Home Office (2004b) *Offender Management Caseload Statistics, 2003*. London: Home Office.
Hough, M., Jacobson, J. and Millie, A. (2003) *The Decision to Imprison: Sentencing and The Prison Population*. London: Prison Reform Trust.
Howard League for Penal Reform (2013) The magistrates courts most likely to send women to prison'. http://www.howardleague.org/magistrates-courts-women/.
Hudson, B. (2002) Gender issues in penal policy and penal theory. In: P. Carlen (ed.)*Women and Punishment: The Struggle for Justice*. Cullompton: Willan.
Jolliffe, D., Hedderman, C., Palmer, E. and Hollin, C. (2011) *Re-offending analysis of women offenders referred to Together Women (TW) and the scope to divert from custody*. Ministry of Justice Research Series 11/11. London: Ministry of Justice.
Magistrates' Association (2010) *Use of Short-Term Custody – Policy Paper*. London: Magistrates' Association.
Mair, G., Cross, N. and Taylor, S. (2008) *The Community Order and the Suspended Sentence Order: The Views and Attitudes of Sentencers*. London: Centre for Crime and Justice Studies.
Malloch, M. and McIvor, G. (2011) Women and Community Sentences. *Criminology & Criminal Justice*, 11: 325–344.
McVeigh, T. (2009) Teenage Girls Driven to Violence by Feuds, Drink and Jealousy. *Observer*, 22 November 2009. http://www.guardian.co.uk/uk/2009/nov/22/teenage-girls-crime-bullying-increase.
Ministry of Justice (2008) *Criminal Statistics, England and Wales, 2007*. London: Ministry of Justice.
Ministry of Justice (2009) *Sentencing Statistics, 2007 England and Wales*. London: Ministry of Justice.
Ministry of Justice (2010) Offender *Management Caseload Statistics 2009*. London: Ministry of Justice.
Ministry of Justice (2011) *Legal Aid, Sentencing and Punishment of Offenders Bill –Sentencing and Punishment of Offenders: Full Equality Impact Assessment*. London: Ministry of Justice.

Ministry of Justice (2012) *Statistics on Women and the Criminal Justice System: A Ministry of Justice Publication under Section 95 of the Criminal Justice Act 1991*. London: Ministry of Justice.

Ministry of Justice (2013a) *Transforming Rehabilitation: A Strategy for Reform*. London: Ministry of Justice.

Ministry of Justice (2013b) *Government Response to the Justice Committee's Second Report of Session 2013–14: Female Offenders*. London: Ministry of Justice. https://www.gov.uk/government/uploads/system/uploads/attachment_data/file/252817/response-jsc-female-offenders.pdf.

Ministry of Justice (2013c) *Annual Tables-Offender Management Caseload Statistics, 2012*. London: Ministry of Justice. https://www.gov.uk/government/uploads/system/uploads/attachment_data/file/218109/omsq-annual-tables-2012.zip.

Ministry of Justice (2013d) *Criminal Justice Statistics Quarterly – December 2012*. London: Ministry of Justice. https://www.gov.uk/government/publications/criminal-justice-statistics-quarterly-update-to-december-2012.

Ministry of Justice (2013e) *Strategic Objectives for Female Offenders*. London: Ministry of Justice.

Open University (2008–9) Endless New Criminal Laws, a Massive Increase in People Jailed, and a Rise in Fear of Crime. *Society Matters*, 11:4.

Player, E. (2005) The Reduction of Women's Imprisonment in England and Wales. *Punishment & Society*, 7: 419–439.

Player, E. (2012) Sentencing women: towards gender equality. In: L. Zedner and J.V. Roberts (eds) *Principles and Values in Criminal Law and Criminal Justice: Essays in Honour of Andrew Ashworth*. Oxford: Oxford University Press.

Sentencing Guidelines Council (2004) *New Sentences:* Criminal Justice Act 2003 *Guideline*. London: Sentencing Guidelines Council.

Stanley, S. (2009) The Use of the Community Order and the Suspended Sentence Order for Women, *Probation Journal*, 56(4): 362–378.

Travis, A. (2006) Fifty Bills Add 700 Offences As Jails Fill Up. *The Guardian*, 26 June. http://www.theguardian.com/politics/2006/jun/24/ukcrime.immigrationpolicy.

Whitehead, T. (2009) Rise of 'Ladette' Culture as 241 Women Arrested Each Day for Violence. *Daily Telegraph*, 1 May. http://www.telegraph.co.uk/news/newstopics/politics/lawandorder/5251042/Rise-of-ladette-culture-as-241-women-arrested-each-day-for-violence.html.

7
Women and Sentencing: Challenges and Choices

Loraine Gelsthorpe and Gillian Sharpe

Baroness Corston's report: *A review of women with particular vulnerabilities in the criminal justice system* made a series of recommendations to bring about improvements in relation to the treatment of women in the criminal justice system. Now, some six years after her report, we find that it is well recognised that women face very different hurdles from men in their journey towards a law abiding life, and that responding appropriately and effectively to the problems that bring women into the criminal justice system require a distinct approach. (Justice Select Committee report: *Women Offenders: After the Corston Report*. Second Report of Sessions 2013–2014. London: House of Commons.)

But how far does sentencing accommodate the need for 'a distinct approach'? *Should* sentencing address such issues? And what particular challenges are there in sentencing women? How far does sentencing achieve justice for women given claims about women being unequal before the law?

Overview

Our aim in this chapter is to prompt critical reflection on a number of themes relating to the sentencing of women. We set the context for considerations of sentencing by looking at previous research and general concerns about women and sentencing. We then identify particular questions which have emerged from legislative and policy developments in England and Wales over the past decade or so, noting steps forwards and backwards in relation to the sentencing of women, and especially the use of custody, notwithstanding public support for less use of custody for women. As part of this, we identify specific challenges for sentencers in terms of women's child care responsibilities and other needs. Although necessarily selective, we conclude with some reflections on what justice might mean for women, and on the nature of gender informed justice, including the possibility of specialist courts. We also conclude that little has been done to correct underlying ideological weaknesses in penal ideology that militate against the equitable treatment of the sexes in sentencing. Instead, as with many aspects of criminal justice policy, the focus has been on issues of procedural justice and outcome evaluation, with scant attention being devoted to substantive factors such as the relationship between social morality and penal policy.

Setting the context

The sentencing of women has been a focus of interest and controversy for some considerable time, as Zedner (1991) vividly describes in an analysis of Victorian responses to them. There was particular interest in the issues following the publication of *Women in Prison* by Ann Smith in 1962, in which she painted a clear picture of the sorry lives of the women within, and an article by Heidensohn in 1968 where she questioned the invisibility of women in the study of crime and deviance. The 1970s produced the publication of Smart's (1976) book *Women, Crime and Criminology*, in which she not only questioned why so many women were being imprisoned for relatively minor crimes, but offered critical reflection on the possibility that there might be a functional equivalent between prisons for men and psychiatric hospitals for women. However, women's predominance in psychiatric hospitals at the time could be explained by any of a number of factors, ranging from women's longevity to psychiatric sexism. But the very questions set in train some critical thinking about the treatment of women in the courts, and a series of empirical studies, many of which focused on the possibility that women were being treated either 'leniently' or 'harshly' compared to men (see Farrington and Morris, 1983; Dominelli, 1984; Edwards, 1984; Heidensohn, 1987; Mair and Brockington, 1988; Moxon, 1988; and Wilczynski, 1997). Notwithstanding some methodological limitations, the various analyses resulted in somewhat conflicting and contradictory conclusions.

There were positive steps forwards when it was recognized that considerations of the social construction of gender appropriate behaviour were as important, if not more so, than analyses of simple sex differences in patterns of sentencing. Hedderman and Gelsthorpe's (1997) Home Office-sponsored study revealed complexity in sentencing decision-making; some women convicted of some offences (shoplifting for example) appeared to be treated more leniently than men, whilst others (recidivist drug offenders) were as likely as men to receive a custodial sentence. In some cases, there was evidence that 'up-tariffing' could occur; women tended to be fined less regularly than men, *and* received a community sentence more frequently than men (although some women received a discharge instead). Interviews with magistrates revealed that family circumstances, appearance and demeanour all seemed to be influential factors in the sentencing of women. Women were also more likely than men to be viewed as 'troubled' rather than 'troublesome', but again all this was contingent on the nature of the offences with which women had been charged (Gelsthorpe and Loucks, 1997).

Concerns and themes

Broadly speaking, four main themes emerged from these various studies of sentencing: pathology, domesticity, respectability and sexuality (the latter was particularly relevant for girls and young women) (Gelsthorpe, 2001). Firstly, a woman who entered the criminal justice system was incongruous or out of place, thus explanations for her presence in the courtroom were sought within the discourse of the pathological (Worrall, 1990). Second, it was thought that judgments of women in terms of marital status and motherhood (and other elements of traditional gender roles relating to domesticity and respectability) influenced sentencing (Carlen, 1983; Worrall, 1990). Carlen (2002) argued that 'women on the margins' who seemingly failed to live in conventional domestic circumstances or who were from minority ethnic groups, were more likely to be processed through the criminal justice system and end up in prison (2002) (see also Loucks, 1998, on women in Scottish prisons). The notion of 'double deviance', whereby women are treated more harshly than men because they have violated both the criminal law and assumptions about what is appropriate and tolerable behaviour for women, seems particularly compelling.

Sentencers may fit punishments less to the crime than to the offender before them, making moral distinctions between who is redeemable and who is not (Tombs and Jagger, 2006), and this seems to be particularly likely where women defendants are concerned (Hudson, 2002). Although women defendants tend to be considered more troubled than troublesome (Gelsthorpe and Loucks, 1997), repeated court appearances may signal to magistrates and judges that a woman has failed to avail herself of the help offered by previous community penalties. This may go some way towards explaining why women are frequently sentenced to imprisonment on account of the persistence of their offending, rather than the seriousness of their current offence(s) (Tombs and Jagger, 2006).[1] At the same time, twice as many women in prison as men have no previous convictions – 28% of those serving under 12 months in 2011, compared with only 12% of men (Ministry of Justice, 2012a, Tables A1.28 and A1.29). But at the same time, twice as many women in prison as men have no previous convictions. Thus, there was a strong critique which revolved around the need for equality in sentencing and the avoidance of inappropriate (gender biased and extra-legal) judgments. At the time of these debates, MacKinnon (1987) alerted audiences to the limitations of such approaches, which somehow assumed that the sentencing of men was right and the appropriate standard against which women should be judged. Interestingly, these same debates led Allen to argue that women should be dealt with more punitively in order to further women's equality. She described 'leniency' as a 'tactic of patriarchal oppression' and argued that women should be exposed to the 'full rigour of penal sanctions' (Allen, 1987).

Three steps forwards, four steps backwards

Rather presciently, in discussion at a 1981 conference, participants drew a distinction between 'paper justice', which would involve giving like penalties to women and men for like offences, and 'real justice', which would involve taking the impact of a penalty into account (the consequences of a woman's imprisonment for her children, for example) (Morris and Gelsthorpe, 1981). Procedural justice and substantive justice are laid bare in this distinction. More recent developments have revolved around the case for substantive justice, taking into account the differential impact of sentencing, especially in regard to imprisonment. The Prison Reform Trust, The Fawcett Society, and The Howard League have taken the lead here (Prison Reform Trust, 2000; Prison Reform Trust 2011; Fawcett Society, 2004; Howard League, 2006), and combined with the gathering momentum of damning prison and probation inspectorate reports throughout the 1990s and early 2000s, reflected concerns about increases in women's imprisonment in England and Wales (Gelsthorpe and Morris, 2002; Deakin and Spencer, 2003; Hedderman, 2004). Similar concerns have been expressed in relation to women's imprisonment in Scotland and indeed, more widely in Western jurisdictions (McIvor, 2010). The key point here is that changes in the use of imprisonment did not reflect changes in offending behaviour but rather greater punitiveness on the part of sentencers, although whether this was specifically aimed at women remains a moot point (cf. Carlen, 2002). The weight of opinion is perhaps that women were caught up in a general 'punitive turn', notwithstanding residual concerns for women's welfare (Gelsthorpe, 2005) as well as there being concerns about a confusion of 'risks' and 'needs', with women offenders being characterized by a low risk of reoffending, but with high needs, and the possibility that women are up-tariffed because of the latter (Hannah-Moffat, 2004).

Increased awareness of the need for gender-appropriate services for women prompted the government in England and Wales to set up a cross-departmental Women's Offending Reduction Programme (WORP) aimed at developing a coordinated response to the characteristics and needs of female offenders (Gelsthorpe, 2007). And more recently, the independent review of vulnerable women in the criminal justice system conducted by Baroness Corston (2007) called for a more focused and gender-appropriate approach to women who offend and those at risk of offending, including the development of women's centres that could provide an integrated, holistic, and accessible service for women at different stages of the criminal justice system. This was seen as a priority in the Government's response and taken forward in the pursuance of the Together Women Programme, which offered a range of services, supports, and activities to women in the form of One Stop shops (Hedderman et al., 2008; 2011) to which women could be referred from a variety of routes, including the police as a diversionary caution (Easton et al., 2010) and as an alternative to imprisonment (Hedderman, 2011).[2]

As noted in Chapter 6 of this volume, the Equality Acts of 2006 and 2010, in particular, also added impetus for change in regard to responses to women. And the Fawcett Society's review of provision for women in the community in 2007 added meat to Corston's 2007 outline of how things might be done differently, by setting out practical possibilities on the ground, and by indicating nine lessons to take forward in developing more gender appropriate responses to women offenders (Gelsthorpe, Sharpe and Roberts, 2007).

Stocktaking

But some stocktaking is due – which leads to the conclusion that for every few steps forwards there have also been some steps backwards. For instance, whilst the Criminal Justice Act 1991 s.95 created a duty to publish information that might help in addressing discrimination, the Criminal Justice Act 2003 led to a situation where the newly created single community order and suspended sentence order were being used for women who did not necessarily deserve such a sentence. Patel and Stanley found that women were more likely than men to have supervision and drug treatment requirements attached to community orders and suspended sentences in England and Wales, while they were less likely to be subject to requirements involving unpaid work and participation in accredited programmes. Given that there were already long-standing concerns about women being given a community sentence instead of a fine with the concomitant risks of imprisonment in cases of breach, Patel and Stanley's (2008) analysis provides some substantiation for this net-widening argument.

What sentencers think about new developments

Following the impetus of the 2007 Corston report and a financial commitment on the part of government in 2009 and again in 2011 to develop community-based resources for women offenders and women at risk of offending, there are, at the time of writing, over 50 women's centres and projects.[3] But provision of such centres has not necessarily reduced the use of imprisonment (Hedderman and Gunby, 2013).

Indeed, an evaluation of Together Women revealed that magistrates in some areas knew very little about the community-based provision for women, a telling finding in itself (Hedderman and Gunby, 2013). Ironically, in light of the current structural changes to probation under the Transforming Rehabilitation initiative,[4] which devolves major responsibility for less serious offenders (tiers one and two) to newly formed community rehabilitation companies, magistrates claimed that what would most encourage them to reconsider sending a woman to custody would be having another option recommended by a probation officer: 'simply knowing of an initiative like Together Women would not influence such a decision, no matter how worthwhile they considered such an intervention to be' (Hedderman and Gunby, 2013, p. 434). In relation to Together Women, for example, sentencers revealed suspicion of the idea of referring women to programmes which cater to *all* women and not just those who have offended (Jolliffe et al., 2011), perhaps because they are seen as not sufficiently tough. Another issue concerns the Magistrates' Association's (2011) notion that if we have community-based services for women we need exactly the same thing for men. This rather misses the point that the centres have evolved out of knowledge based on women's distinctive needs.

There is clearly a need to educate sentencers and to develop their understanding of why generic provision is more suitable for women than offender-specific programmes. This leads us to the legitimacy of claims concerning 'what works' with women and the need to both elucidate theoretical underpinnings of the work and develop consistent ways of measuring impact across programmes which take us beyond simple (and limited) reconviction studies.

Recent developments

Other relevant initiatives include the publication of the 'Government's Strategic Objectives for Female Offenders' (Ministry of Justice, 2013b); there is emphasis on robust community sentences, including the expansion of community support to women on release from short sentences. Also in 2013, the Justice Select Committee published the findings from its inquiry to review progress made since the Corston report (Justice Select Committee, 2013), which makes a series of recommendations to ensure that the distinct needs of women at risk of entering the criminal justice system are recognized and met. The Government's response to this report was published in October 2013, alongside two other documents, the *Women's Custodial Estate Review* (Robinson, 2013) and a *Stocktake of Women's Services for Offenders in the Community* (National Offender Management Service, 2013).

The Ministry of Justice review of the women's custodial estate makes 17 recommendations; ministers have accepted them all. All women's prisons are to be repurposed as resettlement prisons under the Transforming Rehabilitation proposals, with the number of women's prisons being reduced to ten. A simple way of changing sentencing policy, we might think – in terms of fewer prisons and fewer custodial sentences – but this would be a simplistic conclusion, since capacity will be increased in some prisons. The two existing open prisons – Askham Grange and East Sutton Park – are to be closed. (There are, however, plans for the creation of a small open unit linked to HMP Styal). Further, a unit at HMPYOI Peterborough has been established for female foreign national prisoners, with the aim of developing this into a hub for women with identified immigration needs. NOMS's *Stocktake of Women's Services* shows that the spread and availability of community services for women has been increasing and purports to set the groundwork for the expansion of community support for women on release from short custodial sentences in 2014 and beyond. It aims to help new providers (under the Transforming Rehabilitation reforms) to see the possibilities for innovation – particularly through the involvement of organisations from the voluntary and community sector.

Indeed, the Offender Rehabilitation Act 2014 contains provisions which mean that virtually all offenders (male and female) will receive at least 12 months supervision in the community on release from custody. One particular concern here is that this may increase the number of women subject to custody – through increasing the numbers of recalls to prison for breach (see Ministry of Justice, 2012b). How familiar the new community rehabilitation companies will be with skills for effective engagement and development (SEED) initiatives (Sorsby et al., 2013), for instance, remains to be seen. Moreover, it is not clear how far supervision practice is – and will be – gender-informed, yet there are now substantive bodies of work which show precisely what does and does not work with women in terms of suitable approaches (Gelsthorpe, 2010).

Representation and neutrality

We should also think about representation and neutrality. 'The social service which the judge renders to the community is the removal of a sense of injustice', wrote Lord Devlin (1979, p. 3). The concept of impartiality is arguably the foundation stone and guiding philosophy of the English legal system upon which the credibility and legitimacy of the criminal justice system depends; a judicial system which is partial cannot command universal consent or respect. To summarise, there is a popular claim still that the judiciary is elderly, male and white, meaning that justice means 'male justice'. The Government has taken steps to increase the diversity of the judiciary in recent years, including the setting up of a judicial diversity taskforce (Ministry of Justice, 2012c), but of course, the composition of the judiciary inevitably reflects the composition of the legal profession more widely. Here we are alerted to the fact that the most recent available statistics indicated that women comprise 35% of barristers and 45% of private practice solicitors (Ministry of Justice, 2012b, Tables S6.08 and S6.11a, Supplementary Tables).

In terms of court-based judiciary (and excluding Justices of the Supreme Court since data are no longer held centrally), women accounted for 23% of the 3,575 judges in England and Wales in 2012; men made up 77% (Ministry of Justice, 2012b, p. 107). The proportion of women has increased by only four percentage points since 2008. In practice, recorders (part-time judges) account for the largest proportion of the court's judiciary (32%), and comprise 16% women and 84% men. Again, there has been little change since 2008. Women were most represented as deputy masters, deputy registrars, deputy costs judges and deputy district judges, accounting for 39% of the total members of this category.

In 2012, women represented 51% of the 25,170 lay magistrates in post. These proportions have been relatively consistent, despite a 14% reduction in the total number of lay magistrates over this period.[5] But a critical question is whether gender-based representation matters. Some 30 years ago, Farrington and Morris (1983) found that distinctions were made in court between female defendants; decisions were affected by factors such as the involvement of other offenders, marital status, family background and the gender composition of the bench. Controlling for various other factors, women appearing before a bench made up of two women and a man were dealt with more severely than women appearing before benches of two men and a woman. But it was not clear why this was so, beyond speculation that women on the magistrates' bench were more censorious than men in relation to women defendants because they had to show that they could be as tough if not tougher than men.

Simple statistical analyses (whether through central government bodies or research studies) are not able to address the dynamics of courtroom processes or even the dynamics between the players in the courtroom. Moreover, they are not able to address the multiplicity of factors that might shape sentencing outcomes, including pleas in mitigation or the provision of pre-sentence reports. Thus statistical representation alone tells us nothing about the quality of justice within the courtroom, and statistical analyses of outcomes may mask gender-related factors in the process of sentencing. There is scope for further research here in a number of areas: does the gender representation of those in authority in the courtroom have an impact on perceptions of justice? In other words, what symbolic value does representation by women within the judiciary and magistracy have upon perceptions and experiences of justice by both consumers (victims and offenders) and other members of the public?

Equal but different

In the wake of numerous research studies which pointed out that women commit less serious offences than men, that they are less dangerous, and that the social costs of imprisonment are higher than for men, the Prison Reform Trust's 2000 report argued that 'Equal treatment does not mean identical treatment, whether for women, or for members of cultural or ethnic minorities' (2000, para 7.2). The Corston report (2007) rehearsed this central idea, noting that from April 2007 the government would have a statutory duty to take positive action to eliminate gender discrimination and promote equality under the Equality Act 2010. Baroness Corston went on to say that 'I have seen little evidence ... of any real understanding that treating men and women the same results in equality of outcome. Equality does not mean treating everyone the same' (2007, p. 3). Rather, it suggests treatment as an equal. But this subtle difference does present some challenges. The argument has often been that any particular needs of offenders can be taken into account via mitigating factors (Easton and Piper 2012), notwithstanding suggestions that the Sentencing Council's approach to mitigation does not go far enough and does not represent justice (Cooper, 2008; see also Lovegrove, 2010). At the same time, there are arguments against impact mitigation (which is often used in arguments in favour of the differential treatment of women in sentencing), not least because this sets up potential differences in treatment among women, as well as between men and women, creating as much confusion and discrimination as it resolves in terms of differential impact.

Interestingly, notwithstanding Sentencing Advisory Panel (2007) guidance to the Sentencing Guidelines Council on 'Overarching Principles of Sentencing', which gives specific attention to women offenders, the intention is perhaps to inform rather than 'direct'. The section points out that there may be public support for less use of imprisonment, that many women offenders are particularly vulnerable, and that

> sentencing them within a criminal justice system that primarily has been developed to deal with the majority of offenders, who are male, may sometimes result in unfair treatment and outcomes. The Panel, therefore, considers that it is appropriate to recommend a number of principles relating to the way in which the approach to sentencing, whilst remaining faithful to generic values, may need to be slightly adjusted to allow for the particular vulnerabilities of women offenders. (ibid., sec. 3, para. 218)

These principles revolve around the fact that women tend to commit less serious crimes than men; in addition, there are considerations of low culpability, the responsibility for providing childcare or other dependents' care, and behaviour that is sometimes instigated or controlled by men. As the SAP Guidance states,

> By way of conclusion, it is unfair to seek to address any perceived shortfall in the provision of services for women in the community by unnecessarily holding them on remand, or by imposing custodial sentences within which it is hoped that suitable interventions might be provided when this is not commensurate with the seriousness of an offence, and such an approach must be avoided. (ibid., para. 239)

The same principle is rehearsed in relation to custody because of women's particular health vulnerabilities. Recommendation 20 is a statutory requirement that a custodial sentence must not be imposed unless the offence is so serious that neither a fine alone nor a community sentence can be justified and which has a special force in relation to women offenders because of the multiple harms that are likely to result from incarceration (ibid. p. 75). And there is suggestion in Recommendation 21 that the court must always obtain a pre-sentence report before sentencing a woman offender to custody, with the granting of bail while such a report is being prepared (ibid. p. 76).

But we know that there is a difference between rhetoric and reality here, with 65% of women being given short sentences of imprisonment in 2011 (Ministry of Justice, 2012b, p. 75). Indeed, information obtained under a Freedom of Information request shows that in 2011, 2,500 and in 2012 2,458 women were given sentences of under three months (see Table 7.1). The average custodial sentence for women in the magistrates' courts is just two months (Hedderman and Barnes, this volume,

Table 7.1 Female sentence receptions by sentence length* and offence, England and Wales, 2012

	Less than or equal to 6 months	Of which: Less than or equal to 3 months	Of which: Less than or equal to 4 weeks	Of which: Less than or equal to 10 days
Violence Against the Person	617	290	54	1
Sexual Offences	3	0	0	0
Robbery	25	3	0	0
Burglary	81	33	6	1
Theft and Handling	2,159	1,232	231	11
Fraud and Forgery	140	50	7	0
Drug Offences	92	45	7	0
Motoring Offences	96	49	6	0
Other Offences	1,262	743	156	9
Offence Not Recorded	25	13	2	0
All	**4,500**	**2,458**	**469**	**22**

Note: These figures have been drawn from administrative IT systems. Care is taken when processing and analysing the returns, but the detail collected is subject to the inaccuracies inherent in any large-scale recording system, so although shown to the last individual, the figure may not be accurate to that level.

* Receptions are counted in each of the bands into which they fit, e.g. a 10-day sentence will be counted in all four sentence-length bands.

Source: Ministry of Justice (JSAS/FOI) 82495. With thanks to Rona Epstein for these figures.

Chapter 6). These data hardly seem to reflect the notion of the use of custody as a last resort for women, which is implicit in the guidance. Indeed, even if we exclude consideration of women who have committed violent offences, the number of women in custody is still very high.

Concerns about the high use of imprisonment for women are compounded, of course, by the complex issue of sentencing women who are parents, especially since the forcible separation of parent and child via the imprisonment of the parent interferes with the rights of the child under Article 8 of the Human Rights Act 1998 by depriving him or her of parental care. Shona Minson addresses this issue in detail in Chapter 8.

Towards a conclusion

There have been strong arguments regarding the need to reduce the rate of imprisonment for women on grounds of their vulnerability. Indeed, a very high proportion of women lawbreakers have suffered violent and/or sexual victimisation (Prison Reform Trust, 2011). Indeed, for women, it is suggested that victimisation and offending are so frequently intertwined that victimisation might be considered an indirect pathway into crime (Giordano et al., 2006; Rumgay, 2004). The fact that female defendants' past experiences of victimisation have frequently been ignored or minimalized by the police, and rarely brought to the attention of the courts, raises important questions about the legitimacy of punishing their own, usually much less serious, crimes, and indeed about the state's right to punish those women who, as victims, it has denied or ignored (Carlen, 1983). But years of campaigns to reduce women's imprisonment have seemingly borne little fruit. Such campaigns have focused overwhelmingly on women's neediness and vulnerability as well as on the merits of community alternatives to custody. An unintended consequence may have been to raise awareness of women's needs. Moreover, cuts to mainstream health and welfare services in a context of recession (MacLeavy, 2011) may mean that the relatively swift availability of help via criminal justice avenues is particularly attractive to sentencers. (This may explain the high use of imprisonment for women on remand when less than half of those remanded by magistrates' courts and subsequently found guilty [700 of 1,600 in 2011] are given a prison sentence [Ministry of Justice, 2012b, Tables S4.61, S4.62, S4.63]). Whether sentencers really view prisons as modern social services remains an empirical question of course, although, as previously indicated, women defendants tend to be considered more troubled than troublesome (Gelsthorpe and Loucks, 1997).

The evidence of short sentences being given to women (see Table 7.1) seriously undermines popular claims that nothing short of imprisonment is necessary for public protection.

Ways forward?

'Equal but different' could be interpreted as leading to differences in the *form* of penalty rather than the *level* of penalty; this might be perfectly justifiable in light of research evidence concerning women's distinctive needs. In practical terms, this means sentencing both a man and a woman on the basis of the seriousness of their offence (and other sentencing aims) and acknowledging mitigating factors (the potential impact of imprisonment on dependent children) for both. But in a context of promoting the use of alternatives to custody wherever possible, and with recognition that women commit less serious offences than men, and serve shorter sentences (Ministry of Justice 2012a), it is clear that proportionately more women offenders would stand to benefit from this – without having to subvert the principle of desert.

Another possibility concerns limiting magistrates' sentencing powers, so as to avoid the use of short sentences for less serious, and particularly nonviolent offences. This, too, would benefit women in particular, but not exclusively, given that their offences mainly relate to theft and handling. We might also suggest that there is scope to challenge the criminalisation, as well the imprisonment, of women. The announcement, in January 2014, of £25 million of government funding for a national rollout of liaison and diversion schemes – targeting arrestees with mental illness, learning disabilities and substance misuse problems (Department of Health, 2014) is a welcome development and may have an impact on some vulnerable women. However, at the time of writing, there is no clear evidence that schemes will be required to attend to gender in the delivery of services.

Another possibility concerns the structured deferred sentence – a low tariff intervention in Scotland providing structured social work intervention for offenders post-conviction but prior to sentencing. It is intended for offenders with underlying problems such as drug or alcohol dependency, mental illness, learning difficulties or unemployment that might be addressed through social work interventions. Barry and McIvor (2008) maintain that structured deferred sentences are very well suited to women, and indeed, a national evaluation suggests that they have been popular with sentencers in respect of women (Macdivitt, 2008). In England, we might anticipate referrals to community centres for women for suitable interventions or utilisation of the range of services provided by the newly established community rehabilitation companies following a restructuring and privatisation of the probation service (Ministry of Justice, 2013a).

Official statistics consistently demonstrate that, on the whole, women tend to show greater compliance than men (though only marginally so) (Ministry of Justice, 2012b, p. 94), and one particular challenge concerns the use of custody for those in breach of community orders. But arguably it is incumbent upon the criminal justice system to examine the reasons for breaches of orders, whether relating to stigma, child care responsibilities which prevent the completion of requirements, or the gender appropriateness of sentence provision in terms of time, place or content (McCulloch, 2010; Gelsthorpe, 2013). Indeed, it could be considered a public duty under the Equality Act 2010 to make appropriate provision for women. Should the courts therefore have a duty to evaluate the impact of the delivery of interventions (for example, the place, time, childcare arrangements and general appropriateness for women)? Essentially, is there scope to breach the sentence/service providers rather than the sentence/service consumer? Of course, providers are held to account via HM Inspectorates (probation and prisons), but negative reports alone do not always have an impact on practice; it is certainly perceived that such inspectorates lack teeth. Carlen has called for a reimagining of criminal justice

> within a two-dimensional reparative social justice: reparation from all lawbreakers ... to the state in proportion both to the harms committed and the ability to pay; and reparation from the state to those citizens whom it has failed materially and culturally in terms of ensuring satisfaction of their minimum material and cultural needs (2013, p. 100)

This version of 'more sinned against than sinning' is a valid position, but it presents certain challenges: not all of those who are sinned against – or neglected by the state – proceed to commit offences.

One potential way of improving sentencing practice towards women might be the introduction of specialist women's courts, along similar lines to drug courts (Malloch and McIvor, 2011; Ward, 2014). Such a model would facilitate the provision of specialist training for sentencers (and indeed for authors of pre-sentence reports on women) on issues such as avoiding sentencing women to welfare, and tailoring the content of sentences to women's needs without making them more difficult to comply with and thus more punitive. When dealing with breach, courts might consider the appropriateness – taking into account whether any childcare responsibilities have been accommodated, whether women-only provision has been made available, and so on – of orders with which women have not complied. However, responding to women solely on the grounds of gender carries several risks, most notably gender essentialism, or a tendency to ignore differences between women according to age, ethnicity and class.

Concluding Reflections

These reflections aside, it is important to acknowledge that criminal justice has become so politicised that the sustainability of new developments is always at issue. Increasingly, criminal justice developments are driven by economic factors (the need to make financial savings for example) and political factors (an ideological commitment to market competition to deliver services following sentencing for example). Political swings and fiscal controls exacerbate the challenges in addressing women offenders' needs in appropriate and proportionate fashion.

Across different jurisdictions and amongst academics, policy makers, practitioners and campaigners there has been growing recognition that prison is not an appropriate place for women in conflict with the law. The prison has often been a focus for concerns about human rights violation, but a human rights perspective has not brought the much-needed reforms (Moore and Jemphrey, 2013). Moreover, there has been slow attention to the lack of services specifically tailored for women. What is recognised is that women in conflict with the law are often vulnerable, victims of abuse, subject to domestic violence, and poor. As Player (2012, p. 266) suggests, the principle of equality of impact for women in sentencing remains constrained by the proportionality requirements of desert theory. Consequently, the impact of significant sociocultural variables such as women's histories of abuse, their caring responsibility within the family, and the effect their sentences could have on innocent third parties continue to be left to the vagaries of judicial discretion. But movement away from desert principles could delegitimise sentencing. Differential sentencing is not the answer. What is required is an educational programme for sentencers to enhance the capacity of sentencing courts to generate outcomes that engage meaningfully with the social reality of women's lives.

Notes

1. Section 143(2) of the Criminal Justice Act 2003 instructs courts to treat previous convictions as an aggravating factor, thus arguably encouraging progressive sentencing.
2. Importantly, there were similar developments in Scotland during this time with the establishment of Centre 218 in Glasgow in late 2003, involving government funding, providing a range of residential and non-residential

services and adopting a holistic, gender-appropriate approach to women who were at risk of imprisonment (Malloch et al., 2008).
3. http://www.womensbreakout.org.uk.
4. The Transforming Rehabilitation initiative has involved the division of responsibility for offenders between a national probation service and community rehabilitation companies (private and voluntary sector organisations). See Ministry of Justice (2013a).
5. More detailed diversity data can be found at: http://www.judiciary.gov.uk/about-the-judiciary/judges-career-paths/diversity-gender-age-ethnicity/.

References

Allen, H. (1987) *Justice Unbalanced: Gender, Psychiatry and Judicial Decisions*. Milton Keynes: Open University Press.

Barry, M. and McIvor, G. (2008) *Chaotic Lives: A Profile of Women in the Criminal Justice System in Lothian and Borders*. Edinburgh: Lothian and Borders Community Justice Authority.

Carlen, P. (1983) On rights and powers: some notes on penal politics. In: D. Garland and P. Young (eds) *The Power to Punish: Contemporary Penalty and Social Analysis*. London: Heinemann.

——(2002) (ed.) *Women and Imprisonment: The Struggle for Justice*. Cullompton: Willan.

——(2013) Against rehabilitation; for reparative justice. In: K. Carrington, M. Ball, E. O'Brien and J. Tauri (eds) *Crime, Justice and Social Democracy: International perspectives*. Basingstoke: Palgrave.

Cooper, J. (2008) The Sentencing Guidelines Council. A Practical Perspective. *Criminal Law Review*, 4: 277–286.

Corston, Baroness (2007) *The Corston Report: A Review of Women with Particular Vulnerabilities in the Criminal Justice System*. London: Home Office.

Deakin, J. and Spencer, J. (2003) Women Behind Bars: Explanations and Implications. *Howard Journal of Criminal Justice*, 42: 123–136.

Department of Health (2014) Press Release: Extra Funding for Mental Health Nurses to be Based at Police Stations and Courts across the Country. https://www.gov.uk/government/news/extra-funding-for-mental-health-nurses-to-be-based-at-police-stations-and-courts-across-the-country. 6 Jan 2014.

Devlin, P. (1979) *The Judge*. Oxford: Oxford University Press.

Dominelli, L. (1984) Differential Justice: Domestic Labour, Community Service and Female Offenders. *Probation Journal*, 31: 100–103.

Easton, S., Silvestri, M., Evans, K., Matthews, R. and Walklate, S. (2010) *Condition Cautions: Evaluation of the Women Specific Condition Pilot*. Ministry of Justice Research Series 14/10. London: Ministry of Justice.

Easton, S. and Piper, C. (2012) *Sentencing and Punishment. The Quest for Justice*. Oxford: Oxford University Press.

Edwards, S. (1984) *Women on Trial: a Study of The Female Suspect, Defendant, and Offender in the Criminal Law and Criminal Justice System*. Manchester: Manchester University Press.

Farrington, D. and Morris, A. (1983) Sex, Sentencing and Reconviction. *British Journal of Criminology*, 23(3): 229–248.

Fawcett Society (2004) *Women and the Criminal Justice System: A Report of the Fawcett Society's Commission on Women and the Criminal Justice System*. London: Fawcett Society.

Gelsthorpe, L. (2001) Critical decisions and processes in the criminal courts. In: E. McLaughlin and J. Muncie (eds) *Controlling Crime*. London: Sage/Open University.
—— (2005) Back to basics in crime control: weaving in women. In: M. Matravers (ed.) *Managing Modernity. Politics and the Culture of Control*. London: Routledge.
—— (2007) Sentencing and gender. In: R. Sheehan, G. McIvor and C. Trotter (eds) *Working with Women Offenders in the Community*. Cullompton: Willan Publishing.
Gelsthorpe, L. (2010) What works with women offenders? In: M. Herzog-Evans (ed.) *Transnational Criminology Manual*. Vol. 3. Nijmegen, Netherlands: Wolf Legal Publishers.
—— (2013) Working with women in probation: "Will you, won't you, will you, won't you, won't you join the dance?" In: P. Ugwidike and P. Raynor (eds) *What Works in Offender Compliance: International Perspectives and Evidence-based Practice*. Basingstoke: Palgrave Macmillan.
Gelsthorpe, L. and Loucks, N. (1997) Magistrates' explanations of sentencing decisions. In: C. Hedderman and L. Gelsthorpe (eds) *Understanding the Sentencing of Women*. London: Home Office.
Gelsthorpe, L. and Morris, A. (2002) Women's Imprisonment in England and Wales: A Penal Paradox. *Criminal Justice*, 2(3): 277–301.
Gelsthorpe, L., Sharpe, G. and Roberts, J. (2007) *Provision for Women Offenders in the Community*. London: The Fawcett Society. www.fawcettsociety.org.uk/
Giordano, P., Deines, J. and Cernkovich, S. (2006) In and out of crime: a life course perspective on girls' delinquency. In: K. Heimer and C. Kruttschnitt (eds) *Gender and Crime: Patterns in Victimization and Offending*. New York: New York University Press.
Hannah-Moffatt, K. (2004) Criminogenic Need and the Transformative Risk Subject: Hybridizations of Risk/Need in Penalty. *Punishment and Society*, 7: 29–51.
Hedderman, C. (2004) Why are more women being sentenced to custody? In: G. McIvor (ed.) *Women Who Offend*. London: Jessica Kingsley.
—— (2011) Policy developments in England and Wales. In: R. Sheehan, G. McIvor and C. Trotter (eds) *Working With Women Offenders in the Community*. Cullompton: Willan Publishing.
Hedderman, C. and Gelsthorpe, L. (1997) *Understanding the Sentencing of Women*. Home Office Research Study 170. London: Home Office.
Hedderman, C. and Gunby, C. (2013) Diverting Women from Custody: The Importance of Understanding Sentencers' Perspectives. *Probation Journal*, 60(4): 425–438.
Hedderman, C., Palmer, E. and Hollin, C. with the assistance of Gunby, C. (2008) *Implementing Services for Women Offenders and Those 'at Risk' of Offending: Action Research with Together Women*. Ministry of Justice Research Series 12/08. London: Ministry of Justice.
Heidensohn, F. (1968) The Deviance of Women: A Critique and an Enquiry. *British Journal of Sociology*, 19(2): 160–175.
—— (1986) Models of Justice: Portia or Persephone? Some Thoughts on Equality, Fairness and Gender in the Field of Criminal Justice. *International Journal of Sociology of Law*, 14: 287–298.

Howard League for Penal Reform (2006) *Women in the penal system,* Second Report on women with particular vulnerabilities in the criminal justice system. *All Party Parliamentary Group on Women in the Penal system, Chaired by Baroness Corston.* London: The Howard League.

Hudson, B. (2002) Gender issues in penal policy and penal theory. In: P. Carlen (ed.) *Women and Punishment: The Struggle for Justice.* Cullompton: Willan Publishing.

Jolliffe, D., Hedderman, C., Palmer, E. and Hollin, C. (2011) *Re-offending Analysis of Women Offenders Referred to Together Women (TW) and the Scope to Divert from Custody.* Ministry of Justice Research Series 11/11. London: Ministry of Justice.

Justice Select Committee (2013) *Women Offenders: After the Corston Report.* Second Report of Sessions 2013–2014. London: House of Commons.

Loucks, N. (1998) *HMPI Cornton Vale: Research into Drugs and Alcohol, Violence and Bullying, Suicides and Self-Injury, and Backgrounds of Abuse.* SPS Occasional Paper 1/98. Edinburgh: Scottish Prison Service.

Lovegrove, A. (2010) The Sentencing Council, The Public's Sense of Justice, and Personal Mitigation. *Criminal Law Review,* (12): 906–923.

Macdivitt, K. (2008) *An Evaluation of the Structured Deferred Sentence Pilots.* Edinburgh: Scottish Government.

MacKinnon, C. (1987) *Feminism Unmodified: Discourses on Life and Law.* Cambridge, MA: Harvard University Press.

MacLeavy, J. (2011) A 'New Politics' of Austerity, Workfare and Gender? The UK Coalition Government's Welfare Reform Proposals. *Cambridge Journal of Regions, Economy and Society,* 1–13.

Magistrates Association Paper (2011) *Women in the Justice System.* Policy Paper 11/33. London: Magistrates' Association.

Mair, G. and Brockington, N. (1988) Female Offenders and the Probation Service. *Howard Journal of Criminal Justice,* 27(2): 117–126.

Malloch, M., McIvor, G. and Loucks, N. (2008) 'Time Out' for Women: Innovation in Scotland in a Context of Change. *The Howard Journal of Criminal Justice,* 47(4): 383–399.

Malloch, M. and McIvor, G. (2011) Women, drugs and community interventions. In: R. Sheehan, G. McIvor and C. Trotter (eds) *Working with Women Offenders in the Community.* Cullompton: Willan Publishing.

McCulloch, T. (2010) Exploring community service. understanding compliance. In: F. McNeill, P. Raynor and C. Trotter (eds) *Offender Supervision: New Directions in Theory, Research and Practice.* Cullompton: Willan Publishing.

McIvor, G. (2010) Women and crime: The rise in female imprisonment in western countries. In: M. Herzog-Evans (ed.) *Transnational Criminology Manual, Vol. 2,* Nijmegen. The Netherlands: Wolf Legal Publishers.

Ministry of Justice (2012a) *Offender Management Caseload Statistics 2011.* London: Ministry of Justice.

—— (2012b) *Statistics on Women and the Criminal Justice System 2011.* A Ministry of Justice publication under Section 95 of the Criminal Justice Act 1991. London: Ministry of Justice. (Supplementary Tables are indicated by an S).

—— (2012c) *Improving Judicial Diversity: Progress towards Delivery of the Report of the Advisory Panel on Judicial Diversity 2010.* London: Ministry of Justice.

—— (2013a) *Transforming Rehabilitation: A Strategy for Reform.* London: Ministry of Justice.

—— (2013b) *Government's Strategic Objectives for Female Offenders.* London: Ministry of Justice.
Minson, R. (2014) *Mitigating Motherhood: A Study of the Impact of Motherhood on Sentencing Decisions in England and Wales.* London: Howard League.
Moore, L. and Jemphrey, A. (2013) Women's imprisonment in Northern Ireland: social exclusion, punishment and breaches of human rights. In: M. Malloch and G. McIvor (eds) *Women, Punishment and Social Justice: Human Rights and Penal Practices.* Abingdon: Routledge.
Morris, A. and Gelsthorpe, L. (1981) 'Women and Crime'. Papers presented to the Cropwood Round-Table Conference 1980. Cropwood Conference Series No. 13, University of Cambridge: Institute of Criminology.
Moxon, D. (1988) *Sentencing Practice in the Crown Court.* Home Office Research Study 103. London: HMSO.
National Offender Management Service (NOMS) (2013) *Stocktake of Women's Services for Offenders in the Community.* London: NOMS.
Patel, S. and Stanley, S. (2008) *The Use of the Community Order and the Suspended Sentence Order for Women.* London: Centre for Crime and Justice Studies.
Player, E. (2012) Sentencing women: towards gender equality. In: L. Zedner and J.V Roberts (eds) *Principles and Values in Criminal Law and Criminal Justice: Essays in Honour of Andrew Ashworth.* Oxford: Oxford University Press.
Prison Reform Trust (2000) *Justice For Women: The Need For Reform.* The report of the Committee on Women's Imprisonment, Chaired by Professor Dorothy Wedderburn. London: Prison Reform Trust.
—— (2011) *Reforming Women's Justice: Report of the Women's Taskforce.* London: Prison Reform Trust.
Robinson, C. (2013) *Women's Custodial Estate Review.* London, Ministry of Justice: National Offender Management Service.
Rumgay, J. (2004) *When Victims Become Offenders: In Search of Coherence in Policy and Practice.* London: The Fawcett Society.
Sentencing Advisory Panel (2007) *Advice to the Sentencing Guidelines Council. Overarching Principles of Sentencing.* London: Sentencing Advisory Panel.
Smart, C. (1976) *Women, Crime and Criminology.* London: Routledge.
Smith, A. (1962) *Women in Prison. A Study in Penal Methods.* London: Stevens & Sons.
Sorsby, A., Shapland, J., Farrall, S., McNeill, F., Priede, C. and Robinson, G. (2013) *Probation Staff Views of the Skills for Effective Engagement Development (SEED) Pilot.* National Offender Management Service Analytical Summary 2013. London: National Offender Management Service.
Tombs, J. and Jagger, E. (2006) Denying Responsibility: Sentencers' Accounts of Their Decisions to Imprison. *British Journal of Criminology,* 46(5): 803–821.
Ward, J. (2014) *Are Problem-Solving Courts the Way Forward for Justice?* Working Paper 2/2014. London: The Howard League for Penal Reform.
Wilczynski, A. (1997) Mad or Bad? Child-killers, Gender and the Courts. *British Journal of Criminology,* 37: 419–436.
Wilks-Wiffen, S. (2011) *Voice of a Child.* London: The Howard League for Penal Reform.
Worrall, A. (1990) *Offending Women: Female Lawbreakers and the Criminal Justice System.* London: Routledge.
Zedner, L. (1991) *Women, Crime and Custody in Victorian England.* Oxford: Clarendon Press.

8

Sentencing and Dependents: Motherhood as Mitigation

Shona Minson

The impact of imprisonment on women

Studies on the particular characteristics and needs of women offenders (Cabinet Office: Social Exclusion Task Force, 2009; Corston Report, 2007; Commission on Women and the Criminal Justice System, 2009; Women's Justice Taskforce, 2011) have advocated a sentencing approach which acknowledges differences between the male and female sentenced populations and the differing consequential outcomes upon them. The most significant gendered variation is that a greater number of women than men in prison have been the primary caregivers for a child or children prior to their sentence. As women are one of the fastest growing populations within the prison estate, by inference, an ever-increasing number of children are affected by the imprisonment of their primary carer. Between 1995 and 2010, the female prison population more than doubled, from 1,979 to 4,236 (Ministry of Justice, 2014, Table A1.2 Offender Management Statistics Annual Tables 2013), and there was a general increase in the numbers of women sentenced for all offences, rising from 258,600 in 2002 to 299,117 in 2011 (Ministry of Justice, 2012; Statistics on Women and the Criminal Justice System 2011). This increase has taken place despite no corresponding increase in the volume or seriousness of female offending.

Using Gresham Sykes' 1958 'pains of imprisonment' analysis, women suffer the loss of liberty, loss of possessions and loss of autonomy (Genders and Player, 1987, p. 168). Women feel the loss of liberty in the loss of relationships (ibid., p. 170), and as 66% of imprisoned women are mothers of children under 18 (Liebling, 2005, p. 159), many of those are relationships with children. Of those women, 34% have children under 5 and a further 40% have children aged between 5 and 10. The

Social Exclusion Unit report found that women often have no opportunity to discuss how they are going to address childcare issues before they are taken to prison (SEU 2002, p. 112) and the consequence of this on women and children is severe. This contrasts with fathers, whose children are in most cases cared for in the family home by the mother during the period of imprisonment (Gampell, 2003 in Mills and Codd, 2007, p. 686). Additionally, it is difficult for women to receive visits from their children (SEU, 2002), as on average one in five women are placed more than 100 miles from their home (Social Exclusion Task Force, 2009 p. 18). It has been reported that only half of the women who had lived, or were in contact with, their children prior to imprisonment had received a visit since going to prison (SEU, 2002 in PRT, 2010, p. 21). This combination of being held at a significant distance from home and the lack of family / parent carers, does not affect men to the same extent. A third of these mothers are single parents (SEU, 2002, p. 137); only 9% of those children are cared for by their fathers during their mother's imprisonment (Corston, 2007, p. 20), and only 5% remain in the family home (Caddle and Crisp, 1997). Out of 1400 women serving a first sentence in Holloway prison, 42 did not know who was looking after their children (Corston, 2007, p. 16).

Loss of possessions, particularly home and property, affects women more than men, as most men have a female who takes care of their property and possessions while they are in prison (Social Exclusion Unit, 2002, p. 104; Corston, 2007, p. 21). Housing benefits stop at sentence if a prisoner is going to be in prison for more than 13 weeks, so properties are repossessed whilst women are serving their sentence, and often the possessions found at the house are destroyed. Women come out to find themselves 'intentionally homeless' with no personal possessions (Social Exclusion Unit, 2002, p. 98). If children have been taken into local authority care, they will not be returned to the mother until she has suitable housing, and without children she is not prioritised (ibid., p. 104). Housing can also be lost because of poor communication with landlords, and this is more likely to affect women, as they are held further away from their homes (ibid.). Both Dobash and Genders suggested that loss of autonomy is felt in both the areas outlined above as women are powerless to make arrangements about these key areas of their lives and are dependent on others to make arrangements on their behalf. There is a fundamental conflict in the approach to incarcerated women in the expectation that they will use their period of imprisonment to take responsibility and yet the level of control prohibits them from having sufficient autonomy to be self-determining (Dobash, R. Dobash and Gutteridge, 1986, p. 141; Genders, 1987, p. 170).

Judicial discretion in the consideration of motherhood

Sentencing guidelines set out the boundaries within which a judge should sentence, but it is in the consideration of personal mitigation that judges are able to exercise their discretion. At the point of sentence, a judge knows the circumstances of the offence, the plea that was entered, and the details of previous convictions. It is possible that a pre-sentence report may have been prepared and it is likely that the defendant's representative will offer a plea in mitigation.

An important study on personal mitigation in England and Wales used sentencing observation and judicial interviews to gather data (Jacobson and Hough, 2007). It found that in just under 50% of observed cases, personal mitigation was an evident factor in the sentencing (ibid., p. 14), and in 43 of 127 observed cases the judges said the personal circumstances of the offender pulled the sentence back from one of immediate custody (ibid., p. 12). In 61 of 162 cases, information provided to the judges led to a shorter custodial sentence. There was significant variation between the judges in their sentencing behaviours. As part of the study, judges considered three sentencing exercises and in one of these the defendant was a mother of three dependent children. Out of 39 judges, an equal number thought that factor would reduce the sentence from custodial to non-custodial or halve the sentence length as thought that it would have no impact on sentence at all (ibid., p. 16), thus illustrating the subjectivity of the process. The study concluded: 'the significance of mitigation in sentencing is not recognised by policy... the researchers suggest that there is a need for guidance, for example by the Sentencing Guidelines Council, on the principles of personal mitigation that should and should not be incorporated into sentencer's decision making' (2007, p. vii).

Does the impact of sentence on the defendant constitute mitigation?

Within the context of the arguments put forward in this chapter, it is necessary to have a discussion of whether the way in which a defendant will be affected by a sentence should be considered by the sentencing court. This is because a defendant's motherhood will only become relevant as a mitigating factor if the impact of the sentence on their family members or dependents is something which the court should take into account.

The principle of 'equal impact' is that in circumstances where an offender is likely to suffer from the sentence to a significantly different degree than most other people, there is a case for reducing its length (Ashworth, 2010, p. 185). Martin Wasik (2008, p. 216) noted that the guidelines provide for an 'equal decision making process in determining a sentence' rather than providing for an equal outcome. Christine Piper argued for equality of impact (Piper 2007, p. 141) at a time when the factors which influence sentencing policy seemed to be placing significant emphasis on victim impact (see the paper by Easton and Piper 2008, p. 10). Piper's paper argues that only if the offending was less serious would the court consider 'innocent others', such as children, when sentencing. Piper cites the case of Mills which stated that a court should where possible take into account whether the offender is a primary carer for a child. Piper recognised that this approach could be problematic if defendants with children received more lenient sentences, but argued it is better to apply 'retributivist principles to impact factors' as a matter of principle (ibid., p. 155), rather than leaving it to the courts' mercy.

Easton did not disagree with Piper's premise that there was inequality, but argued for the difference to be made not at sentencing but at the point of punishment. She, too, had found that the needs and well-being of dependent children were sometimes taken into account but not always (2008, p. 112). Easton cautioned against idealising family life, and attempting to apply a sentencing philosophy which would require the courts to make judgments about good and bad mothers and which would create absurd and unfair results (ibid. p. 113). Her proposed solution was to address the inequality in punishment at the point of punishment, for example, by giving more support to prisoners' families, or following the Corston report recommendation to house women in smaller local units (2007, p. 5), thus removing the issue of distance from home to prison which causes greater hardship to women. Addressing difference at the point of punishment would be a positive step, but Easton recognised that it was not the whole answer. She wrote that there should be justice in sentencing, and that disparate impact should be avoided (2008, p. 114).

Tanya Loueiro's research in Scotland on the possible introduction of child or family impact statements in court (2009, p. 2) found that participants (key stakeholders) thought an assessment should be made of the impact on all minor children when their primary caregiver was sentenced, and that the government should standardise (i.e., through legislation) how that should be taken into consideration (ibid., p. 57). If these assessments were adopted, a judge could still exercise discretion in the balancing exercise, but the provision of these statements would ensure that all judges were equipped with the relevant information on that particular aspect of mitigation.

The issue, however, may not always be that judges do not have the information about the impact a sentence will have, but that they choose to 'justify and legitimate' their decision to imprison (Tombs and Jagger, 2006, p. 809), using strategies such as 'routinisation' – following a sentencing routine and believing that they need no extra information about the offender (ibid., p. 811) – and 'moral prioritising' – believing that upholding justice is of greater importance than the offender (ibid., p. 814) in order to enable them to continue to use prison as a punishment despite being 'aware of prison's futility as a deterrent, of its detrimental and brutalizing regime, of its negative social and far-reaching consequences for future lives, and of the warehousing role that it has in "managing society's problems"' (ibid., p. 809).

Tombs and Jagger's study (2006) suggested that what needed to be addressed was not a lack of information per se but judicial stereotyping and the unquestioning nature of judicial subjectivity. Both of these issues were explored in the research study referred to later in this chapter (Minson, 2012).

Development of mitigation guidelines

Since the publication of the studies cited above, the Sentencing Council has issued sentencing guidelines which set out a non-exhaustive list of mitigating factors which should be considered within different offence categories. Prior to the promulgation of the sentencing guidelines, the Sentencing Advisory Panel conducted a public consultation on the overarching principles of sentencing and then published an advice to the Sentencing Guidelines Council in which they identified a list of offender factors in mitigation to be considered in every case, although

> the degree to which they influence the severity or choice of sentence, if at all, will depend on the nature and seriousness of the conviction offence(s) and the degree to which failing to adjust the sentence would be likely to result in a disposal that is unduly harsh in the particular circumstances of the individual offender. (Recommendation 11, 2009, p. 49)

The Council has not ranked factors in terms of their relative importance, and the problems of judicial subjectivity and sentencing inconsistency remain.

The guidance made four recommendations specific to women; recommendations 20 and 21 are pertinent to this chapter:

> Recommendation 20: The statutory requirement that a custodial sentence must not be imposed unless the offence is so serious that neither a fine alone nor a community sentence can be justified has a special force in relation to women offenders because of the multiple harms that are likely to result from incarceration.
>
> Recommendation 21: A court always must obtain a PSR before sentencing a woman offender to custody; wherever possible, the defendant should be granted bail whilst the PSR is being prepared. (Sentencing Advisory Panel, 2009, p. 75–76)

These recommendations are in accordance with the research previously referenced by Piper, Easton, and Loueiro, but the Sentencing Council has not yet implemented it, and it remains a matter of judicial discretion whether or not a PSR is requested.

Sentencing scholars have advocated greater guidance on mitigation (Lovegrove, 2010, 2011; Roberts, 2008; Roberts, Hough, Ashworth, 2011). This could take the form of guidance as to the relative weights of different factors (2011, p. 530). Judicial reasoning in the application of mitigation remains under-researched. Fielding's 2011 study found that research on sentencing 'largely addresses outcomes, employing statistical analysis, simulations and econometric modelling. Such research offers limited insight into the play of motivations and values' (p. 97).

The remainder of this chapter describes findings from a study of judicial motivations and values when sentencing mothers (Minson, 2012). The study involved judicial interviews and analysis of sentencing transcripts to create an analytical model which provided insights into sentencing. The interviews focused on the judges' approach to personal mitigation and sentencing and explored the way in which they balanced different factors in mitigation.

Purposive sampling (Silverman, 2010, p. 141) was used to select the judges. As both circuit judges and recorders sit in the Crown Court, four of the sample were full-time circuit judges, and one was a part-time recorder. Gender was another relevant parameter, and because those recommended for judicial appointment at the most recent selection exercise prior to the study, were 92% male and 8% female (with the remainder unknown) (Judicial Appointments Committee, 2012, p.11), the sample consisted of four men and one woman.

Although the sample was small, within the methodological framework it provided sufficient data for this exploratory study, through which a process, rather than a population, was being studied (Mason, 2002, p. 135).

Influences on sentencing decisions

From the data gathered through interviews, the model seen in Figure 8.1 was created to illustrate the different stages which judges seemed to move through prior to deciding upon a sentence for a defendant mother. Judges described themselves as using their discretion, influenced by their personal knowledge and understanding, to determine whether or not to use a PSR to inform their sentencing decision. Judges are influenced by case context, their own view of personal mitigation, their interpretation of the parameters of their discretion, and the boundaries set by sentencing tariffs. The remainder of the chapter will use the interview data to illustrate the main findings of the study.

a) Judicial knowledge of the gendered pains of imprisonment (personal knowledge and understanding) varies significantly between judges.

Through the interviews, it became apparent that the judges' understandings of gender issues in imprisonment varied. Two judges brought a depth of knowledge to the subject. Judge 3 made reference to women being imprisoned more often for first offences, being in prison further from home, suffering from increased mental health issues and separation from children, all of which can mean 'that picking up the threads again is harder when they reemerge.' Judge 4 quoted figures for suicide

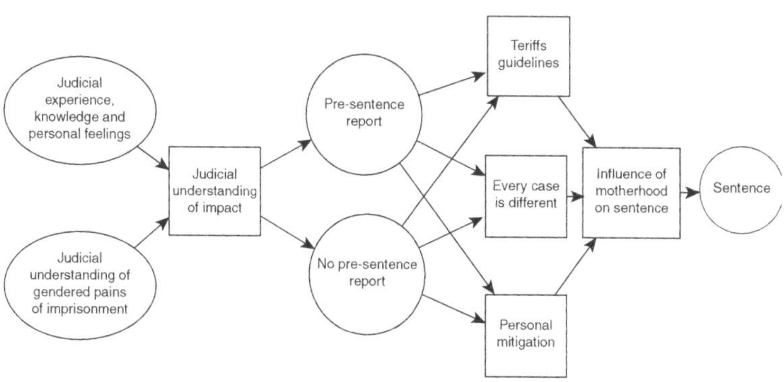

Figure 8.1 Potential influences upon judicial decision-making when sentencing a mother with dependent children

and self-harm among the female prison population, and concluded by saying that 'putting them inside, while it has to happen, and they should be sentenced properly for the offence they committed, can be an extremely harmful thing for them.'

Both of these judges made reference to why they had awareness of gender issues in imprisonment. Judge 4 had studied it at an academic level; Judge 3 said, 'I think I am, again, fairly alive to the knock on effect of this and how destructive short-term, multiple foster care situations can be for children ... because of a good deal of family law experience.' The fact that the others did not mention relevant experience or knowledge did not mean that they did not have any, but it may have influenced them less. The two judges who spoke of their previous knowledge and experience seemed to approach this area of sentencing with some level of emotional response, reflected in their very similar use of language:

> Of course the reality is if someone is a carer on the day *we are straining every sinew* not to punish the children indirectly through the sins of the parents. No, the reality is all the time we are looking – even in serious cases – we are looking to give the maximum achievable weight to those mitigating factors. (Judge 3, emphasis added)

> So, it [motherhood] does have an impact, and it makes — and it *makes me strain* to see if there's an alternative. (Judge 4, emphasis added)

These two judges also talked in terms of being 'desperate to avoid a situation where a parent goes inside', and of the sentencing of parents as a 'troubling' thing to have to do, which could also be 'painful and distressing'.

The other judges seemed to have less awareness, citing separation from children as the main issue for women in prison. Even when they did know about gendered differences, there were also occasions when they lacked confidence in the information. A judge spoke of imprisonment being more difficult for women psychologically, but couched the knowledge in oblique terms, saying,

> It is well known, isn't it, whether rightly or wrongly, but I mean, conventional wisdom is that prison is much harder on women than it is on men. I don't really understand why that should be, but it is thought that a prison sentence is much harder than it is for a man. (Judge 2)

It became clear that some judges had a reluctance to engage with the notion that gender made a difference. Although all of the judges agreed that a woman could suffer potential harm from the loss of her children, they suggested that women should not be given special consideration for this reason:

- Let's not forget: fathers lose children, too, so you know, let's equal it up a bit and not make a sexist point. (Judge 2)
- I generally try to be gender neutral because there are always going to be individual considerations, and they are not purely on a gender basis. (Judge 1)

This approach is contradicted by the literature, which highlights the difficulties, such as the loss of children, that arise when mothers are imprisoned, from which imprisoned fathers are normally shielded (Caddle and Crisp, 1997; Corston, 2007).

Even when the existence of special harms to women was acknowledged, sentencing tariffs and guidelines were given as a reason for not taking gendered differences into account. The distance from home to prison affects the number of visits a prisoner will receive, and this tends to affect women more than men, as there are fewer women's prisons. When this was raised with Judge 1, the judge responded 'I doubt again that it would be appropriate to depart from general guidelines, general principles, just because there are going to be difficulties visiting.' Judge 5 said, 'If I get to the point that the offence is so serious that only a custodial sentence is justified – i.e., I've gone up the league table already – then the offence is so serious, so I'm not actually so concerned about, at that point, impact of multiple harm.' These responses mirrored those found in Millie's 2007 study in which judges were so conscious of the attention which must be paid to sentencing guidelines that they focused on that and paid less attention to mitigation.

b) The interpretation of impact as mitigation is determined by a judge's own knowledge and understanding

The judges acknowledged that their appreciation of the impact of a custodial sentence on a defendant is subjective: 'I suppose the point is that some people may be less aware than others as to what potential impact is; for example on a sole carer,' Judge 4 said. While all of the judges recognised that their mothers going to prison would affect children, their understanding of the extent of the effect varied. Judge 1 took the view that if extended family or people within the community took the children in, then the children 'don't suffer much.' Another realized that separation between mother and child was significant regardless of who cared for them: 'I had to send her inside immediately,' Judge 4 said of a woman at sentencing. 'She had a one-year-old daughter, and I felt terrible. She was going to miss six months of development of her daughter.'

Although (s)he understood that the children would be affected, Judge 5 felt that was not of sufficient importance to make a difference in sentencing: 'I've not ever before weighted that particularly in terms of reduction anywhere.'

The judges interviewed varied in their opinions as to whether the way in which a sentence affected an offenders' family, should be treated as mitigation:

> In any sentencing exercise across a range of judges, certain factors will appear as mitigating elements to some more than others...Some people will take a much tougher line ... 'You've hurt your family, but that is part of the responsibility you must bear'. Others may take the view that, 'I do not want the system to disadvantage these children in the longer term, so I'm therefore going to very significantly mitigate the sentence with the children in mind.' (Judge 3)

In order to gauge the judges' understanding of the consequences of imprisonment on mothers, they were asked about the length of time that housing benefit would be continued to be paid following a prison sentence, as loss of housing whilst in prison affects more women than men. Only one judge (Judge 4) knew the correct timeframe, whilst others thought that the 'safe' period was four times greater than it in fact is.

Judges with greater understanding of the way in which a custodial sentence given to a mother would change her life and the lives of her children, believed that mitigation was relevant even if they intended to impose a custodial sentence (Corston, 2007; Carlen, 2002; Social Exclusion Task Force, 2009; Wilks-Wiffen, 2011). Those who had less understanding of the consequences of the sentence for children did not consider mitigation once the custody threshold had been reached, as they thought that once separation had occurred between mother and child it didn't make any difference how long the separation was for, and this accorded with Piper's 2007 study. Contrary to Tombs and Jagger's argument, this study did not find that the judges had information about families but chose to 'justify and legitimate' their decision to imprison (2006, p. 809). Rather, the judges had differing knowledge about how the imprisonment of their mother alters a child's day to day existence.

c) If a judge has a pre-sentence report (PSR), the defendant's motherhood has a greater likelihood of mitigating the sentence, even if the judge does not agree with the recommendations of the report

The analysis showed that a mother's previous good character has little influence on whether motherhood will be considered as mitigation, and the fact that a defendant is a mother will not be brought to the judge's attention, nor will he or she acknowledge it in all sentencing hearings. However, if a PSR has been prepared, a defendant mother is more likely to have her role as the carer of dependent children acknowledged and given weight as a mitigating factor. It is not necessary for the judge to concur with the recommendations made in the report for motherhood to have an impact on her sentence.

d) Judges with a greater understanding of impact are more likely to order PSRs in the case of all women who are sentenced, and the requesting of reports is not influenced by case context.

The sentencing transcript analysis indicated that the ordering of a PSR has a significant effect on whether motherhood is treated as mitigation, but it gave no explanation as to why that might be. To explore that area further, the interviewees were asked in what circumstances they would ask for a PSR. It was anticipated that there would be variation between the judges, with some, as in Piper's 2007 study, using it only when the offending was less serious, whilst others might have adopted the 2009 recommendation from the Advice to the Sentencing Council: that PSRs should be requested in all cases when a woman is sentenced.

Judges 3 and 4 asked for PSRs in all cases when a custodial sentence was a possibility for a mother. Judges 1, 2 and 5 took the view that PSRs were only necessary if the case was on the edge of the custody threshold:

> If it is at a level where they will be going inside, for example because of statute for a minimum term, it may be obvious from the beginning that it is not necessary to make those enquiries because those consequences are going to flow. (Judge 1)
>
> I would not order a pre-sentence report if it's a very, very serious case when, um, prison is inevitable. (Judge 2)

> You would generally have a pre-sentence report where there's a custody-or-no custody issue. (Judge 5)

Each judge expressed a predetermined and fixed position on their use of PSRs with women offenders. This was the only factor in the study which revealed intrajudicial consistency. The judges who routinely ordered pre-sentence reports for female defendants when custody is a possibility were the same judges who showed greater awareness of the gendered pains of imprisonment, and the impact of imprisonment on a mother; one of them was the judge who knew for how long housing benefit would remain payable.

Their stance may also have been affected by the fact that they felt constrained by sentencing guidelines and tariffs in their use of discretion. All the judges emphasised that the statutory sentencing guidelines, minimum sentences and tariffs constrained their sentencing. 'Very often,' Judge 3 said, 'the difficulty is that you are into an area where the tariff sentencing and the sentencing guidance all but ties your hands.' For Judge 1, minimum custody terms meant that 'their personal mitigation is of minimal significance; the only thing that really counts is the guilty plea.'

Other judges reached the custody threshold and limited the importance that personal mitigation had in their sentencing decisions. According to Judge 5, 'Anything with a statutory minimum, or murder, or a sentence that is lengthy custody with guidelines, anyway – then I don't think it come into it because there's no bit of a sentence you can adjust to fit with the mitigation.' The judges who show greater understanding of impact are also those who request PSRs, even when the likelihood is that the sentence will be custodial, whereas the judges with less understanding of the impact of sentence do not request reports once the custody threshold has been reached.

e) Tariffs, guidelines, 'Every case is different' – Judicial discretion means that there is inconsistency in the application of personal mitigation.

There is both inter- and intrajudicial inconsistency in the application of mitigation to sentencing (Millie, 2007; Jacobson and Hough, 2007; Lovegrove, 2011; Roberts, Hough, Ashworth, 2011). This is due to the fact that every case is different, and each judge will take a slightly different view of the mitigation. However, analysis of the vignettes and weighting exercise showed commonality between the judges with regard to their general approach to personal mitigation and the constraints which can influence its application.

Table 8.1 Ranking of mitigation factors: comparison of responses from the 2007 and 2012 studies

	2012 study	2007 study
Factor	**Rank**	**Rank**
Support from Victim's Family	1	=2
Intense Remorse	2	4
Severe Clinical Depression	=3	1
Isolated Incident	=3	=5
Motivated to Get Drug Treatment	5	=2
Respected Individual	=6	9
Profound Regret	=6	=5
Married with Three Children	=6	7
Support from Defendant's Family	9	10
Steady Job	=10	8
Abused and in Care as a Child	=10	13
Partner and Young Child	12	=11
Functionally Illiterate	13	=11

Table 8.1 compares the way in which the judges in the 2007 study and the 2012 study ranked the significance of mitigating factors in sentencing decisions. Both sets of judges had similar responses to the sentencing exercises, with a common approach to what was more or less significant in mitigation, although with a different ordering of the top and bottom five mitigating categories (see Table 8.1). Through the sentencing exercises, the judges showed themselves to be broadly similar in the way in which they approached personal mitigation to the 2007 Jacobson and Hough judges. They were reluctant to generalise about the kinds of mitigation that influenced them and were unwilling to think about it in terms of general principles, as were the judges in 2007 (p. 14). The judges in both studies held a common view that sentencing was a 'context specific' exercise, as Judge 3 termed it. The categories which produced the widest range of responses in this study, 'married with three children' and 'intense remorse' (Table 2 Vignette 2 [ii], Vignette 2 [iii]) were within the most varied responses in the 2007 study also (p. 18).

Conclusion

This chapter has considered the current practice of the courts when sentencing defendant mothers. The study described was a small-scale exploratory study, and its findings must be viewed in that light. However, where comparison was possible with larger sample populations, the findings were broadly consistent and there may be patterns which need further investigation. The study findings indicate that judges do not approach the sentencing of a defendant mother with an agreed upon and similar understanding of the impact of imprisonment on the family unit. The consequence of this is that the judges who lack this knowledge do not seek pre-sentence reports because they do not know what information they are lacking. The women sentenced by them are therefore doubly disadvantaged: firstly, by the judges' lack of primary knowledge, and secondly by the lack of a pre-sentence report, as the study indicated that its preparation increases the likelihood of a defendant's caring responsibilities being taken into account in sentence length, if not in severity.

This chapter has not touched upon case law or appellate jurisdiction, and the reader may be curious about recent decisions. In the case of *R* (on the application of P and Q) (2001) it was clear that under Article 8 (the right to family life), the human rights of a child are engaged when the court makes a decision to send a parent to prison, and the courts are required to acquire information and balance the rights of the child to family life against the seriousness of the mother's offending. Lord Phillips, Master of the Rolls, said, in his judgment,

> It goes without saying that since 2nd October 2000 sentencing courts have been public authorities within the meaning of section 6 of the Human Rights Act. If the passing of a custodial sentence involves the separation of a mother from her very young child (or, indeed, from any of her children) the sentencing court is bound...to carry out the balancing exercise...before deciding that the seriousness of the offence justifies the separation of mother and child. If the court does not have sufficient information about the likely consequences of the compulsory separation, it must, in compliance with its obligations under section 6(1), ask for more. (EWCA Civ 1151 at paragraph 79) .

In *R v Rosie Lee Petherick* (2012), those principles were restated with nine steps for every sentencing court to consider (EWCA Crim 224, paragraphs 17–25). The case affirmed the principle that the court should seek information about any children who may be affected by a sentence of imprisonment. In the author's own analysis of a sample of 33 appeal court hearings of an appeal against a mother's sentence of imprisonment, it was found that in 26 cases the sentence was reduced or replaced by a suspended or noncustodial sentence. In 20 of the cases, the Court of Appeal stated that the lower court had given insufficient weight to the defendant's motherhood as a mitigating factor. This confirms the patterns of the lower courts found in the study considered in this chapter, where inconsistent considerations were applied by individual judges. Judges in the lower courts do not seem to have the same awareness as the Court of Appeal: that principles have already been established, and certain information should be sought and considered in every case.

In conclusion, I make two proposals for reform. Firstly, the standardisation of approach in this area is important, and I support the recommendation that a pre-sentence report should always be prepared when sentencing a woman. Perhaps the Sentencing Council should consider this suggestion.

Second, whether or not Recommendation 21 is adopted as a guideline, there is a need for judicial education on the impact of imprisonment on mothers. The study I have conducted has shown that there is significant variation in judicial knowledge in this area, and in order to provide more consistent sentencing for women offenders in the absence of pre-sentence reports being considered in all cases, it is important that judges are all similarly well informed when they come to sentencing. The focus on equality has had the effect of discouraging judges from noting gender difference in areas where it has been well documented and its effects are known and unchallenged (Corston, 2007; Codd, 2008). Sentencing judges could achieve greater consistency if judicial education covered in greater depth the relevance of gender and caring responsibilities to sentencing and imprisonment and the need for sentencers to make inquiries about dependents prior to sentence. The judicial college should also integrate this issue into its training for sentencers.

References

Ashworth, A. (2010) *Sentencing and Criminal Justice.* 5th ed. Cambridge: Cambridge University Press.

Caddle, D. and Crisp, D. (1997) *Mothers in Prison.* HO Research and Statistics Directorate Findings, no. 38. London: The Stationary Office.

Carlen, P. (ed.) (2002) *Women and Punishment.* Devon: Willan.

Commission on Women and the Criminal Justice System (2009) *Engendering Justice – from Policy to Practice.* London: Fawcett Society.

Corston, J. (2007) *The Corston Report, A Review of Women with Particular Vulnerabilities in the Criminal Justice System.* London: Home Office.

Criminal Justice Joint Inspection (2011) *Equal but Different? An Inspection of the Use of Alternatives to Custody for Women Offenders. A Joint Inspection by HMI Probation, HMCPSI and HMI Prisons.* London: Criminal Justice Joint Inspection.

Dobash, R.P., Dobash, R.E., and Gutteridge, S. (1986) *The Imprisonment of Women.* Oxford: Blackwell.

Easton, S. (2008) Dangerous Waters: Taking Account of Impact in Sentencing. *Criminal Law Review* 2: 105–120.
Easton, S. and Piper, C. (2008) *Sentencing and Punishment, the Quest for Justice*. Oxford: Oxford University Press.
Fielding, N. (2011) Judges and Their Work. *Social Legal Studies* 20: 97–115.
Gampell, L (2003) *Submission in Response to the Green Paper Consultation 'Every Child Matters'*. London: Action for Prisoner's Families.
Genders, E. and Player, E. (1987) 'Women in prison: the treatment, the control, and the experience'. In: P. Carlen and A. Worrall (eds) *Gender, Crime and Justice*. Milton Keynes: Open University Press.
Jacobson, J. and Hough, M. (2007) *Mitigation: The Role of Personal Factors in Sentencing*. London: Prison Reform Trust.
Judicial Appointments Committee (2012) *Official Statistics 14 June 2012* http://jac.judiciary.gov.uk/static/documents/JAC_publication_2012_06_final.pdf.
Liebling, A. and Maruna, S. (2005) *The Effects of Imprisonment*. Devon: Willan.
Loureiro, T. (2009) *Child and Family Impact Assessments in Court: Implications for Policy and Practice*. Edinburgh: Families Outside.
Lovegrove, A. (2010) The Sentencing Council, the Public's Sense of Justice and Personal Mitigation, *Criminal Law Review*, 12, 906 – 923.
——— (2011) Putting the Offender Back into Sentencing: An Empirical Study of the Public's Understanding of Personal Mitigation. *Criminology and Criminal Justice*, 11: 37–57.
Mason, J. (2002) *Qualitative Researching Second Edition* London: Sage.
Millie, A., Tombs, J. and Hough, M. (2007) Borderline Sentencing: A Comparison of Sentencers' Decision-Making in England and Wales, and Scotland. *Criminology and Criminal Justice*, 7: 243.
Mills, A. and Codd, H. (2007) Prisoner's Families In: Y. Jewkes (ed.) *Handbook on Prisons*. Devon: Willan.
Mills (2002) EWCA Crim 26; [2002] 2 Cr. App. R.(S.) 52 at 232–233, [12] and [15]-[17].
Ministry of Justice (2007) *Offender Management Caseload Statistics 2007*. London: The Stationery Office.
——— (2009) *Statistics on Women and the Criminal Justice System, a Ministry of Justice Publication under Section 95 of the Criminal Justice Act 1991*. London: Ministry of Justice.
——— (2013) *Offender Management Caseload Statistics 2012 Table A2.1c*. London: The Stationery Office.
——— (2014) *Population and Capacity Briefing Week Ending 14 February 2014*. London: The Stationery Office. https//www.gov.uk/government/publications/prison-population-figures-2014.
Minson, S. (2012) *Mitigating Motherhood – A Study of the Impact of Motherhood on Sentencing Decisions in England and Wales*. Guildford: University of Surrey.
——— (2014) *Mitigating Motherhood*. London: Howard League.
Piper, C. (2007) Should Impact Constitute Mitigation? Structured Discretion Versus Mercy? *Criminal Law Review*, (1) 141–155.
Prison Reform Trust (2010) *Bromley Briefings Prison Factfile: December 2010*. http://www.prisonreformtrust.org.uk/Portals/0/ Documents/FactfileDec10small.pdf.
Roberts J. (2008) Aggravating and Mitigating Factors at Sentencing: Towards Greater Consistency of Application. *Criminal Law Review*, (4) 264–276.

Roberts J., Hough, M. and Ashworth, A. (2011) Personal Mitigation, Public Opinion and Sentencing Guidelines in England and Wales 2011. *Criminal Law Review,* (7) 524–530.
Sentencing Advisory Panel (2009) *Overarching Principles of Sentencing – Advice to the Sentencing Guidelines Council.* http://www.banksr.co.uk/images/Guidelines/Advisory%20Panel%20Advice%20to%20the%20Council/Overaching_principles_of_sentencing.pdf
Silverman, D. (2010) *Doing Qualitative Research.* London: Sage.
Social Exclusion Unit (2002) *Reducing Reoffending by Ex-Prisoners.* London: Social Exclusion Unit.
Social Exclusion Task Force (2009) *Short Study on Women Offenders.* London: Cabinet Office http://webarchive.nationalarchives.gov.uk/+/http:/www.cabinetoffice.gov.uk/media/209663/setf_shortstudy_womenoffenders.pdf.
Sykes, G. (1958) *Society of Captives: A Study of Maximum Security Prisons.* Princeton, NJ: Princeton University Press.
Tombs, J., and Jagger, E. (2006) Denying Responsibility: Sentencers' Accounts of Their Decisions to Imprison. *British Journal of Criminology,* 46: 803–821.
Wasik, M. (2001) *Emmins on Sentencing, 4th ed.* Oxford: Oxford University Press.
Wilks-Wiffen, S. (2011) *Voice of a Child.* London: Howard League for Penal Reform.
Women's Justice Taskforce (2011) *Reforming Women's Justice.* London: Prison Reform Trust. http://www.prisonreformtrust.org.uk/Portals/0/Documents/Women's%20Justice%20Taskforce%20Report.pdf.

9

Paying for the Past: The Role of Previous Convictions at Sentencing in the Crown Court

*Julian V. Roberts and Jose Pina Sanchez**

Nigel Walker described prior convictions as 'the most obvious example of aggravation' (1985, p. 44), and there certainly is great intuitive appeal to taking previous convictions into account. Most members of the public believe that offenders with previous convictions should be punished more severely, particularly if the priors are the same as the current conviction. (For findings and discussion, see Roberts and Hough, 2011; Roberts, 2008, chapter 8.) Thus, when asked to sentence offenders with different numbers of prior convictions, the public respond more punitively to recidivists compared to first offenders.

A number of objections may be raised against including prior convictions in the sentencing equation. First, some people argue that once an offender has completed his sentence – whether a term of custody or some non-custodial disposal – the debt to society has been repaid. There may be a 'double punishment' argument at work here: if an offender receives a harsher sentence because of prior convictions, he is being punished twice for the same crime. Offenders may also resent the recidivist sentencing premium since it represents the imposition of additional punishment for crimes he *may* commit, rather than for crimes for which he has actually been convicted. Many practical questions arise: Should *all* prior convictions count, or only some? For example, should sentencers take into account only prior convictions of the same kind as the current offence and disregard all other convictions? Is an offender convicted of assault to be considered a 'first-time offender' if his only previous convictions are for offences of dishonesty? As Wasik (2010) demonstrates, reading a criminal record for the purposes of determining which prior convictions are relevant is a complex and challenging exercise. In short, a number of thorny issues of principle and practice need to be addressed.

Previous convictions, sentencing theories and practices

(a) Crime prevention through deterrence

As might be expected, whether previous convictions should be considered at sentencing depends upon the underlying sentencing philosophy. Sentencers aiming to prevent further offending will argue that repeat offenders pose a higher risk of reoffending, and for this reason a harsher penalty is necessary to deter them from returning to crime. This position carries two assumptions: first, that prior convictions do in fact increase the likelihood that the offender will commit further offences. In general, repeat offenders are more likely than first offenders to reoffend. The relationship between previous and future offending has been demonstrated for decades now. As early as 1948, Grunhut analysed statistics collected in Germany and concluded that 'the probability of recidivism increases with the number of previous sentences' (p. 31). This relationship has been found in many other jurisdictions ever since (see Cunliffe and Shepherd, 2007).

However, this does not mean that all repeat offenders are a greater risk than all first-time offenders. In addition, the nature and timing of previous convictions will be critical. Someone convicted for the first time of assault and who has prior convictions for benefit fraud is not a higher risk for further crimes of violence. Similarly, an offender with a conviction recorded ten years earlier is unlikely to represent a greater risk than someone with no priors (see discussion in Roberts and Yalincak, 2014; Roberts, 2008; Kazemian, 2010). So we should not just assume (and courts *don't* assume) that all prior convictions should always result in a harsher penalty.

The second deterrence-related assumption – that increasing the severity of sentence as the number of prior convictions increases will deter offenders – is also questionable. There is scant evidence that the specific policy of imposing a harsher sentence to reflect an offender's prior convictions will deter offenders more effectively (e.g., Kazemian, 2010). The factors causing reoffending are generally the same ones that predict offending in the first place: drug abuse, economic deprivation, lack of professional opportunities, and the presence of inappropriate role models. More generally, sentencing can play only a limited role in deterring offenders, since most offending is unplanned, and most offenders are unconcerned about future consequences. A policy of imposing harsher penalties to reflect previous convictions may simply result in more punishment for recidivists – but with little actual benefit in terms of lower reoffending rates.

(b) Retributive approaches to previous convictions

The retributive school of thought asserts that factors taken into account at sentencing must affect either the seriousness of the current crime, or the culpability (blameworthiness) of the offender for the current offence. Advocates of the 'just deserts' school take conflicting positions regarding the issue of previous convictions. A small number of scholars believe that courts should ignore all prior convictions – after all they don't make the latest offence worse: an assault does not become more serious because the perpetrator has prior convictions (see Fletcher, 1982; for discussion of competing views, see Roberts, 2008, chapter 3). Conversely, if your car has been stolen, nothing changes if the offender had never committed a crime before – you have still lost your car.

Other sentencing scholars have argued that while the seriousness of the offence may not be affected by the offender's prior convictions, these do influence his level of culpability. Lee (2010), for example, argues that repeat offenders are more blameworthy for having failed to take the necessary steps to address the causes of their offending. For this reason, the state is justified in treating repeat offenders more harshly. Roberts (2010) suggests that first offenders are less culpable than repeat offenders. A person without any prior contact with the criminal justice system may not fully appreciate the wrongfulness of his conduct until he has been charged, convicted and sentenced. On this basis, he should be entitled to be punished less severely.

Then there is an intermediate position. von Hirsch (2010) for example, argues that previous convictions should play a limited role at sentencing. According to this perspective, first offenders are allowed some mitigation to reflect the fact that everyone can err, and that the criminal law should include some forbearance to reflect this. However, the account is not based on diminished culpability, and von Hirsch does not regard repeat offenders as more culpable. First offenders receive a discounted sentence on this account, but once they have lost their status as first offenders, additional convictions do not increase the severity of their sentence. This perspective is represented in the approach described below as 'the progressive loss of mitigation'.

(c) Role of previous convictions in practice

Almost all common and civil law jurisdictions punish offenders with prior convictions more harshly. Beyond this simple fact, arrangements become more complex: An offender's criminal record can affect sentence severity in different ways, depending on the theory underlying sentencing.[1]

Some regimes employ what is termed a 'cumulative sentencing' approach, imposing progressively more severe sentences to reflect the number and seriousness of previous convictions. This approach reflects the preventive purpose we have noted, and carries assumptions that repeat offenders represent a higher risk of reoffending, and/ or are reasonably considered more blameworthy. Many US guidelines – including those found in Minnesota and Pennsylvania – follow this model (see Frase, 2012; Roberts and Yalincak, 2014). For example, consider serious assault under the Minnesota guidelines. Each prior conviction results in the imposition of an additional 12 months of prison time.[2] This approach greatly oversimplifies the consideration of prior convictions at sentencing. The grid creates a scheme whereby each prior conviction represents a uniform quantum of risk or blameworthiness. This is a relatively crude approach to considering prior convictions: two offenders with identical criminal histories (and the same criminal history score) may represent very different risks of reoffending.

Elsewhere, courts apply the principle of the 'progressive loss of mitigation', which, as noted, is associated with the retributive sentencing school. According to this approach, first offenders (and those with minor records) receive significant mitigation, which is progressively withdrawn as they acquire fresh convictions. Eventually the mitigation is exhausted, and the offender receives the fully proportionate sentence: sentences should not escalate in severity beyond this point. This principle has long existed in English sentencing law (see Thomas, 1970; Ashworth, 2010). The principle reflects recognition that most people may lapse into criminality at some point, due to external pressures of one kind or another, and that the criminal law should not respond punitively to the first such lapse.

So there are three principal models for the use of previous convictions at sentencing: (1) cumulative sentencing – sentence severity rises continuously to reflect all previous convictions; (2) flat-rate sentencing – where prior convictions play no role at all; (3) the progressive loss of mitigation – where first offenders receive a reduced sentence; once they accumulate additional convictions, this mitigation is withdrawn, but sentence severity does not increase beyond this point. Figure 9.1 represents these three positions in graphic form.

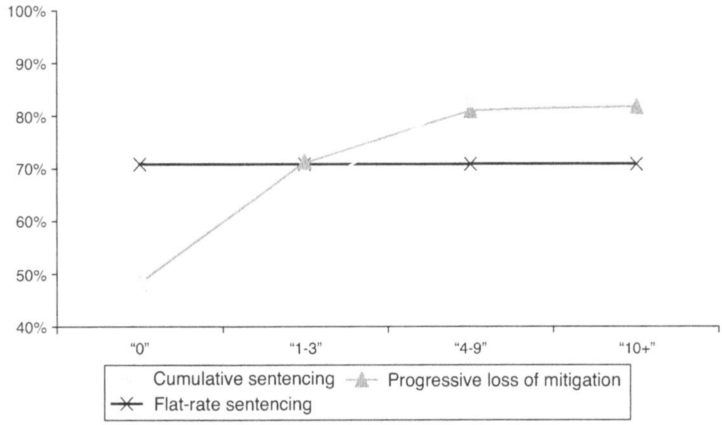

Figure 9.1 Theoretical models for the use of previous convictions at sentencing

Previous convictions in England and Wales: statutory provisions

If sentencing theories approach the issue in different ways, what actually happens in practice? The role of previous convictions at sentencing has evolved significantly over the last 20 years (see Ashworth, 2010, chapter 6). For the purposes of this chapter, we pick up the story with the statutory guidance provided by the Criminal Justice Act 1991. Section 29(1) of this statute restricted the effect of previous convictions at sentencing when it directed courts that an offence was not to be regarded as more serious 'by reason of any previous convictions of the offender'. The provision was amended two years later when the Criminal Justice Act 1993 permitted courts to aggravate sentence on a wider examination of previous convictions. Subsection 29(1) as amended stated that 'In considering the seriousness of any offence, the court *may* take into account any previous convictions of the offender or his failure to respond to previous sentences' (emphasis added).

Legislative guidance came full circle in 2003, when section 143(2) of the Criminal Justice Act 2003 directed courts that

> *In considering the seriousness of an offence... committed by an offender who has one or more previous convictions, the court must treat each prior conviction as an aggravating factor if... the court considers that it can reasonably be so treated having regard to—*

(a) *The nature of the offence to which the conviction relates and its relevance to the current offence, and*

(b) *The time that has elapsed since the conviction.*

The statutory direction thus evolved from *prohibiting* a broad consideration of priors, to *permitting* greater aggravation, to *mandating* such a practice.

Potential threat to proportional sentencing

Some scholars feared that the 2003 provision would greatly increase the aggravating effect of previous convictions by requiring courts to consider each prior conviction as aggravating (unless it would be unreasonable to do so; see von Hirsch and Roberts, 2004). One reason for this is that the provision is reminiscent of many US guidelines where, as noted, sentence lengths are progressively increased to reflect higher numbers of prior convictions. Under these schemes, prior convictions can carry as much weight as the current offence, and if they have a powerful influence on sentence outcomes, offence-based proportionality will be undermined. An example from the state of Minnesota illustrates the danger that a strong recidivist sentencing premium can carry.

Under the Minnesota guidelines, an offender with six or more criminal history points who is convicted of a seriousness level 8 offence is liable to a sentence in the range of 92–129 months, with a midpoint of 108 months. A first offender convicted of the same offence is liable to a range of 41–57 months with a grid midpoint of 48 months. The highest criminal history category midpoint is therefore 225% of the lowest criminal history midpoint provided in the grid. This is a substantial degree of aggravation. It means that offenders with lengthy criminal records will receive much harsher sentences than those imposed on people convicted of more serious crimes but who have no prior convictions. This is a reversal of the principle that sentence severity should track the seriousness of the crime – rather than characteristics of the offender such as his criminal history.

Previous convictions in the definitive English guidelines

Besides the provisions of the Criminal Justice Act 2003 and decisions from the Court of Appeal, there is another source of guidance: the definitive sentencing guidelines. These guidelines create a step-by-step approach which encourages courts to arrive at a sentence by proceeding methodically through the steps (see Roberts and Rafferty, 2011). The first two steps are the most important. At step one, the court establishes a range of sentence and a starting point sentence. At step two, the court moves up or down from the starting point to reflect mitigating and aggravating factors.

Under the Council's guidelines,[3] at step two of the guidelines methodology, a sentencing court considers prior convictions. By placing the factor at step two[4] rather than step one, the Council may have constrained its influence: step two factors affect only the location of the sentence *within* the guideline's category range of sentence. Had the factor been placed at step one, it would have more influence on sentence severity, as it would affect which of three sentence ranges was applied to the case at bar. For example, for the crime of ABH, previous convictions will affect the sentence within a category range – for the intermediate category runs from a low-level community order to 51 weeks custody. If they were considered at step one, they might make the difference between a category upper limit of three years rather than 51 weeks.

The impact of previous convictions may be offence-specific. Although the Council has placed this factor at step two of its methodology, in a number of guidelines issued since the first (assault), Council has seen fit to highlight the importance of prior convictions. In the case of burglary guideline, the Sentencing Council emphasizes the relevance of previous convictions by noting that 'in particular, relevant, recent convictions are likely to result in an upward adjustment' (2011, p. 9), although consideration of the priors is still restricted to step two.[5] A similar feature is found in several other guidelines issued more recently, including the sexual offences guideline (2014).[6]

In this chapter, we address a number of important questions about previous convictions by examining data from the Crown Court Sentencing Survey:

- How many offenders appearing for sentence have prior convictions which are taken into account at sentencing?
- How much variation exists between offence categories?
- Has there been any recent change in the criminal history profiles of offenders appearing for sentencing?
- Which theoretical model of prior offending underpins the use of previous convictions? Is it the cumulative sentencing model which assigns ever-harsher sentences to reflect previous convictions, or the progressive loss of mitigation which limits the extent to which previous convictions aggravate sentence?
- Has the new format of sentencing guideline had any influence on the way that prior convictions affect sentence severity, specifically the probability of a custodial sanction?
- Do previous convictions affect sentence severity in different ways, depending upon the nature of the offence?

Previous research and limitations on annual sentencing statistics

The absence of definitive research on this issue may be explained by the inadequacies of the official statistics. One-off studies conducted over the past 30 years suggested that courts pursued a cumulative approach, with incarceration rates increasing steadily to reflect longer criminal histories (Fitzmaurice and Pease, 1986; Flood-Page and Mackie, 1998; Moxon, 1988). Until now, the only annual, publicly available sentencing data have been the Ministry of Justice sentencing statistics which provide custody rates for categories of offenders with variable criminal histories. The most recent (2013) Ministry of Justice statistics reveal that custody rate rises in a way that is generally consistent with the cumulative sentencing approach:

1–2 priors:	13%
3–6 priors:	18%
7–10 priors:	24%
11 or more priors:	66%[7]

These statistics suffer from an important limitation. The statistics include *all* recorded priors when classifying offenders into categories of criminal history. However, even before, and particularly after the introduction of the 2003 Act, courts may have exercised their discretion to disregard prior convictions if those convictions were old enough or unrelated to the current offence. As noted, the Ministry data include *all prior convictions recorded* in the case file, whether the court took them into account or not. For this reason, a database is needed which includes only those convictions that the sentencer deemed to be relevant – and this is likely, as noted, to represent a subset of all his or her prior convictions.

Findings

Although it has limitations of its own (see Chapter 1 of this volume), the CCSS addresses some of the analytical deficiencies of the Ministry data. Because the sentencing authority is providing this information, the CCSS data permit a more precise estimation of the effect of prior convictions on the severity of sentence imposed, specifically the probability of custody. The Ministry statistics are useful to answer other questions, however. For example, since their limitations are constant over time, we can explore historical trends in the volume of prior convictions as well as other important aspects of criminal history. Accordingly, this chapter draws upon both databases.[8] All CCSS data reported here derive from 2011, the most recent year for which data are currently publicly available.

1. Volume of previous convictions / cautions

The importance of previous convictions as a sentencing factor comes from the fact that according to the Ministry statistics, most offenders appearing for sentence have a criminal record. As can be seen in Table 9.1, only 10% of offenders convicted in 2013 had no prior convictions or cautions for an indictable offence. Fully two-thirds had seven or more prior convictions or cautions. In addition, over the decade 2003–2013, Ministry statistics reveal an increase in the proportion of offenders in the highest criminal history category – rising from 32% to 44% of the total sample. Although these data do not distinguish convictions from cautions, Ministry data on cautions issued for an indictable offence reveal a striking decline in the number of cautions, from 155,000 offenders in 2004 to 98,000 in 2013.[9] This suggests that convictions and not cautions account for the increase in the final column of Table 9.1, which contains the offenders with the most serious criminal histories. However, courts will take only some of these into account at sentencing; only certain priors will justify a harsher sentence. The proportion of cases in which the offender has no relevant prior convictions may be much lower than the percentage in this table with any priors.

Table 9.1 Number of convictions and cautions by year, all offenders, indictable offences, 2003–2013

	0	1–2	3–6	7–10	11 or more
2013	10%	15%	19%	12%	44%
2012	10%	16%	20%	12%	42%
2011	10%	17%	21%	13%	40%
2010	11%	18%	22%	13%	38%
2009	10%	17%	22%	13%	38%
2008	11%	18%	22%	13%	36%
2007	11%	19%	23%	13%	34%
2006	12%	19%	23%	13%	34%
2005	12%	18%	22%	14%	34%
2004	11%	18%	23%	14%	33%
2003	11%	19%	24%	15%	32%

Source: Ministry of Justice, Table Q71 (ii).

Table 9.2 Prior convictions and cautions, all indictable offences and specific offence categories, 2013

	0 priors	1–2	3–6	7–10	11 or more
All indictable offences	10%	15%	19%	12%	44%
Sexual offences	39%	23%	17%	7%	14%
Robbery	17%	18%	20%	12%	32%
Theft	5%	12%	16%	11%	57%
Drug offences	7%	17%	27%	16%	33%
Public order	8%	14%	19%	12%	48%
Fraud	29%	22%	19%	9%	21%
Violence	14%	17%	22%	13%	33%

Source: Ministry of Justice, Table Q71 (ii).

Table 9.2 provides a breakdown of prior convictions and cautions for different offence categories and reveals significant variation in the volume of previous convictions by offence category. Approximately half the offenders convicted of burglary or theft/ handling – but only 14% of sexual offenders – had 11 or more previous convictions or cautions. The variable pattern of previous convictions across offences is relevant to the repeat offender sentencing premium. To the extent that the imposition of a harsher sentence deters reoffending, these data identify which offences have the highest reoffending rates.

Courts might be tempted to impose a greater 'recidivist premium' for offences with the highest reoffending rates, reasoning that offenders committing these crimes repeatedly need an extra degree of punishment for deterrent purposes. Yet adjusting the premium in this way would also be problematic. First, because it means that the less serious offences – which also have the highest reoffending rates – will attract a harsher sentence. If this strategy were adopted, it would undermine offence-based proportionality. Second, increasing sentence severity for the offences with higher reoffending rates would also undermine individualisation in sentencing. The offender convicted of a high reoffending rate crime would be paying a higher price for the reoffending rate of his category – not because he necessarily represents a higher risk.

Crown Court Sentencing Survey data

In contrast to the trends in Ministry data, Table 9.3 provides a breakdown of the volume of prior convictions by offence category derived from the CCSS – those actually taken into account by the sentencer. Direct comparisons between the Ministry and CCSS databases are not

Table 9.3 Volume of previous convictions taken into account by offence category, 2011

	0 Priors	1–3 Priors	4–9 Priors	10 or more Priors
All indictable offences	64%	21%	9%	6%
Sex	80%	15%	3%	2%
Drugs	70%	22%	5%	3%
Assault	69%	20%	8%	2%
Arson	67%	20%	8%	6%
Theft	56%	19%	12%	13%
Driving	53%	28%	11%	8%
Robbery	52%	25%	14%	8%

Source: CCSS.

possible because the Ministry includes prior cautions as well as prior convictions. Nevertheless, some broad conclusions may be drawn. Table 9.3 presents a very different picture, with much higher concentrations of cases in the first offender or modest prior offending categories. For example, approximately two-thirds of the sentenced cases involved offenders without prior convictions.

Table 9.3 suggests that *relevant* prior convictions are a subset of all previous convictions. This is evidence that the courts in England and Wales take a nuanced approach to the issue of previous convictions at sentencing, filtering out prior convictions which, for a variety of reasons, should play no role in the current sentencing exercise. The prior convictions that are disregarded for the purposes of current sentencing are presumably those deemed too old to count or irrelevant to the current sentencing exercise. Sentencers are exercising the discretion created by the Criminal Justice Act 2003 (see above) to take into account only previous convictions which, in the court's view, reasonably should result in a harsher sentence. This places English courts in contrast to other jurisdictions whose less flexible schemes require all previous convictions to be counted at every subsequent sentencing decision.

The pattern of variability in the volume of previous convictions is consistent across offence categories in both databases. Consistent with the Ministry data, offenders sentenced for a sexual offence were significantly less likely than other categories of offenders to have had previous convictions. Thus, fully 80% of the CCSS offenders convicted of a sexual offence, but only approximately half the offenders sentenced for assault, had no prior convictions (see Table 9.3).

2. Models of previous convictions

Table 9.4 summarises custody rates[10] for categories of prior offending and reveals the model underlying previous convictions in the Crown Court. Courts appear to be applying a model which reflects the progressive loss of mitigation. The first time the offender appears for re-sentencing results in a steep escalation in the likelihood of custody; subsequent reconvictions trigger far less significant increments in severity.

Assault provides a good illustration of the trend. As can be seen in Table 9.4, the gap between first two categories of prior convictions (no priors; 1–3 priors) is very striking – the custody rate for first offenders is almost 30 percentage points lower than the second category. However, once the offender has multiple convictions, additional prior convictions make little difference to the custody rate. Sentence severity levels out in a way that reflects the Progressive Loss of Mitigation model (PLM): Across all indictable offences, the custody rate rises from 38% to 65% and then to 77%. Although the cumulative model would predict a further steep increment from the category 4–9 priors to 10 or more priors, no such increase in the custody rate occurs: the custody rate is approximately the same, which reflects the pattern prescribed by the PLM. Approached from the opposite direction, the PLM model prescribes only a very modest difference between the offender who has exhausted all record-based mitigation and offenders who have still some to claim. The same pattern emerges for all indictable offences (see Table 9.4).

The fact that the greatest difference between categories of criminal history is between those with no priors and those in the next category makes sense from many perspectives. The first offender has a very strong claim in mitigation that cannot be made by those who have already been prosecuted,

Table 9.4 Custody rates by number of prior convictions, offence categories, 2011[11]

	0 Priors	1–3 Priors	4–9 Priors	10 or more Priors
All offences	47%	65%	77%	79%
Assault	38%	65%	77%	79%
Drugs	53%	65%	68%	71%
Theft	46%	65%	76%	77%
Arson	45%	67%	60%	76%
Driving	32%	55%	76%	84%
Robbery	76%	91%	95%	97%
Other offences	43%	59%	74%	72%

Source: CCSS.

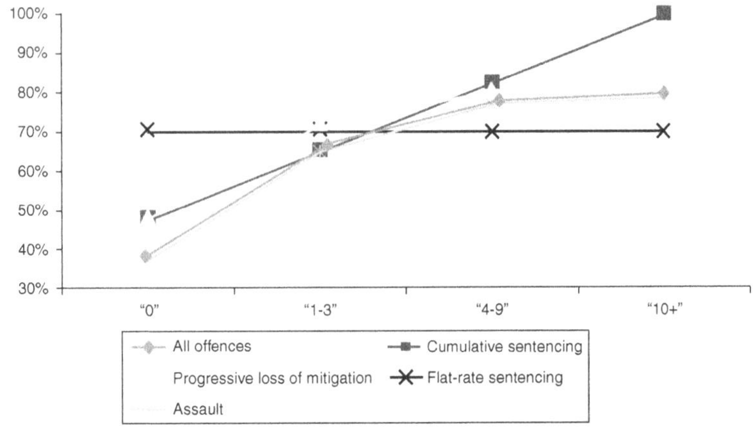

Figure 9.2 Theoretical projections and empirical trends: effects of number of previous convictions on probability of custody

convicted and sentenced (see Roberts, 2010). This has long been recognised by sentencing scholars. In fact as long ago as 1877, the author of the first sentencing text wrote the following: 'I cannot too earnestly urge leniency in the treatment of offenders in this class. A first offence should always be looked upon with pity, as possibly a lapse from virtue, the result more of weakness than wickedness.' (Cox, 1877, p. 133) A century later, Walker observed, 'The argument…is most plausible when used to distinguish the first occasion of sentencing from the second.' (1985, p. 44). Sentencing statutes in a number of jurisdictions also place limits on the powers of a court to sentence first offenders to prison – further evidence that the absence of prior convictions is a powerful mitigating factor.

Figure 9.2 represents this relationship between prior offending and the probability of custody in graphical form. As can be seen, the increase in severity for all offences and all assault offences rises in step with the progressive loss of mitigation – and not the model prescribed by a cumulative sentencing model. There is inevitably a loss of precision in the data as a result of that fact that courts select a category of prior offending rather than recording the exact number of prior convictions taken into account. It is likely that the theoretical and empirical curves would be even closer together if the data were not grouped into four categories on the CCSS form.

Multivariate analyses

As noted earlier, prior research was unable to control for the effect of correlated variables. Using the CCSS data, we conducted multivariate analyses, which revealed the effect of prior convictions on the probability of custody – having controlled for a range of other variables such as plea. These analyses generally confirmed the relationship between the number of prior convictions and the custody rate, although with more variation between offences than was apparent from the previous analysis.

First, in light of the specific reference in the definitive burglary offences guideline to the importance of prior convictions, the trends for this offence are particularly interesting. Figure 9.3 reveals the multivariate pattern for three offences: GBH, burglary in a dwelling, and nondomestic burglary. Once again, the progressive loss of mitigation model fits the data better than the cumulative approach, and this is true even for the domestic burglary cases. However, departures from this pattern did emerge for theft offences. For these cases, the corrected probability of custody rose from .42 for first offenders to .46 for those with modest records to .54 for intermediate records and .61 for the most severe criminal history category. At least with respect to theft offences then, a Cumulative model was in effect, perhaps reflecting the fact that this category of offence contained the highest proportion of offenders in the longest prior conviction categories (as seen in Table 9.2). Courts may be reasoning that a recidivist sentencing premium is more important for offenders with higher recidivism rates.

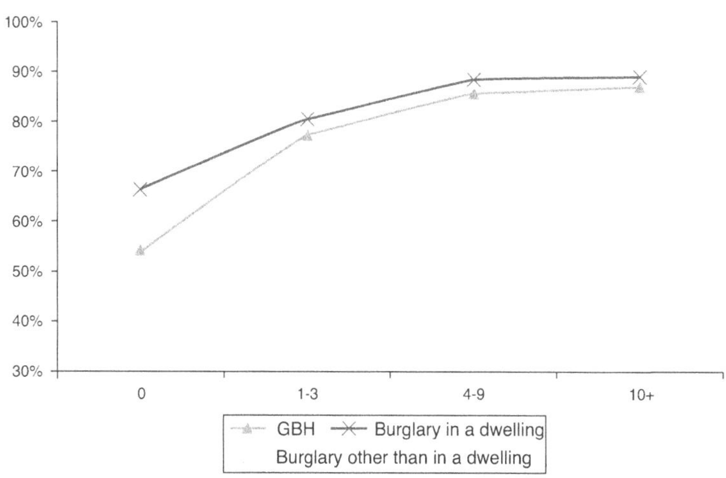

Figure 9.3 Effect of previous convictions on probability of custody controlling for other factors

Source: CCSS.

3. Impact of the new format treatment of previous convictions

Finally, for one particular guideline – the assault offences – it is possible to compare the impact of previous convictions on the custody rate before and after introduction of the new format guideline for assault. As noted, under its new format the Sentencing Council assigned previous convictions to step two of the guidelines methodology. We hypothesised that this may have constrained the aggravating effect of previous convictions. The impact of this change can be evaluated by examining the influence of previous convictions on sentence outcomes before and after the introduction of the new format guideline for the assault offences.

We employed a statistical model predicting the probability of custody, having controlled for the influence of other sentencing factors identified as relevant to the sentencing decision by the sentencer. It is a conservative test of the hypothesis, for two reasons. First, courts sentencing in the period prior to the new guideline coming into effect may have been influenced by the new format, which was apparent from the consultation document issued by the Council. Second, the post-new guideline period captured in the database is relatively brief. Some court locations may have taken time to reflect the new format in their decision-making.

In any event, a clear result emerges from the pre-post guideline comparison. Prior convictions carried less weight in the period in which courts were following the Council's new format guideline. This can be demonstrated by plotting the increase in the probability of custody across all four categories of previous convictions: the slope escalates significantly less steeply in the period after the introduction of the new guideline. Why might this be the case? One explanation that we can readily reject is that there has been a decline in the number of offenders appearing for sentencing with more serious criminal records. As demonstrated earlier in this chapter, the trend has been in the other direction. The most likely explanation is that the decline in the effect of prior convictions reflects the Council's decision to place prior convictions at step two of the guidelines methodology.

The conclusion about the impact of the new format guidelines must be provisional, however, for three reasons relating to data limitations. First, these data derive from a single year, and a multiyear analysis would permit more robust inferences. Second, findings from the before and after the introduction of the guideline only apply to the assault offences. We cannot say if they represent a more widespread trend – an important research question would be whether the highlighted reference to previous convictions in the guidelines issued by the Council after the assault guideline has increased the role of previous convictions for other guideline offences. Nor do we know whether the use of prior convictions is similar in youth courts.

Data limitations and future research directions

Finally, the data reported here derive, by definition, from Crown Courts. We cannot say whether magistrates' courts apply previous convictions in the same way. Another important objective for researchers is to explore the role of prior convictions in sentencing at the magistrates' courts, where most sentencing is conducted by lay magistrates. Although they follow the same definitive guidelines as sentencers in the Crown Courts, lay magistrates may approach the use of prior convictions in a different way. Exploration of sentencing patterns in the magistrates' courts awaits the creation of a database comparable to the survey currently conducted in the Crown Courts. In one of the few studies comparing the impact of prior convictions in the Crown Court and the magistrates' courts, Hedderman and Moxon found the presence of previous convictions had a greater impact on the custody rate in the former (1992, Table 4.2).

Conclusions

A number of conclusions can be drawn from these new findings. First, courts appear to have held the line on the aggravating effect of previous convictions. If the Criminal Justice Act 2003 was designed to promote cumulative sentencing, it has not had that effect on sentencing in the Crown Courts. These data from the CCSS suggest that courts are sensitive to the potential threat that previous convictions carry for offence-based proportionality. For offenders in the more serious criminal history categories, courts are clearly moderating the increase in severity to ensure that previous convictions do not swamp the seriousness of the offence as a determinant of sentence. The principle of the progressive loss of mitigation appears intact, almost a decade after the introduction of the Criminal Justice Act 2003.

The use of previous convictions in English courts seems more reasonable than the approach taken in many US jurisdictions. It is surely overly simplistic to assume that each additional prior conviction warrants an increase in severity, and that each increment should be of the same magnitude. Recall that under the Minnesota guidelines, each prior conviction results in a fixed additional term of imprisonment. The dangers of a very substantial sentencing premium to reflect an offender's previous convictions are not restricted to the threat to proportional sentencing. Frase has demonstrated that much of the difference in sentencing outcomes between black and white offenders in the United States is due to the fact that the former have more extensive criminal histories, and this triggers a harsher sentence (see Frase, 2012). Comparable analyses have not been conducted in England and Wales, but it is comforting to know that if there is a differential impact on visible minority defendants, the effect is likely to be much more modest in this country, as previous convictions do not carry the same weight as in the United States.

Although some penal theorists argue that previous convictions should never count at sentencing, this extreme position has been rejected by almost all jurisdictions. Sentencing statutes and guideline schemes around the world all impose harsher sentences to reflect an offender's prior criminal behaviour, and England and Wales is no exception. Offenders in this country continue to pay for their past misconduct. However, we have argued in this chapter that courts consider prior convictions in a more reasoned and subtle way, taking into account only those priors deemed sufficiently recent and relevant.

Notes

*The views expressed here are solely those of the authors and not those of the institutions with which they are affiliated.

1. Ashworth notes four approaches to punishing persistent offenders: the two identified here as well as flat-rate sentencing (where previous convictions play no role), and a model which employs prior convictions as justifying a rebuttable culpability-based presumption of a harsher sentence. We focus here on the two models which are most applicable to sentencing in common law jurisdictions.
2. See Minnesota Sentencing Guidelines Grid, 2012. Available at: http://mn.gov/sentencing-guidelines/.
3. The first guideline issued by the Council which follows this approach was the assault offences guideline (see Sentencing Council, 2011a). The format created for assault serves as a model for most subsequent offence-specific guidelines. All guidelines are available on the Sentencing Council website.
4. One possible justification for placing priors at the first rather than the second step is that step one factors are described as being relevant to harm or culpability, whereas step two factors are listed under the heading 'Factors increasing seriousness', which more closely reflects the statutory language of s.143 of the Criminal Justice Act 2003. In addition, step one factors are described in the guideline as those which comprise the principal factual elements of the offence, and previous convictions are presumably not a principal element.
5. On this issue, in our analyses, we compared the relationship between the number of priors and the probability of custody for the two offence categories and found no significant differences. On this limited analysis, then, the

highlighted direction to courts with respect to sentencing for burglary appears to have had no demonstrable effect on sentencing practices, at least in the limited time period covered by our analysis.

6. Previous convictions are not highlighted in the drug offences guideline, which became effective in February 2012. The enhanced reference to the significance of previous convictions appears in the following guidelines: burglary; sexual offences and in the proposed guidelines for theft offences.
7. Ministry of Justice data, Table Q7.4.
8. The principal limitation on the CCSS data for the purposes of the present research is that the form requires courts to classify the case as having 0, 1–3, 4–9, or 10 or more previous convictions rather than to record the exact number of prior crimes. This results in certain lack of precision in the resulting analyses.
9. *Source*: Ministry of Justice, Table Q2.3 Offenders cautioned by type of offence.
10. Limitations on length prevent us from discussing the effect of prior convictions on the average sentence length of cases sent to custody, although this would be an interesting focus of research.
11. We exclude sexual offences, as this category contains too many diverse offences.

References

Ashworth, A. (2010) *Sentencing and Criminal Justice*. 5th ed. Cambridge: Cambridge University Press.

Cox, E. (1877) *The Principles of Punishment as Applied in the Administration of The Criminal Law as Applied by Judges and Magistrates*. London: Law Times Office.

Cunliffe, J. and Shepherd, A. (2007) *Re-Offending of Adults: Results from the 2004 Cohort*. Home Office Statistical Bulletin. London: Home Office, Research Development and Statistics Directorate.

Fitzmaurice, C. and Pease, K. (1986) *The Psychology of Judicial Sentencing*. Manchester: Manchester University Press.

Fletcher, G. (1982) The Recidivist Sentencing Premium. *Criminal Justice Ethics*, 1: 54–59.

Flood-Page, C. and Mackie, A. (1998) *Sentencing Practice. An Examination of Decisions in the Magistrates' Courts and the Crown Court*. London: Home Office.

Frase, R. (2012) *Just Sentencing*. New York: Oxford University Press.

Grunhut, M. (1948) *Penal Reform: A Comparative Study*. Oxford: Clarendon Press.

Hedderman, C. and Moxon, D. (1992) *Magistrates' Court or Crown Court? Mode of Trial Decisions and Sentencing*. London: HMSO.

Henham, R. (1995) Sentencing Policy and the Role of the Court of Appeal. *Howard Journal*, 34: 21–31.

Kazemian, L. (2010) Assessing the impact of a recidivist sentencing premium on crime and recidivism rates. In: J.V. Roberts and A. von Hirsch (eds) *The Role of Previous Convictions at Sentencing: Theoretical and Applied Perspectives*. Oxford: Hart Publishing.

Lee, J. (2010) Repeat offenders and the question of desert. In: J.V. Roberts and A. von Hirsch (eds) *The Role of Previous Convictions at Sentencing: Theoretical and Applied Perspectives*. Oxford: Hart Publishing.

Minnesota Sentencing Guidelines Commission (2013) *Sentencing Guidelines Grid.* Available at: http://mn.gov/sentencing-guidelines/.
Moxon, D. (1988) *Sentencing Practice in the Crown Court.* HORS 103. London: Home Office.
Roberts, J.V. (1997) Paying for the past: the role of criminal record in the sentencing process. In: M. Tonry (ed.) *Crime and Justice.* Chicago: University of Chicago Press.
——— (2008) *Punishing Persistent Offenders.* Oxford: Oxford University Press.
——— (2010) Re-examining first offender discounts at sentencing. In: J.V. Roberts and A. von Hirsch (eds) *The Role of Previous Convictions at Sentencing: Theoretical and Applied Perspectives.* Oxford: Hart Publishing.
Roberts, J.V. and Hough, M. (2011) Custody or Community? Exploring the Boundaries of Public Punitiveness in England and Wales. *Criminology and Criminal Justice,* 11: 185–202.
Roberts, J.V. and Pina-Sanchez, J. (2014) Previous Convictions at Sentencing: Exploring Empirical Trends in the Crown Court. *Criminal Law Review,* 8: 575–589.
Roberts, J.V. and Rafferty, A. (2011) Sentencing Guidelines in England and Wales: Exploring the New Format. *Criminal Law Review,* 9: 680–689.
Roberts, J.V. and Yalincak, O. (2014) Risk, Retribution, and Prior Record Enhancement Provisions in State Sentencing Guidelines. *Federal Sentencing Reporter,* 26: 177–190.
Sentencing Council (2011a) *Assault Offences. Definitive Guideline.* London: Sentencing Council.
——— (2011b) *Burglary Offences. Definitive Guideline.* London: Sentencing Council.
——— (2014) *Sexual Offences. Definitive Guideline.* London: Sentencing Council.
von Hirsch, A. (2010) Proportionality and the progressive loss of mitigation. some further reflections. In: J.V. Roberts and A. von Hirsch (eds) *The Role of Previous Convictions at Sentencing: Theoretical and Applied Perspectives.* Oxford: Hart Publishing.
von Hirsch, A. and Roberts, J.V. (2004) Legislating Sentencing Principles: The Provisions of the Criminal Justice Act 2003 Relating to Sentencing Purposes and the Role of Previous Convictions. *Criminal Law Review,* August: 639–652.
Walker, N. (1985) *Sentencing. Theory, Law and Practice.* London: Butterworths.
Wasik, M. (2010) Dimensions of criminal history: reflections on theory and practice. In: J.V. Roberts and A. von Hirsch (eds) *Previous Convictions at Sentencing. Theoretical and Applied Perspectives.* Oxford: Hart Publishing.

10
Penitence and Persistence: How Should Sentencing Factors Interact?

Hannah Maslen

The English sentencing guidelines list multiple factors for judges to take into account at different steps to determine the appropriate sentence. Some of these factors aggravate the seriousness of the offence, whilst others mitigate its seriousness; additional factors are to be taken into account in personal mitigation. The idea that aggravating factors should increase the severity of the offender's punishment and that mitigating factors do the opposite is straightforward. However, aside from the guilty plea discount (Sentencing Guidelines Council, 2007), there is no direction in the guidelines (and few attempts in the sentencing literature) to suggest how factors should be weighted or how they may interact (see Roberts, 2011).[1] The only distinction in the guidelines is between factors taken into account at step one (when determining the offence category) and factors considered at step two, which serve to modify the assessment of overall seriousness *within* the range of the offence category. In the new format guidelines, judges are instructed as follows:[2]

> The table below contains a non-exhaustive list of additional factual elements providing the context of the offence and factors relating to the offender. Identify whether any combination of these, or other relevant factors, should result in an upward or downward adjustment from the starting point. In some cases, having considered these factors, it may be appropriate to move outside the identified category range.

Whilst the aggravating or mitigating force of specific factors may be obvious, how different factors should interact is much less clear. For example, should aggravating and mitigating factors simply be weighed against each other, each aggravator cancelling out each mitigator? Or should mitigating factors have diminishing force as the number of aggravating factors increases? Or is there a more nuanced relationship between some particular factors, given what they imply about the offender or the offence?

Overview

In this chapter I explore the relationship between two sentencing factors that may interact in complex ways: previous convictions and remorse. Previous convictions appear in the new guideline format as a statutory aggravating factor at step two. Remorse appears as a factor reflecting personal mitigation, also at step two. As a very rough indication of the effect of previous convictions on sentence outcome, the Crown Court Sentencing Annual Publication, 2012 (Sentencing Council, 2013) reported that 'for offences of assault and public order, 77% of offenders with ten or more previous convictions taken into account were sentenced to immediate custody, compared to 34% of offenders with no previous convictions taken into account' (ibid., p. 21). The same report also revealed that remorse was the mitigating factor most frequently taken into account for all offences other than sexual offences and robbery (ibid., p. 31). Both of these factors might influence the severity of an offender's sentence: previous convictions pulling in one direction and remorse pulling in the other.

However, the relationship between remorse and previous convictions could be more complex than crudely balancing one against the other. An offender's previous convictions may *contextualise* her remorse: the nature of her response to her own crime is made clearer when we understand the history of this wrongdoing and, perhaps, her responses to earlier criminal convictions. This contextualising relationship is not present, for example, when we consider the aggravating factor of targeting a vulnerable victim and the mitigating factor of playing a subordinate role in a group or gang. The addition of either factor says nothing about the effect of the other: both seem to retain their intuitive pull when considered in combination. An increasing number of previous convictions, however, could be seen to put pressure on the mitigating force of remorse. The argument might be evidentiary – previous convictions make claims of remorse look dubious – or, notwithstanding the genuineness of an offender's remorse, previous convictions may preclude it from being relevant, or *as* relevant at sentencing.

To begin to explore the relationship, I first provide an overview of why remorse and previous convictions are important to sentencing, summarising the justifications for their influence within a retributive framework. Previous convictions have received more attention than most other sentencing factors (see Roberts, 2008; Roberts and von Hirsch, 2010; Tamburrini and Ryberg, 2012), and there are a number of competing models that have been put forward in defence of their aggravating effect. Remorse has received much less attention, and accounts intended to justify its role as a mitigating factor are less developed (but see Tasioulas, 2006; Tudor, 2008; Maslen, 2014).

I will then consider what the two principal justifications for the effect of previous convictions might say about their interaction with remorse. In particular, I contrast the 'progressive loss of mitigation' model with 'enhanced culpability' models. How remorse and previous convictions *should* interact will depend upon the theoretical justifications underlying their independent effects: different accounts, involving different underlying tenets, generate different predictions. Finally, I present analysis of data from the Crown Court Sentencing Survey to test whether the interactions predicted in theory in fact play out in practice. I focus on assault offences, as they were the first to be covered by the new format sentencing guideline and therefore constitute the largest data set collected under the new format. The analysis conducted should be seen as exploratory: although the individual level data are available, many of the variables are divided into ordinal categories such that precision is not possible. These limitations notwithstanding, the results provide an interesting picture of current practice and a springboard for further theoretical discussion.

The importance of remorse

Remorse is generally regarded as a powerful source of personal mitigation at sentencing. There are a number of areas which support this general proposition: some sentencing laws identify remorse as a statutory factor for courts to consider; remorse has repeatedly been cited in sentencing judgments from courts across the common law world; research with sentencers and other criminal justice professionals has demonstrated the significance of remorse; and when members of the public are asked to impose sentence, they often take this factor into account. Research into sentencing decisions underscores the importance of remorse. In borderline cases, remorse often tips the balance towards a noncustodial sentence (Tombs and Jagger, 2006) and in the United States, it can make

Table 10.1 Percentage of cases where remorse was noted by sentencer, 2011[3]

Offence Category	Percentage of all cases in which remorse was noted
Offences Causing Death	39%
Assault (old form)	37%
Arson and Criminal Damage	36%
Driving Offences	34%
Robbery	32%
Assault (new form)	31%
Drugs	28%
Sexual Offences	28%
Other Offences	28%
Theft	27%

Source: CCSS.

the difference between a sentence of life or death; jurors often cite the absence of remorse as a significant factor in their decision to impose the death penalty in capital cases (Sundby, 1998, p. 1558).

In 2012, the Sentencing Council released the first annual wave of data from the Crown Court Sentencing Survey, and results confirm the importance of remorse as a sentencing factor.[4] Although the number and nature of mitigating factors varies significantly across offences, one feature is consistent: In 2011, for eight of the ten offence categories, remorse was the most frequently cited mitigating factor, and was the second most frequent factor for the remaining two offence categories (robbery and sexual offences). Table 10.1 summarises the proportion of cases in which the court cited remorse as a mitigating factor. The category where remorse appeared most frequently – cited by the court in 39% of sentences imposed – was for offences causing death.

A theoretical justification for the mitigating effect of remorse

In order to decide how remorse and previous convictions should interact in theory, we need accounts of why their independent effects are justified.[5] I here present a summary of one justification for the mitigating role of remorse, which I have developed in full elsewhere (Maslen, forthcoming). The account focuses on the idea of Responsive Censure.

Modern desert theories emphasise the censuring function of punishment (particularly von Hirsch, 1993 and von Hirsch and Ashworth, 2005;

see also Duff (2001)). What is deserved is not punishment per se but censure – an expression of disapprobation from the state – communicated through punishment. It can be argued that the legitimacy of this state censure is maximised when a dialogical approach is taken in which the message of censure *responds to* the offender's expressions of remorse. This is particularly attractive given that, according to von Hirsch and Ashworth (2005), sentences are supposed to address offenders as moral agents who have the capacity to evaluate and respond to an official evaluation of their conduct. They write:

> Penal censure has important moral functions that are not reducible to crime prevention. A response to criminal wrongdoing that conveys disapprobation gives the individual the opportunity to respond in ways that are typically those of an agent capable of moral deliberation: to recognise the wrongfulness of the action; to feel remorse; to express regret; to make efforts to desist in future – or else to try to give reasons why the conduct was not actually wrong. (2005, p. 92)

Within a responsive censure model, an expression of remorse constitutes a significant, relevant contribution to the dialogue about the offence: it is the offender's freely expressed condemnation of his own wrongdoing. Censure that ignored the offender's remorseful communication would fail to optimally appeal to the offender's reason and insight because it would not address him in his present state of understanding. Instead, it would merely seek the response it should have already heard. Communication gains greater legitimacy when it is tailored to its recipient. If it is not also listening, the state's sentencing process becomes an asymmetric exercise in penal communication: the state broadcasts its censure, and the offender passively absorbs the consequent punishment.[6]

So if, as von Hirsch and Ashworth argue, the offender's reflective process is important to the rationale underlying the censuring response, then an offender who independently engages with the reflective process should be censured in light of this. Adopting a limited dialogical model of censure achieves this by making room for input from the offender on the subject of his wrongdoing. Of course, this does not mean that censure is inappropriate in cases where the offender demonstrates remorse. The censure still needs to reiterate and confirm the wrongfulness of the offence, but the offender's mind does not need to be drawn to the conclusion. Consequently, the magnitude of the censure required in response is altered. Failing to moderate the degree of censure would be to address the offender as if she lacked any appreciation of the seriousness of the offence. To address her in this way would demonstrate deficient communication on the part of the state.

The importance of previous convictions

Roberts and Pina Sanchez (Chapter 9, this volume) explore the role of previous convictions in the Crown Court. They note that prior convictions are considered differently in different jurisdictions and report that sentencers in England and Wales consider previous convictions in a more reasoned and nuanced way, taking into account only priors deemed sufficiently recent and relevant. Since Roberts and Pina Sanchez provide a comprehensive discussion of patterns and practice, I shall not repeat this exercise here. I shall, however, reexamine two of the theoretical justifications for this established practice in close detail.

Previous convictions have received considerable attention from sentencing theorists (see Roberts and von Hirsch, 2010 for recent discussion). As with remorse, it should be noted that commentators are not always convinced of the relevance of previous convictions to desert-based sentencing. Theorists who argue that the offender's desert should be proportionate to the seriousness of the current offence and nothing else, see no role for previous convictions. To take prior convictions into account, it is argued, is to punish the offender for who he is, rather than what he has done, and results in double punishment (see, for example, Bagaric, 2000; Davis, 1992). However, as I will now discuss, other commentators disagree and propose arguments derived from retributive theory to support a principled approach to taking previous convictions into consideration. The arguments of these theorists are considered in what follows.

Progressive loss of mitigation and the lapse theory

Andreas von Hirsch has defended the progressive loss of mitigation model of the apparent aggravating effect of previous convictions (1985; 1991; 1993). The phrase 'progressive loss of mitigation' describes the manner by which an offender's sentence will become more severe each time he reoffends, until the full, unmitigated sentence is justified. The initial mitigation is not earned; it is an expression of tolerance which the state extends to those who may have lapsed into offending – a sort of benefit of the doubt, until it becomes clear that the offender's conduct is more than a mere lapse. The following passage from Wasik and von

Hirsch (1994) explains the rationale underlying the progressive loss of mitigation model:

> Our everyday moral judgments include the notion of a lapse. A transgression (even a fairly serious one) is judged somewhat less strictly when it occurs against a background of prior compliance. The idea is that even an ordinarily well-behaved person can have his or her inhibitions fail in a moment of wilfulness or weakness. Such a temporary breakdown of self-control is the kind of frailty for which some understanding should be shown. In sentencing, the relevant lapse is an infringement of criminal law, rather than a more commonplace moral failure, but the logic of the first offender discount remains the same—that of dealing with a lapse more tolerantly. A reason for so treating a lapse is respect for the process by which people attend to, and respond to, censure for their conduct. A first offender, after being confronted with censure or blame, is capable—as a reasoning human being presumed capable of ethical judgments—of reflecting on the morality of what he has done and of making an extra effort to show greater restraint. What we do, in granting the discount, is to show respect for this capacity—and thereby give the offender a so-called 'second chance'. With repetitions, however, the discount should diminish, and eventually disappear. (1994, p. 410)

The practical ramifications of this theory are that previous convictions will remove a quantum of mitigation for the first two, three or four convictions, but then further convictions will have no additional, aggravating effect on the offender's sentence (Ashworth (2005) suggests the mitigation is lost after the second offence; Wasik (1987) suggests that the mitigation may extend to the fifth conviction). Some theorists have questioned whether the progressive nature of the loss of mitigation is at odds with the core rationale of tolerating a lapse and giving an offender a second chance (Roberts, 2008, p. 58). Should the offender be given a third and fourth chance? Does the idea of a 'temporary breakdown of self-control' seem plausible once an offender has repeatedly broken the law? Thus, although those who expound the lapse theory suggest that the loss of mitigation is progressive, others have suggested that the underlying notion of lapse points more coherently to a dichotomous effect, whereby offenders are given the benefit of the doubt the first time they offend, but thereafter should receive the proportionate sentence (see, for example, Adler, 1991). In contrast to the next set of theories discussed, the mitigation afforded to first (and second) time offenders is not a direct function of desert; rather, it derives its justification from broader principles relating to anticipation of effective censure and the appropriate attitude the state should have to occasional weakness.

Enhanced culpability perspectives on previous convictions

There are various versions of the enhanced culpability argument for a recidivist premium. In contrast to the progressive loss of mitigation approach, which the lapse theory seeks to justify, enhanced culpability accounts seek to demonstrate why previous convictions aggravate the offender's sentence. Although the precise details of the accounts vary, the underlying tenet in each is that previous convictions are relevant to the repeat offender's desert because they make him more blameworthy in some way. Accordingly, even if the material acts and resulting harms of two offences are otherwise identical, an offender who has previous convictions can deserve more punishment than an offender with no or fewer previous convictions because of the way they are implicated in his degree of culpability for the offence.

According to Lee (2009), the repeat offender should have come to learn that exposure to certain people, situations or activities increases their likelihood of reoffending. For example, a person who is likely to commit an assault when drunk should avoid drinking to excess; a person who feels attracted to children should avoid being alone with them. A failure to avoid criminogenic triggers and contexts, if they do in fact lead to reoffending, constitutes an omission which increases the offender's culpability for the ensuing offence. Having been convicted and punished, the offender finds himself in a relationship with the state that confers on him the obligation to attempt to steer his life in a direction that reduces the likelihood that he will reoffend.

There are other versions of the enhanced culpability argument. Roberts (2008) proposes an account according to which previous convictions speak to the state of mind of the offender in a similar way to premeditation. The comparison is made as follows:

> Premeditation bespeaks a disregard for legality, and a commitment to offending that is not true of spontaneous offending. Having been charged, convicted and punished, repeat offenders also share a state of mind that renders them more blameworthy than first-time offenders. Both considerations speak to the relationship between the offender and the offence and constitute legitimate grounds for aggravating the severity of sentence. (p. 85)

According to this view, the repeat offender commits the offence knowing more, and this has parallels with the notion of forethought (essential to premeditation). MacPherson (2002) also proposes an account according to which recidivism should have an aggravating effect on punishment to reflect the offender's additionally culpable choice to act in the present without regard for society's past censure. The offender's decision not to react to society's message of blame, by again committing the same crime, is a culpable choice in itself.

Common to all three proposals is the idea that recidivism is a culpability enhancer that derives its relevance from the offender's decisions to act (or not act), having been exposed to the message communicated by censure and to the harmful consequences resulting from prior offending. If previous convictions increase culpability, then increasing the severity of the recidivist's punishment is a requirement of justice. This aggravation operates more internally to desert than does the progressive loss of mitigation that the lapse theory promotes. None of these theorists proposes that previous convictions should outweigh the seriousness of the offence, nor do any propose that each previous conviction should result in the same increase in sentence indefinitely. This mirrors the judicial approach that Roberts and Pina Sanchez report in Chapter 9: the practice in England and Wales seems to be to consider previous convictions in a nuanced way, and courts moderate the increase in sentence severity to ensure that previous convictions do not swamp the seriousness of the offence.

The penitent recidivist: what do the theoretical models predict?

Remorse and previous convictions according to the lapse theory

If the lapse theory were to be the correct justification for the effect of previous convictions on the severity of the sentence, then how should the mitigating effect of remorse interact? The lapse theory essentially extends the benefit of the doubt to all first offenders to assume that their offending was a temporary breakdown of self-control and that they will be responsive to the reasons embodied in the censure to refrain from further offending. The censure is attenuated to reflect this assumption of understanding and future compliance. This is, then, very similar to attenuating censure to address the offender who already appears to have internalized its message, as evidenced by his remorse. On the lapse theory, it is as if the mitigation afforded to the first time offender treats him as if he were remorseful. Interestingly, it would seem that a *lack* of remorse might be particularly relevant to sentencing when the offender has not yet exhausted the mitigation extended to him, on the assumption that his offending constitutes a lapse. It is difficult to present the offender who does not denounce his behaviour as one who suffered a weakness of self-control, even if his offence occurred against a background of relative compliance: the lapse theory extends the benefit of the doubt to the offender, but a lack of remorse may reveal that the offender's conduct is more than a mere lapse.

Does this mean a lack of remorse should result in the offender being denied a first offender discount since it makes the idea of a lapse seem far-fetched? If we accept the lapse theory, there are still reasons to retain the mitigation even for the remorseless offender. First, an offender can consistently intend to make extra effort to show greater restraint without feeling remorse. He might intend to do so for prudential reasons rather than moral reasons: he might intend to stay out of trouble. Second, the language used by Wasik and von Hirsch (1994) is prospective: even if an offender is not remorseful prior to sentencing, he should be considered capable of reflecting on the morality of what he has done once he has been confronted with censure or blame. Thus, the benefit of the doubt errs on the side of assuming that the first time offender is or will become remorseful.

This still leaves an interesting interaction between the mitigating effect of remorse and the aggravating (or progressively less mitigating) effect of previous convictions on this account. If the message embodied in the reduced censure is one that treats the offender as if he does, or at least will, understand the wrongfulness of what he has done, then it would be duplication to further attenuate the censure on the grounds of remorse: it is essentially the same message. If the argument is that remorse changes the quality of the censure to respect moral agency and the offender's ability to accept the message, then this is already the starting point for first offenders on the lapse theory. First-time offenders are treated as if they do not need the full message: they get a benefit which we later only afford the remorseful offender.

The upshot of this is that remorse should have no mitigating effect until the first offender discount has been lost.[7] Since previous convictions do not aggravate on this theory, remorse is not in tension with them once the full sentence is active, and its effect is actually very similar to that of giving first offenders the benefit of the doubt that they do or will reflect sufficiently on the message embodied in the censure. Thus, if we accept the lapse theory, lack of previous convictions mitigates until the offender has three or four convictions, but remorse does not mitigate until this same point (or at least until some of the quantum of mitigation has been lost). After the full sentence is activated, previous convictions should not aggravate further, and genuine remorse can mitigate to any amount up to that granted to the first-time offender.

Remorse and previous convictions according to the enhanced culpability model

If previous convictions enhance culpability because of what they imply about the offender's culpability, what role does remorse play? I have argued that the mitigating effect of remorse is justified on the grounds of the reduced censure that becomes appropriate in light of the offender's understanding and rejection of his wrongful conduct. In presenting the enhanced culpability model, I argued that previous convictions, whilst themselves being antecedent, tie the blameworthy element more closely to the primary determinants of desert. This was seen to have similarities to planning, which occurs prior to the actual act but is relevant to the offender's culpability at the time of its commission. The offender with previous convictions decides to commit the offence in full knowledge of the harm he will cause and/or under the influence of factors he was culpable in failing to avoid. Remorse, on the other hand, is not constitutive of the offender's state of mind at the time of the offence and thus not relevant to the assessment of culpability. Remorse therefore is offender-related, whilst the relevance of previous convictions might be offence-related in the same way as is premeditation (Roberts, 2008), or in analogy to failing to intervene to prevent a harm (cf. Lee, 2009). This is important when considering the interaction, as it situates the influence of previous convictions and remorse at different points in the sentencing decision, rather than at the same point where they might appear more directly in tension.

Being remorseful does not change the offender's state of mind at the time of the offence, nor undo any culpable decisions or omissions that facilitated it. Thus, for the assessment of offence seriousness – an assessment that takes into account the culpability of the offender – previous convictions will always have an aggravating effect to the extent that the previous convictions gave the offender insight into the factors that make him more likely to reoffend; he is culpable to the extent he failed to avoid them. Remorse, having a role to play after the seriousness of the offence has been established, will justify attenuating the censure to address the offender in the context of his understanding of the wrongfulness of his conduct. Since, on this model, previous convictions affect the offender's culpability for the offence and are therefore arguably offence-related, they should carry more weight than remorse, which is not part of the assessment of the seriousness of the offence. This will especially be the case where there are a number of previous convictions which have cumulatively aggravated the offence and corresponding proportionate punishment.

However, even on this model, it could still be argued that there is room for remorse and previous convictions to interact, and Roberts (2008) makes some claims which suggest this. Even though previous convictions and remorse theoretically operate at different points in the sentencing decision (if previous convictions are of consequence for the offender's culpability), remorse may have an *evidentiary* role to play in providing evidence of attempts at desistance. The criminogenic factors of which prior offending makes the offender aware are not always easy or even possible for the offender to avoid, and this should be taken into account when assessing the extent to which failing to avoid them enhances culpability. Roberts (2008) says 'consideration of the offender's previous convictions requires a more multidimensional approach, one which incorporates the individual's efforts to achieve desistance, even if these efforts are ultimately unsuccessful' (p. 89–90). The offender's response to his own wrongdoing may reveal frustration over his repeat offending, which he has attempted to stop. Lee (2009) makes a similar point, saying that inferences that the offender failed to reform can be rebutted by the offender: 'Repeat offenders ought to be able to present the ways in which they have tried to steer clear of criminality and, depending on the reasonableness and sincerity of their attempts, receive a reduction in the recidivist premium' (p. 616). In this way, recidivism may render the offender only slightly more culpable if he is remorseful. But this will be the case only to the extent that remorse is associated with sincere attempts at desistance, attenuating the culpability associated with failing to take steps to prevent reoffending.

The relationship between remorse and previous convictions is complex according to this model. Previous convictions alone have more weight than remorse alone due to their being tied to the offender's culpability for the offence. However, when previous convictions and remorse are present, it may be the case that remorse has an evidentiary role to play in indicating that the offender is not as culpable for failing to avoid known criminogenic factors, but only where the remorse indicates that attempts to avoid them have been made. Where this is the case, the aggravating effect of previous convictions may be somewhat reduced. Since remorse is relevant to the communicative context of the censure, it will continue to have mitigating force which is independent of any evidence it provides, suggesting a lesser aggravating role for previous convictions in such cases. To repeat, remorse does not dilute the aggravating effect of previous convictions on culpability, rather it reveals that the offender's failure to avoid known criminogenic factors was not as culpable as it otherwise would be: the offender, remorse might reveal, was not unconcerned about putting himself in situations where he is likely to reoffend, but he may have found doing this incredibly difficult.

Persistence and penitence in practice

To explore the effects of remorse and previous convictions on sentence, binary logistic analysis was conducted on a sample of 5405 offenders sentenced for an assault offence using custodial or non-custodial sentence outcome as the dependent variable. In addition to remorse and previous convictions,[8] offence seriousness,[9] number of aggravating factors (excluding previous convictions) and number of mitigating factors (excluding remorse) were also included in the model to control for their independent effects on sentence outcome. All five independent variables were statistically significant predictors of whether the sentence outcome was custodial or non-custodial. Although plea should be related to sentence outcome, its inclusion did not strengthen the model, and its effect was not significant. (This could be a result of a high number of missing values for this variable.) The inclusion of the interaction between remorse and previous convictions was also not significant. Table 10.2 shows the output of the logistic regression analysis.

Table 10.2 Logistic regression model showing the extent to which variables predict whether the offender receives a custodial sentence for an assault offence

	Beta Weight	Standard Error	Wald	Degrees of Freedom	Significance Level	Exponentiated Beta
Remorse	−.693	.082	72.346	1	.000	.500
Previous Convictions	.212	.016	174.868	1	.000	1.236
Offence Seriousness	.584	.024	596.076	1	.000	1.794
Mitigating Factors	−.483	.029	283.299	1	:000	.617
Aggravating Factors	.361	.019	342.196	1	.000	1.434
Constant	−3.997	.167	573.149	1	.000	.018

The model predicted 81% of the sentence outcomes correctly. From the table, we can observe that if an offender is *not* remorseful (the inverse of the result shown in the table, which gives the odds of a custodial sentence when the offender *is* remorseful), the odds of her receiving a custodial sentence for an assault offence are twice as large as for the remorseful offender. The non-remorseful offender is more likely to receive a custodial sentence than the remorseful offender. We can also see that for every additional previous conviction, the odds of receiving a custodial sentence are 1.2 times as large, and thus every additional previous conviction increases the odds of receiving custodial sentence by a factor of 1.2. (This should be treated as a rough estimate, as previous convictions were measured by way of ordinal ranges).

Significant contributions are also made by the seriousness of the offence, number of aggravating and mitigating factors, with offence seriousness making the greatest contribution. This last finding reflects the proportionality-based framework of sentencing for this and other offences. We can also note that previous convictions had a greater impact than remorse on the likelihood of custody: although significant, remorse contributes least to the predictive power of the model. Figure 10.1 represents the relationship between previous convictions, remorse and the likelihood of a custodial sentence. The number of previous convictions is plotted against the predicted probability of a custodial sentence. Separate lines for remorseful and non-remorseful offenders are presented.

The graph clearly shows that both previous convictions and remorse influence the likelihood of custody. In general, the more previous convictions an offender has, the more likely it is that she will receive a custodial sentence. Further, being remorseful makes it less likely that an offender will receive a custodial sentence: for any number of previous convictions, the remorseful offender is less likely to receive a custodial sentence than the non-remorseful offender. This means that (controlling for other factors) the mitigating influence of remorse remains even as previous convictions increase to the higher numbers. The graph also shows a plateauing of the effect of previous convictions – a finding consistent with the analyses reported by Roberts and Pina-Sanchez in this volume.

Further logistic regression analysis revealed significant interactions between remorse and offence seriousness, and between previous convictions and offense seriousness. Graphical representations of these interactions showed a common feature: as offence seriousness increases, the effects of the respective sentencing factors gradually decrease to

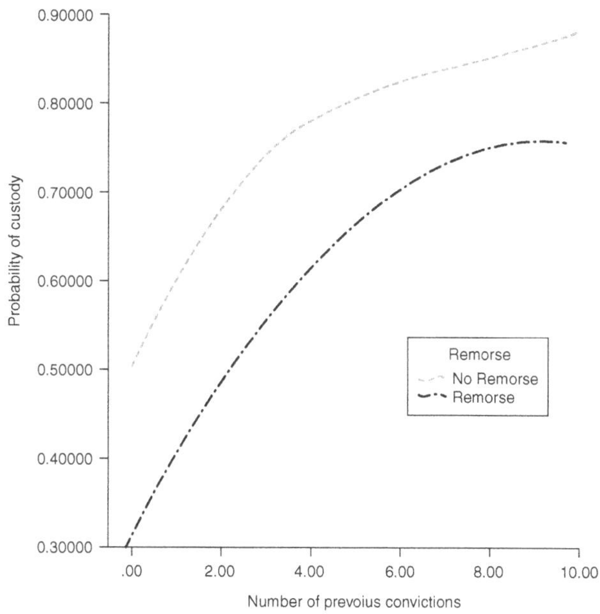

Figure 10.1 Relationship between number of previous convictions and the probability of custody for an assault offence, by remorse[10]

zero. In general, as the seriousness of the offence increases, the probability of custody increases for all offenders. Relating to the interaction between offence seriousness and remorse, the separate lines showing the probability of custody for the remorseful and non-remorse offenders began to converge at sentences rated 7 (out of 11) on the adapted seriousness scale, and overlapped completely for offences of seriousness 10 and 11. This convergence shows that as offence seriousness increases, the impact that remorse has on the likelihood of custody diminishes to zero. At the lower end of the seriousness scale, remorse has the largest mitigating effect, and this diminishes as the seriousness of the offences increases. Remorse eventually ceases to exert any effect on the sentences passed for the most serious assault offences.

Further graphical analysis showed that this diminishing influence was also true of the aggravating effect of previous convictions: previous convictions significantly interact with offence seriousness such that as the seriousness of the offence increases, previous convictions have less and less effect on the likelihood of custody. For the most serious offences, having fewer previous convictions does not make a custodial sentence less likely. These findings are consistent with the principle that offence seriousness should be the primary determinant of sentence, and that as seriousness increases, aggravating and mitigating factors should cease to perceptibly affect the sentence. However, it should be noted that the dependent variable used in this analysis only captured the likelihood of custody, and did not distinguish between longer and shorter prison terms.

Summary and conclusions

This chapter has explored the interaction between two important and common sentencing factors: criminal history and remorse. The following findings emerged:

- Remorse mitigates the offender's sentence. Controlling for offence seriousness and other variables, the remorseful offender is less likely than the non-remorseful offender to be committed to custody.
- Previous convictions aggravate the offender's sentence, although the aggravating effect of previous convictions tapers off after about 6–7 previous convictions. The effect of previous convictions is greater than the effect of remorse.
- Previous convictions and remorse do not interact. Both exert independent effects on the likelihood of custody. The mitigating effect of remorse is not diminished as the number of previous convictions increases.
- Remorse interacts with offence seriousness. As offences become more serious, the mitigating effect of remorse diminishes, eventually appearing to have no effect on the likelihood of custody for offenders sentenced for the most serious offences.
- Previous convictions interact with offence seriousness. As offences become more serious, the aggravating effect of priors diminishes, eventually having little or no effect on custody rate at the highest levels of seriousness.

The data revealed a pattern consistent with an approach to previous convictions which either reflects a limited enhanced culpability model (whether priors aggravate up to a point) or a progressive loss of mitigation model on which the mitigation is exhausted after a number of convictions: the analysis showed that the likelihood of a custodial sentence continued to rise beyond the second and third convictions but levelled off after about the sixth. It also revealed a pattern consistent with a model which does not support an interaction between previous convictions and remorse: the effect of remorse was significant even when offenders had ten prior convictions. The pattern observed is also consistent with an account that puts more emphasis on previous convictions than remorse. A model that ties previous convictions (but not remorse) to culpability thus fits the data.

The interaction between offence seriousness and remorse, and offence seriousness and previous convictions reveals a pattern consistent with a model that places limits on the influence of sentencing factors: the weight of individual factors should not eclipse the seriousness of the offence. This finding is consistent with a general trend for aggravating and mitigating factors to play a lesser role when the offence is particularly serious (Ashworth, 2010).

Whether the mitigating power of remorse is outweighed by the effect of the seriousness of the most serious offences (i.e., its influence is imperceptible in the face of the gravity of the offence), or whether it ceases to be justified as a mitigating factor in such serious cases is an interesting theoretical question (see Maslen and Roberts, 2013). It could be argued that it is not just that the mitigating effect of remorse is swamped when it comes to the most serious offences, but rather that some offences are too serious for a mitigating effect even to be justified (regardless of whether it would be swamped in practice). The aggravating power of previous convictions, in contrast, will have some normative force at all levels of seriousness – it is not that the seriousness of the offence makes their relevance theoretically uncertain – but the effect on the offender's sentence is likely to be eclipsed as seriousness increases.

A further interesting question is how, if it were possible, previous remorse should be taken into account alongside repeat offending, especially in an evidentiary capacity. Does a history of expressing remorse make the latest expression of remorse more plausible and thus underscores its relevance, or do previous expressions of remorse undermine the proposal that the currently remorseful offender accepts the message of censure? How many times can you be sorry before the claim loses force? It is possible that the answers to these questions will differ depending on the type of offending and the offender's degree of control over it.

Implications for sentencing guidelines

The discussion at the beginning of the chapter argued that the way in which previous convictions and remorse should (or should not) interact would depend on the theoretical model adopted. Due to the underlying justifications, lapse theory may have more scope for interaction than an enhanced culpability model, although it was suggested that both have room for remorse to play an evidentially role in different ways. The data shows that they do not interact in practice. This finding will be of interest to those constructing sentencing guidelines. If the Sentencing Council considers the lack of interaction to be correct, then it may wish to officially endorse this practice. However, if the Council is of the opinion that there should be an interaction – for example, that recidivists should receive no mitigation on the grounds of their remorse – then specific direction could be given in the guidance to correct the approach observed in current practice.

The new format guidelines in England and Wales cite previous convictions as an aggravating factor and lack of previous convictions as a mitigator. This conflates the progressive loss of mitigation and enhanced culpability model and indicates that the guidelines (at least in their presentation) are not committed to one over the other (or perhaps are committed to a hybrid account). Attempting to add theoretical precision to an approach that currently fails to adjudicate between the main competing models would thus be inadvisable, although a general statement could be made about whether there are limits to the mitigating effect of remorse.

I have tried to demonstrate that the choice of model would have consequences for the shape of the interaction between previous convictions and remorse such that weighing them against each other would proceed differently in both theory and practice depending on the preferred model. I have demonstrated the general patterns observable in current practice. This practice is either justifiable or not. In order for sentencing to be principled, penal theorists and those constructing guidance need to consider whether particular factors should affect sentence, as well as whether factors should interact in the ways they influence sentencing.

Notes

1. Roberts (2008, p. 264) describes the lack of guidance on sentencing factors as 'regrettable', saying, 'Most guideline schemes around the world adopt a laissez-faire approach to the use of sentencing factors. Guidance regarding the application of these factors is usually quite limited, possibly reflecting the view that consideration of mitigation and aggravation is more properly left to the exercise of judicial discretion, with only minimal direction from the legislature, the guidelines authority, or the Court of Appeal.'
2. See, for example, the definitive guideline for assault offences (Sentencing Council, 2011).

3. *Source*: Sentencing Council (2012).
4. See Sentencing Council, *Crown Court Sentencing Survey* (2012).
5. It should be noted that there are penal theorists who argue that remorse should not have a mitigating effect on the offender's sentence. Such theorists argue that since remorse does not change the state of mind of the offender at the time of the offence, it cannot be relevant to desert; that taking remorse into account unjustifiably brings in consideration of the offender's character; or that the difficulty of assessing whether an offender is genuine in his expression of remorse precludes its consideration (see, variously, Murphy, 2006; Ward, 2006; Bagaric and Amarasekara, 2001). Whilst these arguments deserve careful consideration, for the purposes of this paper, I assume that the sentencing guidelines are not erring in their inclusion of remorse as a mitigating factor.
6. Further, whilst I have suggested that this argument has force on a minimally communicative account such as von Hirsch's, it has even greater force where *dialogue* between the state and offender is emphasized. Duff (1996, p.33), for example, argues that the offender should not merely be a 'passive recipient' but should actively participate in the dialogue.
7. It should be noted that there are versions of this model that treat the first offender mitigation as an *entitlement*. On these accounts, the potential receptiveness or otherwise of the offender to the message of censure, or how realistic it was that the offence was a temporary lapse, would have no bearing on whether the mitigation should be granted (see Roberts, 2010).
8. In the original data, the values denoting previous convictions were organised as ordinal categories: 'None', '1 to 3', '4 to 9' and '10 or more'. Since these categories extend over different ranges, a decision had to be made about how to code previous convictions for analysis. Although it is impossible to add precision back into the data, it was decided that the categories should be recoded according to the midpoint of the range. 'None' became '0', '1–3' became '2', '4–9' became '6.5' and '10 or more' became '10'. The decision to code '10 or more' as 10 was made due to the plateauing effect that was evident in the CCSS report: precision in the number of previous convictions above ten is unlikely to affect the analysis.
9. Values for offence seriousness were determined by creating an ordinal ranking of all sentence starting points across all assault offences. This generated an 11-point scale of offence seriousness. The seriousness of an individual offender's sentence was then determined by identifying the starting point associated with the offence category for the particular offence type and translating it to the corresponding number on the 11-point scale.
10. Variables controlled for: offence seriousness, number of aggravating factors (excluding previous convictions), number of mitigating factors (excluding remorse). Due to the way in which the previous convictions variable was measured (via ordinal categories), the lines were interpolated to appear continuous through all possible values of previous convictions.

References

Adler, J. (1991) *The Urgings of Conscience: A Theory of Punishment*. Philadelphia: Temple University Press.

Ashworth, A. (2005) *Sentencing and Criminal Justice* (4th edn). Cambridge: Cambridge University Press.
Bagaric, M., and Amarasekara, K. (2001) Feeling Sorry? – Tell Someone Who Cares: The Irrelevance of Remorse in Sentencing. *The Howard Journal of Criminal Justice*, 40 (4): 364–376.
Bagaric, M. (2000) Double Punishment and Punishing Character: The Unfairness of Prior Convictions. *Criminal Justice Ethics*, 19(1): 10–28.
Davis, M. (1992) *To Make the Punishment Fit the Crime: Essays in the Theory of Criminal Justice*. Boulder, CO: Westview Press.
Duff, R.A. (1996) Penal Communications: Recent Work in the Philosophy of Punishment. *Crime and Justice*, 20: 1–97.
Lee, Y. (2009) Recidivism as Omission: A Relational Account. *Texas Law Review*, 87(3): 571–622.
MacPherson, D.L. (2002) The Relevance of Prior Record in the Criminal Law: A Response to the Theory of Professor von Hirsch. *Queen's Law Journal*, 28: 177–219.
Maslen, H (forthcoming) *Remorse, Penal Theory and Sentencing*. Oxford: Hart Publishing.
Maslen, H., and Roberts, J.V. (2013) Remorse and sentencing: an analysis of sentencing guidelines and sentencing practice. In: A. Ashworth and J.V Roberts (eds) *Sentencing Guidelines: Exploring the English Model*. Oxford: Oxford University Press.
Murphy, J.G. (2006) Well Excuse Me – Remorse, Apology, and Criminal Sentencing. *Arizona State Law Journal*, 38: 371–386.
Roberts, J. V. (2008) Aggravating and Mitigating Factors at Sentencing: Towards Greater Consistency of Application. *Criminal Law Review*, (4): 264–276.
——— (2008) *Punishing Persistent Offenders: Exploring Community and Offender Perspectives*. Oxford: Oxford University Press.
——— (2010) Re-examining first offender discounts at sentencing. In: J.V. Roberts and A. von Hirsch (eds) *The Role of Previous Convictions at Sentencing: Theoretical and Applied Perspectives*. Oxford: Hart Publishing.
——— (ed.) (2011) *Mitigation and Aggravation at Sentencing*. Cambridge: Cambridge University Press.
Roberts, J. V. and von Hirsch, A. (eds) (2010) *Previous Convictions at Sentencing: Theoretical and Applied Perspectives*. Oxford: Hart Publishing.
Sentencing Guidelines Council (2007) *Reduction in Sentence for a Guilty Plea. Definitive Guideline*. London: Sentencing Council of England and Wales.
Sentencing Council (2011) *Assault. Definitive Guideline*. London: Sentencing Council of England and Wales.
——— (2013) *Crown Court Sentencing Survey: Annual Publication, 2012*. London: Sentencing Council of England and Wales.
Sundby, S. (1998) The Capital Jury and Absolution: The Intersection of Trial Strategy, Remorse, and the Death Penalty. *Cornell Law Review*, 83: 1557–1598.
Tamburrini, C. and Ryberg, J. (2012) *Recidivist Punishments. The Philosopher's View*. New York: Lexington Books.
Tasioulas, J. (2006) Punishment and Repentance. *Philosophy*, 81(2): 279–322.
Tombs, J. and Jagger, E. (2006) Denying Responsibility: Sentencers' Accounts of Their Decisions to Imprison. *British Journal of Criminology*, 46: 803–821.

Tudor, S.K. (2008) Why Should Remorse Be a Mitigating Factor in Sentencing? *Criminal Law and Philosophy*, 2(3): 241–257.
von Hirsch, A. (1985) *Past or Future Crimes: Deservedness and Dangerousness in the Sentencing of Criminals*. New Brunswick, NJ: Rutgers University Press.
——— (1991) Criminal Record Rides Again. *Criminal Justice Ethics*, 10: 55–57.
——— (1993) *Censure and Sanctions*. Oxford: Clarendon Press.
von Hirsch, A. and Ashworth, A. (2005) *Proportionate Sentencing*. Oxford: Oxford University Press.
Ward, B.H. (2006) Sentencing Without Remorse. *Loyola. U. Chi. LJ*, 38: 131–895.
Wasik, M. (1987) Guidance, guidelines and criminal record. In: M. Wasik and K. Pease (eds) *Sentencing Reform: Guidance or Guidelines?* Manchester: Manchester University Press.
Wasik, M. and von Hirsch, A. (1994) Section 29 Revised: Previous Convictions in Sentencing. *Criminal Law Review*, June: 409–418.

11

Exploring the Impact of Sentencing Factors on Sentencing Domestic Burglary

Keir Irwin-Rogers and Thomas W. Perry

Introduction

When an offender is sentenced in the criminal courts of England and Wales, the primary factor that determines the severity of the sentence is the seriousness of the offence. This principle has been firmly established in statute by the Criminal Justice Act 2003. In section 143(1) of this act, courts are instructed to determine the seriousness of an offence by considering the offender's culpability in committing the offence and any harm which the offence caused, was intended to cause, or might foreseeably have caused. The principle that the seriousness of the offence should be the primary basis for the severity of the sentence is further reinforced by the Sentencing Council for England and Wales, an independent, nondepartmental body of the Ministry of Justice, established by the Coroners and Justice Act 2009. The Council puts this principle into practice in a number of ways, one of which is the provision of offence-specific sentencing guidelines that operationalise the concept of offence seriousness. (see Ashworth and Roberts, 2013 for discussion of the format of sentencing guidelines.)

The English sentencing guidelines provide the courts with a step-by-step process for determining the seriousness of an offence and consequently the type and severity of a sentence. In the first step of most guidelines, the Council identifies a set of sentencing factors that it regards as the principal factual elements of the offence (see Sentencing Council, 2011a, p. 8). Using these factors, the court places the offence into one of three categories of seriousness: category one, for the most serious offences; category two, for offences of mid-level seriousness; and category three, for the least serious offences (see Appendix A). For each category of seriousness, the Council has assigned a starting point sentence. So, for example, if an offender is found guilty of a domestic burglary, and the court decides that the case constitutes a category one offence, the starting point sentence in the current guideline is three years' custody (see Appendix B).

At step two, the court is given the opportunity to adjust the sentence either upward or downward within a prescribed category range, depending on a second set of sentencing factors that constitute the additional factual elements of the offence (see Appendix B). The step two set of sentencing factors is non-exhaustive, meaning that the courts have the discretion to consider any other relevant factors that have not been listed in the guideline. Step two sentencing factors are intended to be less significant than the sentencing factors listed in step one. In the domestic burglary guideline, for example, the step one factors – violence used or threatened against the victim and soiling, ransacking or vandalism of property – are considered by the Council to be more significant than the step two factors: offence was committed at night or demonstration of remorse by the offender. Sentencing factors, therefore, play an important role in determining the seriousness of an offence and consequently the severity of sentence.

Data source: the Crown Court Sentencing Survey

On 1 October 2010, the CCSS began operating across all Crown Court centres in England and Wales. Each time a sentence is passed, the courts complete a survey form that records which sentencing factors were considered relevant to the case in question (Appendix C). At the time of writing, the CCSS had collected data on a number of different offence types, including arson, assault, burglary, driving offences, drug offences, robbery, sexual offences and theft. In this chapter, we focus on one particular offence: domestic burglary. This offence was selected for two reasons. First, domestic burglaries are a relatively common offence in England and Wales. This is reflected in the CCSS data set for 2012, which contains 4,645 cases of domestic burglary, compared to, for example, only 192 cases of aggravated burglary. Second, domestic burglary cases resulted in the imposition of a high proportion of sentences of immediate imprisonment, as opposed to other disposals such as suspended sentence orders (SSOs), community orders (COs) or fines. From a statistical perspective, this is preferable because ranking the severity of prison sentences is relatively straightforward – it can be based solely on the length of the sentence. The severity of COs or SSOs, on the other hand, is less straightforward – it depends not only on the length of the sentence, but also on the number and types of requirement that are attached to them (see Mair, 2011; cf. Rex and von Hirsch, 1998).

Findings

Summary statistics

Cases and sentencing outcomes

The data used in this chapter are drawn from the 2012 dataset for domestic burglary cases, the most recent dataset that the Sentencing Council had released to members of the public at the time of writing. It provided information on 4,645 domestic burglary cases in total. Before we begin our analysis, we should note two caveats. First, in 2011, the CCSS had a response rate of 61% (Pina-Sanchez and Linacre, 2013). We cannot rule out the possibility that the sentencing decisions of courts that filled in and returned the CCSS forms might have been systematically different somehow from those that did not. Therefore, we would expect there to be some degree of difference between the statistics presented and the corresponding figures for all sentencing cases. Nevertheless, we expect that the general trends presented in this chapter will largely apply to the remaining 39% of cases for which data were unavailable. Second, external researchers are currently unable to access the full CCSS database in its raw state.[1] The datasets made available to the public have been edited so that exact sentence lengths have been replaced by ten sentence categories.[2] While this prevented us from analysing the precise impact of sentencing factors on sentence severity, we considered these ranked sentence categories to be a good substitute for exact sentence lengths.

Over three-quarters of all cases of domestic burglary in 2012 resulted in a sentence of immediate imprisonment. Although the majority of these sentences ranged between twelve months and three years' imprisonment, a sufficiently large number of cases fell within each sentence category for us to conduct our analysis exploring the associations between sentencing factors and sentence severity.

Sentencing factor frequencies

In steps one and two of the domestic burglary guideline, the Council lists 39 different sentencing factors relevant to a particular case. Table 11.1 reveals the percentage of cases in which the courts cited each sentencing factor.

The courts cited each sentencing factor listed in the domestic burglary sentencing guideline at least once. Nevertheless, there are

Table 11.1 Domestic burglary – percentage of cases in which sentence factor was cited

Previous relevant convictions	71%	Age/lack of maturity affecting responsibility	8%
Victim on/returns to premises while offender present	35%	Child at home/returns	7%
Committed at night	28%	Offence committed on bail	6%
Member of group or gang	24%	Subordinate role in group or gang	5%
Remorse	23%	Good character/exemplary conduct	4%
Theft of/damage to property causing significant degree of loss	23%	Weapon present on entry or carried	4%
Deliberately targeted	22%	Violence used/threatened particularly involving a weapon	4%
Limited damage/disturbance to property	18%	Offender exploited by others	3%
Offender was under the influence of alcohol/drugs	17%	Established evidence of community impact	2%
Significant degree of planning	16%	Mental disorder/learning disability where not linked to the commission of the offence	2%
Nothing stolen or of very low value	15%	Sole/primary career for dependant relatives	2%
Soiling/ransacking/vandalism of property	13%	Mental disorder/learning disability where linked to the commission of the offence	2%
Failure to comply with current court orders	12%	Serious medical conditions	1%
Offence committed on impulse/limited intrusion	12%	Victim compelled to leave home (domestic violence in particular)	1%
Equipped for burglary	11%	Made voluntary reparation	1%
No previous relevant convictions	11%	Lapse of time not fault of offender	1%
Significant physical/psychological injury or trauma	10%	Gratuitous degradation	1%
On licence	10%	Steps taken to prevent reporting of offence	0.3%
Determination/demonstration to address addiction/behaviour	10%	Context of general public disorder	0.2%
TICs	8%		

clear differences in the frequency with which the factors were cited. For example, the most commonly cited sentencing factor, 'previous convictions', appeared in over two-thirds of all cases, whereas the least frequently cited sentencing factor, 'context of general public disorder', appeared in only 0.2% of cases (about one in every 663 cases).

At step one – the step in which each case is assigned a sentence category that reflects the seriousness of the offence – the courts cited a total of 7,500 aggravating factors, compared to only 2,310 mitigating factors (over a total of 4,645 cases).[3] Given this disparity, if these factors had been assigned an equal weight by the courts, we would expect to see a much greater proportion of cases being classified as category one (the most serious category of offences) than as category three (the least serious category of offences). The data did indeed reveal that the courts classified more cases as category one than category three: 1,097 category one cases compared to 637 category three cases. The difference between the numbers of cases in each of these categories, however, was less pronounced than the 3:1 ratio of aggravating to mitigating factors suggests. This reflects, at least in part, the courts' discretion to allocate different weights to individual sentencing factors. For example, a case that involved a greater number of step one aggravating factors than mitigating factors could, nevertheless, be classified as category three if the court decided that the mitigating factors were more significant than the aggravating factors in defining the seriousness of the offence.

At step two – the step in which sentence severity is adjusted on the basis of additional sentencing factors – the courts cited a total of 7,275 aggravating factors, compared to 3,135 mitigating factors. Unlike at step one, the difference between the total number of aggravating factors and mitigating factors could not have been due to the difference in the number of factors provided in the guideline lists: the Sentencing Council stipulates twelve possible step two aggravating factors and eleven possible step two mitigating factors in the domestic burglary guideline. Much of the difference, however, was the result of one particular aggravating factor – previous relevant convictions – which accounted for 3,298 of the total number of aggravating factors. Due to the replacement of precise sentence lengths with sentence categories in the CCSS dataset, we were unable to analyse the extent to which the cases that fell within Categories 1 and 3 were aggravated/mitigated at step two. Fortuitously, however, one of the sentence categories in the dataset (12 months' imprisonment) corresponded to the sentence starting point for Category 2 offences. Therefore, we were able to calculate the proportion of Category 2 cases which were aggravated at step two (47.6%), the proportion that were mitigated (41.8%), and the proportion that were neither aggravated nor mitigated (10.7%). Despite judicial discretion to allocate different weights to sentencing factors, given the considerable difference between the numbers of aggravating and mitigating factors that were cited by the courts, it seems likely that Category 1 and 3 cases were also more likely to be aggravated than mitigated at step two.

Sentencing factors and sentence severity

In the following sections, we consider the impact of selected sentencing factors on sentence severity. Although we included all sentencing factors in our initial data analysis, we decided to limit the number discussed in this chapter in order to provide a more detailed level of analysis. Therefore, a subset of factors was selected that we thought readers would consider most interesting from an analytical perspective. For example, we chose to focus on a number of sentencing factors that have been the subject of recent publications, including remorse (Maslen and Roberts, 2013; Tudor, 2008), intoxication (Padfield, 2011; Dingwall and Koffman, 2008), and previous convictions (Roberts and von Hirsch, 2010; Roberts, 2008). Moreover, we selected factors from steps one *and* two of the domestic burglary guideline, so that we could scrutinise the principle that step one factors ought to have more of an impact on sentence severity than step two factors.

Bivariate and multivariate analyses

The bivariate analysis presented in this chapter compared the distribution of sentencing outcomes for cases in which a particular sentencing factor was cited by the courts with (i) the overall distribution of sentencing outcomes, and (ii) the distribution of sentencing outcomes associated with other sentencing factors. The advantage of this approach is that it can generate clear, easily interpretable results which show the link between individual factors and sentence severity. From an analytical perspective, however, there are clear limitations to a bivariate analysis: First, by definition, this type of analysis considers the links between sentence severity and sentencing factors one at a time. In practice, we think it is more likely that the courts make collective judgements about multiple sentencing factors simultaneously. Second, although an initial correlational analysis did not reveal any strong associations between factors, some moderate associations were discovered. Therefore, the estimated impact of individual factors will be biased to some degree by the impact of other factors with which they were associated. In short, the problem with considering the impact of individual sentencing factors using bivariate analysis is that factors neither operate nor occur independently in practice.

To address these issues, we also conducted a multivariate analysis. Specifically, an ordinal logistic regression model was run to estimate the individual impact of each sentencing factor while controlling for the impact of all other factors.[4] Analysis of this type, however, has a cost: that of simplicity and transparency for readers unfamiliar with this statistical approach. To decide whether this trade-off was worthwhile, we assessed the consistency between the results of both analyses. With some notable exceptions, the results from the multivariate analysis were consistent with those that emerged from the bivariate analysis. Because of this consistency, we decided that our bivariate results – presented in the form of figures and tables – provided a clearer and more useful mode of communication than the odds ratios that were generated by our multivariate analysis. Therefore, it is primarily these bivariate results that we use to discuss the relationship between sentencing factors and sentence severity in the following sections. When the results from the multivariate analysis did not support the results from the bivariate analysis, however, we have highlighted this inconsistency and directed the reader to the odds ratios that provide a more robust indication of the impact of each sentencing factor on sentence severity.

For readers who are not familiar with interpreting the results of ordinal logistic regression, the essential point, at least for the purposes of the current chapter, is that the odds ratio for each sentencing factor compares the proportion of cases equal to or below a particular sentence severity category with the proportion of cases in all higher sentence severity categories, while controlling for other factors included in the model. Therefore, if a sentencing factor has an odds ratio greater than one, this indicates that an offence characterised by this factor is more likely to result in a more severe sentence than an offence that is not characterised by the factor. Conversely, if a sentencing factor has an odds ratio below one, this indicates that an offence characterised by this factor is more likely to result in a less severe sentence than an offence that is not characterised by the factor. The further the sentencing factor odds ratio is above one, the greater the chances of a more severe sentence if that factor is present; the further the ratio is below one, the greater the chances of a less severe sentence if that factor is present (see Garson, 2014).[5]

On a final note, we would reiterate that both analytical approaches are correlational in nature. Relationships between factors and sentence severity are necessary but not sufficient in establishing causal links between factors and sentence outcomes (Gorard, 2013). In other words, while differences in sentencing outcomes based on the presence/absence of a particular sentencing factor provide a good indication of the impact of each factor on sentence severity, these differences may partly reflect unobserved variation in the underlying cases rather than independent, causal factors per se. Moreover, it is our view that lists of sentencing factors can only imperfectly capture the complexity of sentencing. As a result, there will inevitably be some gap between the picture presented by the data and the underlying reality of sentencing decisions.

Mitigating factors and sentence severity

In this section, we address the following questions:

- What is the relationship between each selected mitigating factor and sentence severity in practice?
- To what extent does the data support or contradict the principle that step one mitigating factors ought to mitigate sentence severity more than step two mitigating factors?

Consider Figure 11.1 and Table 11.2. In order to improve the clarity of our analysis, we collapsed the ten sentence categories in the CCSS dataset into five categories, which are organised in order of sentence severity: (i) Noncustodial sanction/SSO; (ii) Low severity (below 12 months' imprisonment); (iii) Medium-low severity (12 months' up to 18 months' imprisonment); (iv) Medium-high severity (18 months' up to 4 years' imprisonment); and v) High severity (4 years' imprisonment and above).

Figure 11.1 compares the sentencing outcomes for cases in which a particular mitigating factor was identified as relevant with the distribution of outcomes for all domestic burglary cases (top bar). In general terms, it shows that the presence of each mitigating factor was associated with an increase in the proportion of lenient sentences (noncustodial sanctions / SSOs – the section that is furthest left on each bar), and a decrease in the proportion of medium-high severity and high severity sentences (18 months' to 4 years' imprisonment and 4 years' imprisonment and above – the two sections that are furthest right on each bar).[6] In short, our theoretically grounded expectations about mitigating factors were supported by the empirical data; so far, so good. With this in mind, consider Table 11.2, which allowed us to make some more precise comparisons.

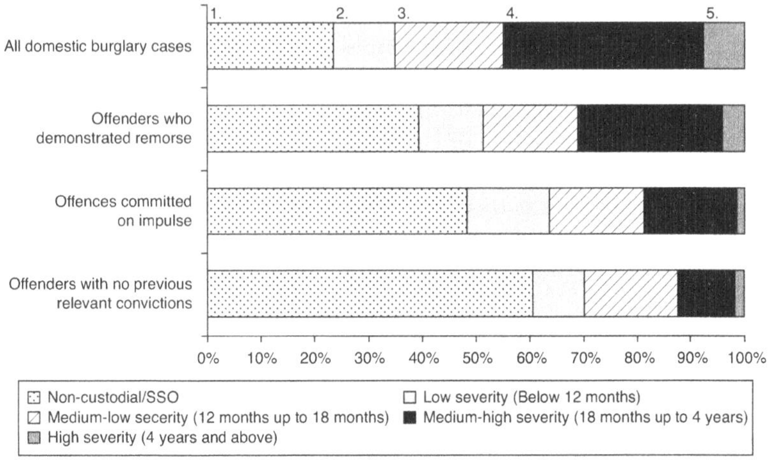

Figure 11.1 Sentence severity by mitigating factor

Table 11.2 Percentage of offenders within sentence category by mitigating factor

Mitigating Factor	Noncustodial sanction/ SSO	Low severity (Below 12 months)	Medium-low severity (12–18 months)	Medium-high severity (18 months–4 years)	High severity (4+ years)
All domestic burglary cases	24%	11%	20%	38%	7%
Remorse	39%	12%	17%	27%	4%
Committed on impulse	48%	15%	18%	17%	1%
No previous relevant convictions	61%	9%	18%	10%	2%

Let us begin by focusing on the step two mitigating factor, 'remorse'. Although one might question the relevance of remorse within a primarily retributivist sentencing framework, Maslen and Roberts (2013) have outlined two arguments in favour of it being considered a relevant sentencing factor by the courts. The first is grounded in the concept of mercy, and the second in the value of a responsive censure model in sentencing (ibid., p. 125–126). In any case, given that remorse is listed as a step two mitigating factor in the domestic burglary guideline, one would expect that, on the whole, compared to the overall distribution of sentencing outcomes for domestic burglary cases, offenders demonstrating remorse would receive less severe sentences. Indeed, this is what the data revealed. While 24% of all domestic burglary cases resulted in the imposition of a noncustodial sanction, a greater percentage of domestic burglary cases in which the offender demonstrated remorse – 39% – resulted in this relatively lenient sanction. Moreover, at the other end of the severity scale, remorse was associated with a decrease in the proportion of severe sentences. While 45% of all domestic burglary cases resulted in either a medium-high or high severity sentence (18 months' imprisonment or more), only 31% of cases in which the offender demonstrated remorse resulted in these relatively severe sentences.

Next, consider the step one mitigating factor, 'offence committed on impulse'. If an offender commits their offence on impulse, this is considered to be a mitigating factor because it implies that the offender is less culpable than they would have been had they engaged in some degree of planning (Ashworth, 2010). Therefore, we would expect those offenders who committed their offences on impulse to have (on average) less severe sentences in comparison to the overall distribution of sentencing outcomes. Again, the data supported this hypothesis. While less than one quarter of all domestic burglary cases resulted in a noncustodial sanction, 48% of cases in which the offender committed the offence on impulse resulted in these relatively lenient sentences – an even higher percentage than the percentage related to remorse (39%).

Moreover, at the other end of the severity scale, 'committed on impulse' was associated with a decrease in the proportion of severe sentences. While almost half of all domestic burglary cases received either a medium-high or high severity sentence (18 months' imprisonment or more), only 18% of cases in which the offender committed the offence on impulse resulted in these relatively severe sentences – an even lower percentage than the percentage related to remorse (31%). This is consistent with the sentencing guidelines: both the step two mitigating factor 'remorse' and the step one mitigating factor 'committed on impulse' were associated with a decrease in sentence severity. The step one factor, however, had a stronger mitigating effect on sentence severity than the step two factor. The odds ratios generated by the multivariate analysis provided further evidence for this finding (see Appendix D). This is precisely what the Sentencing Council intends by distinguishing between principal sentencing factors in step one and additional sentencing factors in step two.

The step one – step two principle for mitigating factors

The principle that a step one mitigating factor should have a greater impact on sentence severity than a step two mitigating factor was largely supported by the results of both the bivariate and multivariate analyses. The bivariate results, however, identified some step two factors which had stronger mitigating associations with sentence severity than step one factors. For example, consider the mitigating factor 'subordinate role in a group or gang'. The courts might consider that an offender who had a subordinate role in a group or gang during the commission of an offence was less culpable than someone who played a more dominant role (see Ashworth and Roberts, 2013). This was indeed reflected by the data. In terms of the step one – step two principle, however, a straightforward comparison between the bivariate results associated with this sentencing factor and the factor 'committed on impulse' might lead one to conclude that 'subordinate role in a group or gang' (a step two factor) had a greater mitigating association with sentence severity than the step one factor. For example, while 48% of cases in which offenders committed their offence on impulse resulted in noncustodial sanctions / SSOs being imposed, an even higher proportion of cases in which offenders had a subordinate role in a group or gang (53%) resulted in the imposition of these relatively lenient sanctions.

This is one example, however, in which the results from the multivariate analysis did not fully support those from the simple bivariate analysis. The odds ratio for 'committed on impulse' was 0.474 compared to 0.565 for 'subordinate role in a group or gang' (see Appendix D). As outlined above, the further away the odds ratio is from one, the greater the supposed impact on sentence severity (ratios smaller than one are indicative of a mitigating relationship, and those greater than one are indicative of an aggravating relationship). We hypothesised that this difference might have been due to the correlation between the sentencing factor 'subordinate role in a group or gang' and some other mitigating factors. For example, we predicted that if an offender had a subordinate role in a gang, then the court was also likely to consider that this offender had been 'exploited by others' (a step one sentencing factor). The presence of this latter factor might have resulted in the mitigating effect of 'subordinate role in a group or gang' being exaggerated by the bivariate analysis (which does not control for other sentencing factors). Indeed, the data supported this theoretical speculation. A basic cross-tabulation revealed that in 26.5% of cases in which an offender had a subordinate role in a group or gang, the courts also considered that the offender had been exploited by others. In contrast, in only 1.7% of cases in which an offender was *not* deemed to have had a subordinate role in a group or gang, did the courts consider that others had exploited the offender. We consider this association to be a good example of factor association of a sufficient magnitude to explain the discrepancy between the results of the bivariate and multivariate analyses. It is also likely that associations with other sentencing factors were also present and contributed to the observed discrepancy between the two analytical approaches.

In summary, the results from our multivariate analysis on the selected mitigating factors provided evidence that the step one – step two principle regarding the relative importance of sentencing factors was largely consistent with sentencing practice: Factors from step one exercise a greater effect over sentence severity.

Aggravating factors and sentence severity

In this section, we address the following questions:

1. What is the relationship between each selected aggravating factor and sentence severity in practice?
2. To what extent does the data support or contradict the principle that step one aggravating factors ought to aggravate sentence severity more than step two aggravating factors?

Consider Figure 11.2 and Table 11.3, which show the associations between four aggravating factors and sentence severity. As was the case with Figure 11.1, the horizontal bars in Figure 11.2 show the distribution of sentencing outcomes depending on the presence of the four aggravating factors that we selected for analysis. A comparison of these distributions with one another, and with the overall distribution for all cases (top bar) provides a good overall impression of the shift in the distribution of sentence severity for cases in which each factor is applicable. In general terms, it shows that, compared to the distribution of sentence outcomes for all domestic burglary cases, the presence of each aggravating factor was associated with a decrease in the proportion of lenient sentences (noncustodial sanctions/SSOs – the section that is furthest left on each bar), and an increase in the proportion of medium-high severity and high severity sentences (18 months' to 4 years' imprisonment and 4 years' imprisonment and above – the two sections that are furthest right on each bar). In other words, our theoretically grounded expectations about aggravating factors were supported by the empirical data.

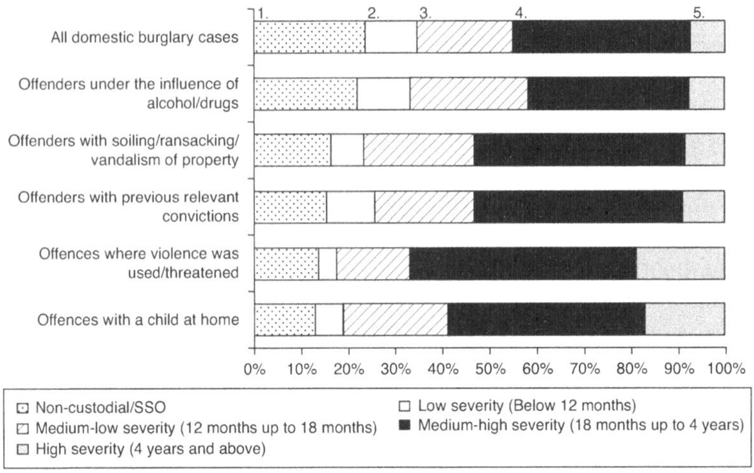

Figure 11.2 Sentence Severity by aggravating factor

Table 11.3 Percentage of offenders within sentence category by aggravating factor

Aggravating Factor	Noncustodial sanction/ SSO	Low severity (Below 12 months)	Medium-low severity (12–18 months)	Medium-high severity (18 months – 4 years)	High severity (4+ years)
All domestic burglary cases	24%	11%	20%	38%	7%
Under the influence of alcohol/drugs	22%	11%	25%	34%	8%
Soiling/ ransacking/ vandalism	16%	7%	23%	45%	8%
Previous relevant convictions	15%	10%	21%	44%	9%
Child at home	13%	6%	22%	42%	17%
Violence used/ threatened	14%	4%	15%	48%	19%

With this in mind, consider Table 11.3, which allowed us to make some more precise comparisons. Let us begin by focusing on the step two aggravating factor, 'under the influence of alcohol/drugs'. In the academic literature, this is considered to be one of the most controversial sentencing factors (see Padfield, 2011; Dingwall and Koffman,

2008). Historically, the courts in England and Wales have sometimes treated voluntary intoxication as a mitigating factor (Walker, 1999). Moreover, Padfield (2011) has argued that the aggravating/mitigating effect of intoxication ought to depend on the particular circumstances of the offence and/or the offender. For example, one issue that might influence whether the courts should regard intoxication as an aggravating or mitigating factor is whether the offender is considered to be someone who has the ability/willingness to address his or her alcohol problems (ibid., p. 93).

In light of this controversy, we were particularly interested to find out about the role of this factor in sentencing practice. The data revealed that 'under the influence of alcohol/drugs' had one of the weakest associations with sentence severity of all the sentencing factors. Perhaps this is most clearly illustrated by Figure 11.2, in which the bars representing all domestic burglary cases and this aggravating factor are almost identical. This means that offenders who were intoxicated were not much more or less likely to receive any particular category of sentence than the overall population of domestic burglary offenders. In fact, our multivariate analysis revealed that 'under the influence of alcohol/drugs' had a very weak mitigating association with sentence severity (odds ratio = 0.936; however, note that this association was not statistically significant: p = .407; see Appendix D).

We think there are two potential explanations for this finding. The first is that the courts might not have regarded intoxication as a particularly important factor in determining the culpability of the offender. The second is that the courts might have regarded intoxication as an aggravating factor in some cases and as a mitigating factor in others. For two reasons, we think that the first of these explanations is more likely. First, intoxication is listed in the domestic burglary sentencing guideline as an aggravating factor. Therefore, we consider it unlikely that the courts would have sentenced contrary to the guideline by treating intoxication as a mitigating factor in certain cases. Second, for the latter explanation to hold, the impact of intoxication as an aggravating factor must have roughly balanced the impact of intoxication as a mitigating factor across the total number of cases. While this is possible, it seems improbable. Either way, the CCSS data revealed that the ambiguity present in the academic literature about what the relationship between intoxication and sentence severity ought to be is also present at the level of judicial decision-making.

Next, consider the step one aggravating factor 'soiling/ransacking/vandalism of property'. If a burglary involved soiling/ransacking/

vandalising a victim's property, it was presumably more harmful (all other things being equal) than burglaries in which property was not soiled/ransacked/vandalised. One would expect, therefore, that offenders who had soiled/ransacked/vandalised property would receive more severe sentences (on average) than offenders who had not soiled/ransacked/vandalised property. Indeed, this is what the CCSS data revealed. While 24% of all domestic burglary cases resulted in the imposition of a noncustodial sanction, only 16% of offenders who had soiled/ransacked/vandalised property received this relatively lenient sentence outcome. Moreover, while 45% of all domestic burglary cases resulted in either a medium-high or high severity sentence (18 months' imprisonment or more), an even greater percentage of offenders who had soiled/ransacked/vandalised property (53%) received these relatively severe sentences.

A similar picture was created by the results from the bivariate analysis on the step one aggravating factor, 'violence used or threatened'. Comparing the bars in Figure 11.2 and figures in Table 11.3, one can see that 'violence used or threatened' had the greatest aggravating association with sentence severity of all the aggravating factors that were selected.

The step one – step two principle for aggravating factors

The principle that a step one aggravating factor should have a greater impact on sentence severity than a step two aggravating factor was generally supported by the results of both the bivariate and multivariate analyses. We found, however, that there was one notable exception: previous convictions. The presence/absence of previous convictions, it may be argued, is a good indicator of the likelihood of an offender reoffending. Previous convictions demonstrate an offender's propensity to break the law; therefore, harsher sentences may be warranted on the grounds of deterrence (although see Kazemian, 2010, for a critical discussion of this issue). Alternatively, the presence/absence of previous convictions may reveal something about an offender's culpability (see Lee, 2010). For example, it may be argued that an offence committed by an offender with no previous convictions does not reflect the otherwise law-abiding behaviour of that offender. Consequently, an offender with previous convictions ought to be given a more severe sentence than an offender without previous convictions (all other things being equal) in order to reflect their different levels of culpability.

Whatever the rationale for imposing more severe sentences on those with previous convictions, the data from the CCSS indicated that this factor had a strong aggravating relationship with sentence severity. The full strength and nature of this relationship is not immediately apparent from the data shown in Figure 11.2 and the figures in Table 11.3. These estimates are based on a binary previous convictions variable (in other words, whether offenders were considered to have previous relevant convictions, or not), which was included on the CCSS forms. We predicted that the aggravating effect of previous convictions, however, might depend not only on their absence/presence, but on their quantity. Consequently, we split the variable 'previous convictions' into three separate variables: (i) 1 to 3 previous convictions; (ii) 4 to 9 previous convictions; and (iii) 10 or more previous convictions. Based on this breakdown of the variable 'previous convictions', Figure 11.3 provides a more useful indication of the bivariate associations between previous convictions and sentence severity.

In contrast to the bivariate analysis, the results from our multivariate analysis estimated the aggravating effect of the (binary) 'previous relevant convictions' sentencing factor to be higher than the effect of the factor 'violence was used or threatened' – the odds ratios were 2.38 and 1.56 respectively.[7] As has been shown, however, this overall figure disguises substantial variation in relation to the relevant number of previous convictions. In this respect, both analyses were extremely clear: larger numbers of previous convictions were associated with considerably more severe sentences. When the distinction was made between the numbers of previous convictions in the multivariate analysis, the estimated odds ratios for 1 to 3 previous convictions, 4 to 9 previous convictions and 10 or more previous convictions were 1.538, 2.724 and

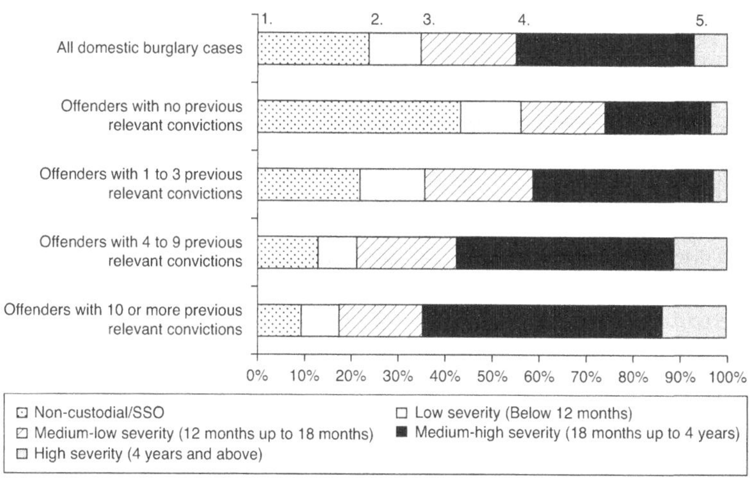

Figure 11. 3 Sentence severity by number of previous convictions

3.650 respectively (see Appendix D). The estimated aggravating effect of 1 to 3 previous convictions was therefore smaller than the effect of the step one sentencing factor 'violence was used or threatened' – 1.538 compared to 1.563. However, the estimated aggravating effects of the higher two categories on sentence severity (2.724 and 3.650) were considerably stronger than that of the step one factor. This may reflect the fact that the burglary guideline contains an enhanced reference to the role of precious convictions. (For further discussion, see Roberts and Pina-Sanchez in this volume, Chapter 9.)

Summary and conclusions

Our analysis of the data generated by the CCSS indicated that all of the sentencing factors on the domestic burglary guideline had the type of relationship with sentence severity that one would expect. In other words, aggravating factors were associated with an increase in sentence severity and mitigating factors were associated with a decrease in sentence severity. One notable exception to this was the sentencing factor 'under the influence of alcohol/drugs', which although very weak, had a *negative* association with sentence severity (see Appendix D). More importantly, we found that the CCSS generated some interesting data about the relative strength of the associations between sentencing factors and sentence severity. The results of our bivariate and multivariate analyses provided a strong indication that the courts were sentencing in a manner that was generally consistent with the domestic burglary sentencing guideline and, in particular, the principle that the factors in step one of the guideline should have more of an influence on sentence severity than the factors in step two. There was, however, at least one significant exception: the step two aggravating factor, 'previous convictions'.

We think that there are a number of ways in which the Sentencing Council might find the CCSS data useful in terms of the development of future guidelines. First, we note a suggestion made by Roberts (2013, p. 13–14; cf. Young and King, 2013) that sentencing guidelines might be developed by moving beyond the provision of unranked lists of sentencing factors. If the Council were to consider providing more guidance on the relative weight of the sentencing factors outlined in the lists of steps one and two, then we think that this consideration could be well-informed by the CCSS data.

For example, consider the step two aggravating factor, 'under the influence of alcohol/drugs'. Our data revealed that this factor had a mitigating association with sentence severity in practice (albeit this association was very weak and statistically insignificant). It seems that in most cases the courts do not attach much weight to this factor in terms of determining sentence severity. Moreover, there seems to be some ambiguity in the academic literature concerning the role that this sentencing factor ought to have in sentencing (see Padfield, 2011; Dingwall and Koffman, 2008). Given this ambiguity, we think that a good case could be made for providing the courts with additional guidance about the typical weight this sentencing factor ought to be given when determining the seriousness of the offence, compared to other step two sentencing factors. Or, if guidance on a typical weight is thought to be inappropriate, then perhaps the Sentencing Council could expand on the circumstances in which this factor ought/ought not to play a role in aggravating sentence severity.

Double counting the same factor is a potential problem of which the Council is aware (see Sentencing Council, 2011b). In other words, a given factor is sometimes being used to mitigate a sentence both at step one and at step two. There is some evidence that certain factors might have been double-counted in sentencing practice. Somewhat ironically, it was the simple bivariate analysis of the CCSS data that drew our attention to this issue. The bivariate analysis suggested that the step two factor 'subordinate role in group or gang' had a stronger mitigating association with sentence severity than most other sentencing factors, including those from step one such as 'committed on impulse'. The multivariate analysis, however, generated results that were more in line with our theoretically grounded expectations: 'subordinate role in a group or gang' had an odds ratio closer to one than 'committed on impulse', indicating that when other sentencing factors were controlled for, the mitigating impact of the step two factor was not as strong as the mitigating impact of this step one factor.

There is good evidence to suggest that the strong mitigating relationship between 'subordinate role in a group or gang' and sentence severity in our bivariate analysis was the result of its correlation with other mitigating factors, such as the step one factor 'exploited by others'. Arguably, both of these factors refer to a similar aspect of an offence, and therefore mitigation should occur *either* at step one or at step two (but not at both). Our cross-tabulation of these factors showed that in 26.5% of cases in which offenders' sentences were mitigated at step two because of their subordinate roles in a group or gang, these sentences were also mitigated at step one because these offenders were deemed to have been exploited by others. Whether or not one accepts the argument that this particular example constitutes evidence of double counting, the CCSS data seems to provide a useful tool for detecting possible instances of double counting in sentencing practice.

Third, the reader might recall that the courts cited considerably more step two aggravating factors than step two mitigating factors (7,275 aggravating factors compared to 3,135 mitigating factors). Given the format of the domestic burglary guideline, we see no reason why this is a problem per se. However, given that a greater proportion of Category 2 cases were aggravated rather than mitigated at step two (and the likelihood that a similar finding would apply in relation to Categories 1 and 3), the Sentencing Council might regard this as a relevant consideration when deliberating about appropriate sentence starting points and ranges for each of its categories in future versions of the guideline.

Finally, our results are based on the 61% response rate of the CCSS in 2011. Our findings might be useful for considering ways in which to increase this rate. It seems possible that some courts might consider the current sentencing guidelines overly onerous – particularly, for example, in terms of the 39 sentencing factors that courts are asked to consider in the domestic burglary guideline. If this is the case, we believe that our analysis – which reveals the citation frequency of each sentencing factor and the apparent impact of these factors on sentence severity – provides a good indication of which factors might usefully be removed from future versions of the guideline (at least, that is, the sentencing factors in step two). As the Council's lists of sentencing factors in step two are not exhaustive, any factors that had been removed could still be taken into account by the courts if/when they were deemed applicable to an individual case. But their removal might go some way towards improving response rates by simplifying the guidelines and making them more streamlined and user-friendly.

Conclusion

While we acknowledge the complexity of establishing an appropriate balance between judicial discretion and consistency in sentencing, CCSS data seem to offer one good reference point for decisions concerning the development of sentencing guidelines. Our intention in this chapter has been to provide readers with an exploratory insight into the way that sentencing in England and Wales operates in practice, focusing in particular on the relationship between sentencing factors and sentence severity. This analysis has only scratched the surface of the available data. The CCSS dataset provides researchers with the opportunity to conduct in-depth explorations of many other issues that have been beyond the purview of this chapter. Furthermore, given that the collection of data by the CCSS is ongoing, there is ample scope for researchers to monitor and analyse changes in sentencing practice over time. We end by reiterating our opening observation: despite there being much debate in recent years about the impact that sentencing factors ought to have on sentence severity, little empirical research has explored the impact of these factors on sentence severity in practice. We hope that the reader will consider the empirical findings and analysis provided in this chapter to be a valuable complement to these important normative debates.

Appendix A: Domestic Burglary Guideline – Step One

STEP ONE
Determining the offence category

The court should determine the offence category using the table below

Category 1	Greater harm **and** higher culpability
Category 2	Greater harm **and** lower culpability **or** lesser harm **and** higher culpability
Category 3	Lesser harm **and** lower culpability

The court should determine culpability and harm caused or intended, by reference **only** to the factors below, which comprise the principal factual elements of the offence. Where an offence does not fall squarely into a category, individual factors may require a degree of weighting before making an overall assessment and determining the appropriate offence category.

DOMESTIC

Factors indicating greater harm

Theft of/damage to property causing a significant degree of loss to the victim (whether economic, sentimental or personal value)

Soiling, ransacking or vandalism of property

Occupier at home (or returns home) while offender present

Trauma to the victim, beyond the normal inevitable consequence of intrusion and theft

Violence used or threatened against victim

Context of general public disorder

Factors indicating lesser harm

Nothing stolen or only property of very low value to the victim (whether economic, sentimental or personal)

Limited damage or disturbance to property

Factors indicating higher culpability

Victim or premises deliberately targeted (for example, due to vulnerability or hostility based on disability, race, sexual orientation)

A significant degree of planning or organisation

Knife or other weapon carried (where not charged separately)

Equipped for burglary (for example, implements carried and/or use of vehicle)

Member of a group or gang

Factors indicating lower culpability

Offence committed on impulse, with limited intrusion into property

Offender exploited by others

Mental disorder or learning disability, where linked to the commission of the offence

Source: Sentencing Council of England and Wales.

Appendix B: Domestic Burglary Guideline – Step Two

Offence Category	**Starting Point** *(Applicable to all offenders)*	**Category Range** *(Applicable to all offenders)*
Category 1	3 years' custody	2–6 years' custody
Category 2	1 year's custody	High level community order – 2 years' custody
Category 3	High Level Community Order	Low level community order – 26 weeks' custody

The table below contains a **non-exhaustive** list of additional factual elements providing the context of the offence and factors relating to the offender. Identify whether any combination of these, or other relevant factors, should result in an upward or downward adjustment from the starting point. **In particular, relevant recent convictions are likely to result in an upward adjustment**. In some cases, having considered these factors, it may be appropriate to move outside the identified category range.

When sentencing **category 2 or 3** offences, the court should also consider the custody threshold as follows:

- has the custody threshold been passed?
- if so, is it unavoidable that a custodial sentence be imposed?
- if so, can that sentence be suspended?

DOMESTIC

Factors increasing seriousness

Statutory aggravating factors:

Previous convictions, having regard to a) the nature of the offence to which the conviction relates and its relevance to the current offence, and b) the time that has elapsed since the conviction*
Offence committed whilst on bail
Other aggravating factors include:
Child at home (or returns home) when offence committed
Offence committed at night
Gratuitous degradation of the victim
Any steps taken to prevent the victim reporting the incident or obtaining assistance and/or from assisting or supporting the prosecution
Victim compelled to leave their home (in particular victims of domestic violence)
Established evidence of community impact
Commission of offence whilst under the influence of alcohol or drugs
Failure to comply with current court orders
Offence committed whilst on licence
Offences Taken into Consideration (TICs)

Factors reducing seriousness or reflecting personal mitigation

Offender has made voluntary reparation to the victim
Subordinate role in a group or gang
No previous convictions or no relevant/recent convictions
Remorse
Good character and/or exemplary conduct
Determination, and/or demonstration of steps taken to address addiction or offending behaviour
Serious medical conditions requiring urgent, intensive or long-term treatment
Age and/or lack of maturity where it affects the responsibility of the offender
Lapse of time since the offence where this is not the fault of the offender
Mental disorder or learning disability, where not linked to the commission of the offence
Sole or primary carer for dependent relatives

Source: Sentencing Council of England and Wales.

Appendix C: Crown Court Sentencing Survey Form – Burglary Offences

Part B: To be completed by the sentencing Judge/Recorder for the PRINCIPAL OFFENCE ONLY — SEE NOTES OVERLEAF

1. Type of offence *FOR BREACHES, SEE NOTES OVERLEAF*

- ☐ Single offence
- ☐ Multiple offences - *ANSWER FOR THE PRINCIPAL OFFENCE ONLY*
- ☐ Aggravated Burglary
- ☐ Domestic Burglary
- ☐ Non-domestic Burglary
- ☐ Other (please specify in box below)

2. Sentence outcome (for the PRINCIPAL OFFENCE ONLY)

SEE NOTES OVERLEAF. TICK ALL THAT APPLY

(a) Custodial Sentence

- ☐ Determinate
- ☐ Extended
- ☐ Life
- ☐ Hospital Order

(b) Suspended Sentence Order or Community Order

- ☐ SSO
- ☐ Community Order

Requirements of Suspended Sentence Order or Community Order
TICK ALL ADULT REQUIREMENTS GIVEN OR NEAREST YRO EQUIVALENT

- ☐ Supervision
- ☐ Unpaid work
- ☐ Curfew
- ☐ Activity
- ☐ Prohibited activity
- ☐ Exclusion
- ☐ Residence
- ☐ Foreign travel prohibition
- ☐ Attendance centre
- ☐ Mental health treatment
- ☐ Drug rehabilitation
- ☐ Alcohol treatment
- ☐ Alcohol abstinence and monitoring (pilot scheme)
- ☐ Programme(s) (please specify in box below)

(c) Other outcome

- ☐ Fine
- ☐ Conditional discharge
- ☐ Absolute discharge

RECORD COMPENSATION, CONFISCATION & COSTS IN SECTION 7

3. Definitive guideline - Step 1

(a) Factors indicating greater harm

- ☐ Theft of/damage to property causing significant degree of loss
- ☐ Soiling/ransacking/vandalism of property
- ☐ Victim on/returns to premises while offender present
- ☐ Significant physical/psychological injury or trauma
- ☐ Violence used/ threatened particularly involving a weapon
- ☐ Context of general public disorder

(b) Factors indicating lesser harm

- ☐ No physical/psychological injury or trauma
- ☐ No violence used/threatened and a weapon not produced
- ☐ Nothing stolen or of very low value
- ☐ Limited damage/disturbance to property

(c) Factors indicating higher culpability

- ☐ Deliberately targeted
- ☐ Significant degree of planning
- ☐ Equipped for burglary
- ☐ Weapon present on entry or carried
- ☐ Member of group or gang

(d) Factors indicating lower culpability

- ☐ Offender exploited by others
- ☐ Offence committed on impulse/limited intrusion
- ☐ Mental disorder/learning disability where linked to the commission of the offence

4. Offence seriousness *SEE NOTES OVERLEAF, INCLUDING GUIDANCE ON OFFENCES THAT FALL BETWEEN TWO CATEGORIES*

☐ Category 1 (Most serious) ☐ Category 2 ☐ Category 3 (Least serious) ☐ No guideline

5. Definitive guideline - Step 2

(a) Factors increasing seriousness

Statutory aggravating factors

- ☐ Previous relevant convictions ☐ 1-3 ☐ 4-9 ☐ 10+
- ☐ Offence committed on bail

Other aggravating factors include

- ☐ Child at home/returns
- ☐ Committed at night
- ☐ Abuse of power/trust
- ☐ Gratuitous degradation
- ☐ Steps taken to prevent reporting/assisting prosecution
- ☐ Victim compelled to leave home (domestic violence in particular)
- ☐ Established evidence of community impact
- ☐ Offender was under the influence of alcohol/drugs
- ☐ Failure to comply with current court orders
- ☐ On licence
- ☐ TICs
- ☐ Other factors (please specify in box below)

(b) Factors reducing seriousness or reflecting personal mitigation

- ☐ Subordinate role in group or gang
- ☐ Injuries caused recklessly
- ☐ Nothing stolen or of very low value
- ☐ Made voluntary reparation
- ☐ No previous relevant convictions
- ☐ Remorse
- ☐ Good character/exemplary conduct
- ☐ Determination/demonstration to address addiction/behaviour
- ☐ Serious medical conditions
- ☐ Age/lack of maturity affecting responsibility
- ☐ Lapse of time not fault of offender
- ☐ Mental disorder/learning disability where not linked to the commission of the offence
- ☐ Sole/primary carer for dependent relatives
- ☐ Other factors (please specify in box below)

6. Indication of guilt/guilty plea *SEE NOTES OVERLEAF*

Was guilt indicated at police station?

☐ Yes ☐ No ☐ Don't know

Was a guilty plea entered for the principal offence?

☐ Yes ☐ No

Where was guilty plea entered?

- ☐ At magistrates' court
- ☐ At early guilty plea hearing
- ☐ Prior to PCMH
- ☐ At PCMH
- ☐ After PCMH/prior to day of trial
- ☐ At/after day of trial

Was the guilty plea entered at the first reasonable opportunity?

☐ Yes ☐ No

Approximately what guilty plea discount was given?

7. Additional factors

Were any of the following other factors present or stated to have influenced the sentence imposed?

DO NOT INCLUDE ANYTHING THAT IS COVERED ELSEWHERE ON THIS FORM

- ☐ Totality principle
- ☐ Consecutive sentence
- ☐ Concurrent sentence
- ☐ Multiple defendants
- ☐ Ancillary Order
- ☐ Compensation Order
- ☐ Confiscation Order
- ☐ Costs
- ☐ Serving another sentence
- ☐ Other factors that you stated and are relevant to the sentencing decision, for example S 116 Return to Custody (please specify in box below)

Appendix D: Results from Ordinal Logistic Regression[8]

	Odds Ratio	Hypothesis Test		
Ordinal Logistic Regression Output Dependent variable: Sentence Severity (Ordinal variable, 5 categories)	**Exp(B)**	**Wald Chi- Square**	**df**	**Sig.**
Theft of/damage to property causing significant degree of loss	1.679	49.25	1	.000
Soiling/ransacking/vandalism of property	1.288	7.70	1	.006
Victim on/returns to premises while offender present	2.092	116.34	1	.000
Significant physical/psychological injury or trauma	2.156	55.74	1	.000
Violence used/threatened particularly involving a weapon	1.563	7.86	1	.005
Context of general public disorder	1.237	.06	1	.806
No physical/psychological injury or trauma	.773	5.56	1	.018
No violence used/threatened and a weapon not produced	1.127	1.42	1	.233
Nothing stolen or of very low value	.541	37.80	1	.000
Limited damage/disturbance to property	.790	6.86	1	.009
Deliberately targeted	1.679	48.00	1	.000
Significant degree of planning	1.693	34.77	1	.000
Equipped for burglary	1.563	22.15	1	.000
Weapon present on entry or carried	1.315	3.51	1	.061
Member of group or gang	1.086	1.21	1	.270
Offender exploited by others	.568	8.62	1	.003
Offence committed on impulse/limited intrusion	.474	56.54	1	.000
Mental disorder/learning disability where linked to the commission of the offence	.493	6.84	1	.009
Offence committed on bail	1.237	3.22	1	.072
Child at home/returns	1.652	13.05	1	.000
Committed at night	1.243	9.16	1	.002
Abuse of power/trust	.701	4.44	1	.035
Gratuitous degradation	1.435	.98	1	.321
Steps taken to prevent reporting/assisting prosecution	1.615	.65	1	.417
Victim compelled to leave home (domestic violence in particular)	.949	.03	1	.851
Established evidence of community impact	2.618	21.85	1	.000
Offender was under the influence of alcohol/drugs	.936	.68	1	.407
Failure to comply with current court orders	.913	1.02	1	.311
On licence	2.573	85.69	1	.000
TICs	2.812	91.58	1	.000
Subordinate role in group or gang	.565	14.45	1	.000
Made voluntary reparation	.364	8.55	1	.003
No previous relevant convictions	.421	49.99	1	.000
Remorse	.760	12.84	1	.000
Good character/exemplary conduct	.467	18.14	1	.000
Determination/demonstration to address addiction/behaviour	.410	72.54	1	.000
Serious medical conditions	.844	.33	1	.561
Age/lack of maturity affecting responsibility	.549	27.71	1	.000
Lapse of time not fault of offender	.439	5.55	1	.018
Mental disorder/learning disability where not linked to the commission of the offence	.472	10.96	1	.001
Sole/primary career for dependant relatives	.416	11.78	1	.001
Previous Convictions = 1 to 3	1.538	27.29	1	.000
Previous Convictions = 4 to 9	2.724	125.09	1	.000
Previous Convictions = 10 or more	3.650	195.04	1	.000

Number with factor applicable in each sentence category				
Non-Custodial /SSO	Low-severity (Below 12 months)	Med-Low (12 months up to 18 months)	Med-high (18 months up to 4 years)	High severity (4 years and above)
144	83	238	449	139
99	42	140	270	51
241	121	360	706	186
42	20	88	214	100
25	7	28	87	34
2	0	1	3	1
260	109	125	177	13
322	127	201	271	34
282	122	133	144	14
332	139	155	212	17
154	100	207	407	161
78	64	144	319	128
66	49	102	225	88
32	13	44	86	16
195	103	238	450	110
83	12	26	18	2
267	84	97	96	7
39	4	2	21	2
27	38	78	116	31
41	19	69	131	54
234	108	283	533	149
44	22	37	41	4
3	2	8	11	7
169	88	191	264	60
12	6	3	19	11
9	3	9	54	24
169	88	191	264	60
60	90	146	217	40
24	19	72	244	105
29	18	63	209	65
129	29	43	37	7
29	6	4	7	0
301	47	88	51	8
425	130	186	294	44
129	25	14	20	6
226	38	70	109	12
28	4	9	10	3
165	44	78	75	6
18	4	7	5	2
50	8	13	17	4
43	7	7	13	1
277	175	292	485	42
124	79	205	446	111
87	77	170	482	133

Notes

1. We were informed by the Office of the Sentencing Council that members of the public had access to a modified dataset in order to ensure that the identities of individual offenders were protected.
2. The ten sentence categories are as follows: up to three months' imprisonment; over three months' and up to six months' imprisonment; over six months' to less than twelve months' imprisonment; twelve months' imprisonment; over twelve months' and up to eighteen months' imprisonment; over eighteen months' and up to three years' imprisonment; over three years' and less than four years' imprisonment; four years' imprisonment; over four years' and up to five years' imprisonment; over five years' and up to ten years' imprisonment.
3. On a point of terminology, we should point out that the Sentencing Council does not refer to the sentencing factors in their guidelines simply as 'aggravating' or 'mitigating' factors. In step one of the domestic burglary guideline, for example, sentencing factors are referred to as factors indicating greater harm/lesser harm and factors indicating higher culpability/lower culpability. In step two, they are referred to as factors 'increasing seriousness' and 'reducing seriousness or reflecting personal mitigation' (Sentencing Council 2011a: 9). Essentially, however, each factor either aggravates or mitigates the seriousness of the offence and consequently the severity of the sentence. Therefore, for the purposes of analysis, we have collapsed these distinctions into the two categories of aggravating and mitigating factors.
4. We considered the prediction accuracy of our ordinal logistic regression model to have been reasonable (78.4% of all cases were predicted within one sentence category of the actual sentence category they received in practice) but not optimal from a technical perspective (10.2% of all cases were predicted three or four categories away from the actual sentence category they received in practice). Given that our intention was to keep the analysis simple and reach broad conclusions about factor impact across the overall range of sentence outcomes, we did not pursue more sophisticated modelling approaches – partial proportional odds models, for instance. Nor did we think it was necessary to expand on issues relating to the model's ability to discriminate between custodial categories and between qualitatively different noncustodial/SSO and custodial outcomes. Therefore, there is scope for future research to reach more precise impact estimates through a more nuanced analysis of the CCSS data.
5. One technical point to add to this interpretation is that the assumption of 'proportional odds' is made, meaning that the factors are assumed to have the same aggravating or mitigating impact across the range of sentence categories. In our analysis, however, it was found that there were slight differences in the parameter estimates across the sentence severity range. Detailing these minor differences in a more fine-grained analysis is beyond the purview of this chapter and not a decisive factor in the conclusions presented here. Nevertheless, future studies may wish to consider the implications of these differences.
6. The use of terms such as 'lenient' and 'severe' is for analytical purposes only. A sentence category that we describe as lenient, for example, was one that

was less severe than the average severity of sentences imposed for this offence type; the terms, therefore, are not a product of our own value judgements about the severity of sentences.

7. These odds ratios were estimated in a preliminary model using the binary variable for previous convictions included on the CCSS form. The final model presented in Appendix D included three variables in place of previous convictions: (i) 1 to 3 previous convictions; (ii) 4 to 9 previous convictions; and (iii) 10 or more previous convictions. All other parameters of this earlier model were closely in line with those of the final model.
8. *Model estimated using SPSS, Ordinal regression using Logit link function. -2LogLikelihood = 9310.513, $\chi 2(46) = 2363.038$, $p < .001$*

References

Ashworth, A. (2010) *Sentencing and Criminal Justice.* 5th ed. Cambridge: Cambridge University Press.

Ashworth, A. and Roberts, J.V. (2013) The origins and nature of the sentencing guidelines in England and Wales. In: A. Ashworth and J.V. Roberts (eds) *Sentencing Guidelines: Exploring the English Model.* Oxford: Oxford University Press.

Cooper, J. (2013) Nothing personal: the impact of personal mitigation at sentencing since creation of the council. In: A. Ashworth and J.V. Roberts (eds) *Sentencing Guidelines: Exploring the English Model.* Oxford: Oxford University Press.

Dingwall, G. and Koffman, L. (2008) Determining the Impact of Intoxication in a Desert-Based Sentencing Framework. *Criminology and Criminal Justice,* 8: 335–348.

Dolinko, D. (2000) Justice in the Age of Sentencing Guidelines. *Ethics,* 110: 563–585.

Garson, D.G. (2014) *Ordinal Regression (Statistical Associates 'Blue Book' Series).* Asheboro: Statistical Associates Publishing. Kindle edition.

Gorard, S. (2013) *Research Design: Robust Approaches for the Social Sciences.* London: Sage.

Jacobson, J. and Hough, M. (2007) *Mitigation: The Role of Personal Factors in Sentencing.* London: Prison Reform Trust.

Kazemian, L. (2010) Assessing the impact of a recidivist sentencing premium on crime and recidivism rates. In: J.V. Roberts and A. von Hirsch (eds) *The Role of Previous Convictions at Sentencing: Theoretical and Applied Perspectives.* Oxford: Hart Publishing.

Lee, J. (2010) Repeat offenders and the question of desert. In: J.V. Roberts and A. von Hirsch (eds) *The Role of Previous Convictions at Sentencing: Theoretical and Applied Perspectives.* Oxford: Hart Publishing.

Mair, G. (2011) The Community Order in England and Wales: Policy and Practice. *Probation Journal,* 58: 215–232.

Maslen, H. and Roberts, J.V. (2013) Remorse and sentencing: an analysis of sentencing guidelines and sentencing practice. In: A. Ashworth and J.V. Roberts (eds) *Sentencing Guidelines: Exploring the English Model.* Oxford: Oxford University Press.

Padfield, N. (2011) Intoxication as a sentencing factor: mitigation or aggravation? In: J.V. Roberts (ed.) *Mitigation and Aggravation at Sentencing*. Cambridge: Cambridge University Press.

Pina-Sanchez, J. and Linacre, R. (2013) Sentence Consistency in England and Wales. *British Journal of Criminology*, 53: 1118–1138.

Rex, S. and von Hirsch, A. (1998) Community Orders and the Assessment of Punishment Severity. *Federal Sentencing Reporter*, 10: 278–282.

Roberts, J.V. (2008) Punishing Persistence. *British Journal of Criminology*, 48: 468–481.

——— (2011) Sentencing Guidelines and Judicial Discretion. *British Journal of Criminology*, 51: 997–1013.

——— (2013) Punishing, more or less: exploring aggravation and mitigation at sentencing. In: J.V. Roberts (ed.) *Mitigation and Aggravation at Sentencing*. Cambridge: Cambridge University Press.

——— and von Hirsch, A. (2010) *Previous Convictions at Sentencing: Theoretical and Applied Perspectives*. Oxford: Hart Publishing.

Sentencing Council (2011a) *Burglary Offences: Definitive Guideline*. London: Sentencing Council.

——— (2011b) *Assault Guideline: Response to Consultation*. London: Sentencing Council.

Tudor, S. (2008) Why Should Remorse be a Mitigating Factor in Sentencing? *Criminal Law and Philosophy*, 2: 241–257.

Walker, N. (1999) *Aggravation, Mitigation and Mercy in English Criminal Justice*. London: Blackstone.

Young, W. and King, A. (2013) Addressing problematic sentencing factors in the development of guidelines. In: J.V. Roberts (ed.) *Mitigation and Aggravation at Sentencing*. Cambridge: Cambridge University Press.

12
More Than One Crime: Sentencing the Multiple Conviction Offender

Natalia Vibla

Multiple-offence sentencing can take many forms; there is no common profile to multiple-offence offenders. These cases can consist of two or many more crimes; the offences may have been committed within a short or longer period of time; they could be the product of a single criminal undertaking or several; they could be of the same type or of different types; they could be of very different degrees of seriousness; they could have been committed within the same geographical area or not; they could involve one or many victims. What all multiple conviction cases have in common, however, is that the offences are distinguished, charged, and convicted separately but sentenced in the same hearing. The importance of studying multiple-offence cases is highlighted by the fact that, unsurprisingly, the number of offences is highly correlated with the severity of sentence.[1]

Members of the public generally conceive of a sentencing hearing as a proceeding in which an individual offender is sentenced for a single conviction, resulting in the imposition of a single sentence. Reality is more complex: While it is widely acknowledged among judges, justice professionals and academics that multiple-offence cases occur frequently, there is a dearth of statistical evidence on the subject. One explanation for the lack of statistics on multiple-offence cases is to be found in the way sentencing statistics are recorded and published by the Ministry of Justice. Statistical data in such reports generally relate to the 'principal' offence and not to other related and associated offences included in a case (e.g., Sentencing Statistics Quarterly Brief, 2010). The principal offence is usually defined as the one with the most severe sentence imposed or, in a case of two or more equal sentences, the one for which the statutory maximum is the most severe.

Volume of multiple-offence cases

In 2010, the Sentencing Council launched a consultation on a guideline on totality and related issues. As will be discussed later in this essay, the principle of 'totality' is usually applied whenever a court sentences an offender convicted of multiple crimes. The consultation noted that Totality was invoked in 24% of all cases and was more frequently applied in the Crown Court (in 48% of cases versus 22% in the magistrates' courts). A breakdown of custodial and noncustodial sentences demonstrates that the principle of totality was applied in 22% of the noncustodial and in 56% of custodial cases.[2] Thus multiple-offence cases represent approximately half the cases sentenced in the Crown Court and, consistent with previous findings, were more likely to be associated with the imposition of custody. In light of the volume of multiple convictions – and their impact on sentence severity – it is clearly important for the courts to have guidance in this area. The application of totality was more frequent for certain offences. For example, where the principal offence was arson and criminal damage, totality was invoked in 32% of cases; where the principal offence was assault with intent to resist apprehension, it was applied in 44% of cases; when driving while disqualified was a principal offence, totality was applied in 45% of cases; in rape of a male aged 16 and over, totality was applied in 67% of cases.[3]

The problem of sentencing multiple-offence cases

When faced with a multiple-offence case, the task for a sentencing court is complex. The offence-specific guidelines issued by the Sentencing Council (e.g., Sentencing Council, 2011) all apply to a single conviction for the offence under consideration. According to the offence-specific guidelines, courts should follow a step-by-step process in order to determine the sentence for a particular offence, and the guideline provides sentencing ranges and starting point sentences as reference points. In multiple-offence cases, due to the variety of offences and diversity of circumstances, such ready reference points are not available.

The problem created by multiple-offence sentencing...

The problem of considering multiple crimes principally arises in the context of convictions, each of which results in a term of custody. For example, imagine an offender is to be sentenced for eight commercial burglaries, all committed during the course of a single night. If the typical sentence for this offence were one year in prison, simply imposing eight one-year sentences would mean that the offender would receive eight years in prison for one night's criminality. Such a sentence would mean that he was punished more severely than an offender convicted of manslaughter or rape – crimes of far greater seriousness. This outcome might violate offence-based proportionality, according to which the severity of the sentence should rise in direct correspondence to the seriousness of the crime. This case illustrates a second potential problem arising from multiple conviction cases: An eight-year sentence may have a crushing effect, ruining the offender's life chances – all for a single night's crime spree. The sentencing system attempts to avoid this simplistic and punitive response to multiple crimes by adjusting the sentence in a way which moderates the total impact of the sentences on the offender.

...And the potential solutions

Courts generally follow one of two approaches to dealing with such multiple-offence cases. The first is the imposition of a sentence for each crime but making the sentences of custody run *concurrently*: separate sentences are served at the same time. This means that the total sentence for a case equals the sentence for the most serious offence (the one resulting in the longest term). In the example above, the offender may receive eight one-year sentences of custody, but they will all be discharged at the same time, meaning that he will serve a single year under the warrant of the court. This may seem unfair when an offender convicted of a single crime also receives a sentence of one year. In order to distinguish these two cases, a court may impose a longer sentence for one crime (say two years) and then a single year for all the other convictions, with all sentences being served concurrently. In this way, the multiple offender serves more than the single conviction offender, but not the eight years that would have been the case had he been required to serve one sentence after the other.

The second possible judicial response is to make the individual sentences *consecutive*: separate sentences are calculated for the individual offences and made to run one after the other. In the above example, the offender may receive eight sentences, each to be served one after the other. If this approach were followed, the total would be regarded as excessive, so in order to mitigate the severity of the total sentence, the court may reduce the length of each individual term. In addition, a court may combine the sentences, ordering some to be served concurrently, others to be served consecutively. The definitive guideline issued by the Sentencing Council (discussed later in the essay) provides guidance as to the conditions under which sentences should be imposed to be served concurrently or consecutively.

The common denominator in both examples – sentences to be served concurrently or sentences to be served consecutively but for shorter periods – is that a total sentence for a case constructed out of aggregating separately calculated sentences for the individual offences is discounted. This discount contrasts with sentencing in cases in which the offender has multiple crimes for which he has been sentenced in the past: the repeat offender. The repeat offender pays a heavier price for his multiple crimes (see Chapter 9 of this volume) while the multiple conviction offender receives a discount in the sense that his crimes do not simply result in the accumulation of sentences.

The difference between the repeat and the multiple offender cases can be illustrated in another simple example. Consider two offenders who commit three burglaries. The first is sentenced on three different occasions, each followed by separate punishment (the repeat offender). The second is sentenced on a single occasion for three burglaries followed by a combined punishment (the multiple offender). Imagine that burglary carries a six-month period of custody as a penalty. The repeat offender may receive six months for the first burglary, seven for the second and eight for his third – the increase from one sentencing hearing to another reflects the 'recidivist premium' discussed in Chapter 9 of this volume. This amounts to a total of 21 months of imprisonment for the three crimes. In contrast, the multiple offender may receive six months of custodial sentence for the first burglary, six months consecutive for the second, and six months concurrent for his third burglary. His total sentence to be served in custody would be twelve months – nine months less than the sentence of the repeat offender. Thus, while both offenders committed exactly the same number of offences, their total sentences (and amount of time in prison) will differ substantially. In other jurisdictions the difference between the treatment of repeat and multiple offenders can be even greater than suggested by this simple example. Reitz (2010) provides examples from Washington State's guidelines where the difference in sentencing between repeat and multiple offenders is even more striking.

So how does the sentencing system justify such divergent approaches to multiple convictions, depending upon whether they were sentenced over time or sentenced on a single occasion?

Theoretical propositions on justifying the discount in multiple-offence sentencing

Sentencing scholars – whether utilitarian or retributive – have devoted insufficient attention to the study of multiple-offence cases. The lack of interest from utilitarian theorists is consistent with their general stance towards the goals of punishment. Bottoms remarks that since the consequentialist approach is concerned with the consequences of punishment, whether the case consists of one or many crimes is irrelevant: 'it should not matter whether a given offender is before the court for one offence, for twenty, or for two hundred; what is important is whether the sentence to be passed on this offender will have the appropriate effect of deterring him and others from future offending, reforming him, or producing appropriate incapacitation from likely future offending' (Bottoms, 1998, p. 64).

Retributive scholars who are more concerned with proportional sentencing and less concerned with preventing future crime should be more interested in the problem of sentencing multiple-offence cases. Despite the relevance of the issue, few such scholars have addressed the problem. The scant attention towards the issue of multiple-offence sentencing paid by retributive and desert scholars is more troublesome, however, as it undermines the foundation of the theory aimed at designated 'appropriate punitive responses' to sentencing problems (for discussion, see Ryberg, 2005, p. 214; Lippke, 2011; Reitz, 2010; Bennett, 2012).

The first significant scholarly attempt to study multiple-offence sentencing is found in Thomas's comprehensive analysis of the English and Welsh Court of Appeal cases (Thomas, 1979). He identified two major approaches that the Court relies upon for sentencing multiple offenders: the concept of a 'single transaction' rule and the 'Totality' principle.

The single transaction rule

The concept of a single transaction concerns offences that are committed sufficiently close together to be regarded as a single criminal transaction. The idea here is that four offences arising out of the same incident should be regarded differently from the same four offences committed on four separate occasions. Offences arising from a single incident or encounter should be sentenced according to a single transaction rule: 'The essence of the one-transaction rule appears to be that consecutive sentences are inappropriate when all the offences taken together constitute a single invasion of the same legally protected interest' (Thomas, 1979, p. 53). A single transaction can broadly be interpreted as concerning offences committed closely together in terms of temporal proximity in time, type of offences, and committed against the same victim, although such definition is rather vague.

For practical purposes, the concept of a single transaction is not always helpful. Ashworth notes that: 'It is very difficult to construct a workable definition of a 'single transaction', especially since it seems to be little more than a pragmatic device for limiting overall sentences rather than a reflection of a sharp category distinction' (Ashworth, 2010, p. 266). In addition, Thomas's analysis of the Court of Appeal cases demonstrated that the single transaction rule is subject to numerous exceptions; it is often invoked for offences committed in close temporal proximity to each other and which seemingly form a single transaction but whose separate sentences are then made to run consecutively, rather than concurrently. Wasik also demonstrated divergent approaches the courts take with regards to offences arising out of a single transaction (2012). Since the concept of a single transaction confuses as much as it clarifies, suggestions have been made to abandon it in England and Wales; Sweden did exactly that over 70 years ago (Jareborg, 1998).

The Totality principle

The second principle identified by Thomas on the basis of analysis of the Court of Appeal decisions is the 'Totality' principle. This applies to situations in which separate sentences for the individual offences forming a single case are served consecutively. The Totality principle attempts to ensure that the total sentence for a multiple-offence case, constructed according to the rules of governing consecutive sentences, is 'just and appropriate' (Thomas, 1979, p. 56).

Ensuring that the sentence is just and proportionate usually entails adjusting the total sentence for a case, and if necessary, reducing its severity. The Totality principle precludes the court from purely mathematical calculations when passing a sentence in a multiple-offence case: 'When cases of multiplicity of offences come before the court, the court must not content itself by doing the arithmetic and passing the sentence which the arithmetic produces. It must look at the totality of the criminal behaviour and ask itself what is the appropriate sentence for all the offences' (Barton, 1972, cited in Thomas, 1979, p. 57). The questions arising out of the principle of totality are what constitutes a just and proportionate total sentence for a case, and how to justify the discount allocated to the total sentence as a result of totality application.

The Totality principle is founded, in Thomas's words, in two limbs. The first of these is the idea that the total sentence for a case should not exceed the upper sentencing ranges provided for the most serious offence in the case: 'The aggregate sentence should not be longer than the upper limit of the normal bracket of sentences for the category of cases in which the most serious offence committed by the offender would be placed.' (Thomas, 1979, p. 59) Thomas remarks, however, that at times the Court of Appeal upholds sentences in excess of the normal bracket for the most serious offences – when the purpose is preventive custody for dangerous offenders, for example.

The Totality principle and the application of a sentence 'discount' for multiple crimes undermine the traditional application of the principle of proportionality, which is to observe proportionality between a specific offence and its sentence. Therefore, Ashworth (2010) suggested a different kind of proportionality, namely the overall proportionality between categories of crimes, which refers to the relativity between a total sentence for a case and a sentence for a more severe category of crime than the ones comprising the case: 'This intuition may lead to assertions such as "no number of offences of taking cars can be regarded as morally so heinous as a middle-range rape" or "no number of non-violent middle range burglaries can be regarded as the moral equivalent of a single unprovoked serious wounding"' (p. 272).

The second limb of the Totality principle is rooted in the idea of mitigation and avoiding a 'crushing effect' that a sentence might have on an offender. It therefore concerns his or her rehabilitative prospects: 'This part of the principle appears to require a sentencer who imposes a series of consecutive sentences to consider the mitigating factors in relation to the totality of the sentence, even though they have already been considered in relation to the individual component parts' (Thomas, 1979, p. 59). The second limb was shown to apply to categories of offenders such as young offenders facing their first sentences of imprisonment; mature offenders receiving their first lengthy sentence; and other cases in which the life prospects of offenders might be very adversely affected by lengthy total sentences. In Australia, a similar principle is referred to as the 'enough is enough' principle (Wells, 1992; Bottoms, 1998; Lovegrove, 2004).

To summarise, the 'discount' in multiple-offence cases (compared to the 'premium' imposed in the repeat offender example) is justified on the basis of the principle of totality –the proposition that the addition of separate sentences for the individual offences in a consecutive manner would lead to a sentence normally applicable for more severe crimes. In addition, concerns about offenders' life prospects provide a basis for mitigating long sentences via the exercise of mercy. The discounted sentence can be seen as proportionate according to the concept of overall proportionality, namely proportionality between categories of crimes rather than individual offences.

But what happens in practice? How do judges decide on multiple-offence cases in court, and how do they apply the discount?

Empirical research on sentencing for multiple convictions

Surprisingly, in light of the volume of such cases, there is very little research on the ways that courts sentence multiple-offence offenders; the few studies on the topic come from foreign jurisdictions. Albrecht (1994) devotes a section to the analysis of multiple-offence cases in Germany. In Australia, Lovegrove (2004; 2008) used hypothetical scenarios to explore the issue. Lovegrove constructed a decision-making model for sentencing multiple-offence cases. Australian judges impose separate sentences for the individual offences and then arrange those sentences via the rules of concurrency, consecutiveness and, most frequently, a complex combination of two approaches. Lovegrove concludes that the principal reason judges reduce sentences in multiple-offence cases is grounded in an attempt to avoid the harsh effect of large total sentence upon offenders and their rehabilitative prospects.

Vibla (2014) studied multiple-offence sentences in Sweden where, like England and Wales, sentencing is guided by the principle of proportionality. The goal was to explore the reasons, principles and values underpinning sentencing decisions. The task of a Swedish judge dealing with a case consisting of more than one offence is to construct a single total sentence for the whole case, thus the rules of concurrency and consecutiveness are not applicable. The decision process leading to the construction of the total consists of several steps. First, separate sentences for the individual offences are identified, and the most severe of those is taken to form the basis of the total sentence. Then proportions of the sentences for the secondary offences are added in the order of their relative seriousness. The exact proportions depend upon the seriousness of the worst offence: the more serious the principal offence, the lower the proportions of the secondary sentences. They also depend on the circumstantial factors of the case, such as the number of offences, their type, seriousness, the time span between the offences, the presence of victims, co-defendants and other relevant factors.

With regards to the reasoning for providing discounts or, in other words, imposing proportions of the sentences for the secondary offences rather than their full sentences, judges rely upon several grounds, two of which are the so-called comparative and humanitarian grounds. The comparative ground relates to comparing the total sentence for a case to sentences for more serious categories of crimes. The humanitarian ground relates to the aspiration of avoiding excessive suffering by the offenders. Thus, when sentencing multiple-offence cases, both Swedish and Australian judges pay considerable attention to the effect of a lengthy sentence upon an offender and thus try to reduce it upon that ground, an approach which closely resembles Thomas's second limb of the Totality principle. Swedish judges in particular attempt to compare their sentencing decisions to sentences for the more serious categories of crimes, which closely resembles Ashworth's concept of overall proportionality. The two approaches described above provide a relatively straightforward way of constructing a total sentence in correspondence with the principle of totality and overall proportionality.

Concurrent and consecutive sentences within the framework of totality and overall proportionality

As demonstrated by Thomas in his analysis of the Court of Appeal cases, sentences imposed for crimes viewed as part of a single transaction are usually ordered to run concurrently to each other, although there are exceptions to that general rule. When offences that arise from a single transaction result in a total sentence which appears inadequate under the concurrent approach, the offences may each attract separate sentences which are then served consecutively. The situation becomes more complicated if the offences do not arise out of the same transaction or episode. Under these conditions, the sentences should be made to run consecutively, but this may lead to total sentences that are too onerous. A choice must be made in such situations: whether to impose concurrent sentences but inflate them in order to reflect the total offending behaviour, or to impose consecutive sentences but reduce them in order to avoid lengthy excessive sentences.

Wasik considers concurrent and consecutive sentences to constitute tools to help judges in their imposition of the total sentences: 'These principles actually have little importance in driving sentence outcome but, rather, provide judges with options within which multiple-offence sentencing can be presented within totality' (2012, p. 294). He further suggests that instead of reducing consecutive sentences, which ultimately would lead to under-sentencing, making the sentences concurrent better reflects proportionality as it allows the imposition of proportionate sentences for the individual offences. The advice from courts, as has been noted by Thomas (1979) earlier, is that in situations when the total sentence needs to be reduced, it is preferable to arrange sentences as concurrent rather than reduce the individual sentences and make them consecutive. Concurrent sentences may at times be increased in length in order to fully reflect the offending behaviour. There are situations though when even such aggravation would not reflect the offending behaviour and consecutive sentences are needed: for example, as stressing additional punishment for certain offences, such as firearms offences.

Having identified theoretical justifications for discounts in multiple conviction cases, what guidance is available to courts in England and Wales? Limitations on space preclude a discussion of the appellate caselaw, but it is important to note the statutory basis for the practice as well as the definitive guideline in effect.

Legal guidance on sentencing multiple-offence cases

The Criminal Justice Act 2003 contains a section that governs sentencing cases consisting of more than one offence. While it does not contain precise guidance, it does provide the direction taken when dealing with such cases, which is by way of mitigation:

> Nothing ... prevents a court – (a) from mitigating any penalty included in an offender's sentence by taking into account any other penalty included in that sentence, and (b) in the case of an offender who is convicted of one or more other offences, from mitigating his sentence by applying any rule of law as to the totality of sentences. (Section 166 (3))

Definitive guideline on totality

The Council's offence-specific guidelines touch upon the issue of totality. For example, according to the definitive guideline for assault offences, a court proceeds through a series of nine steps to ultimately determine the sentence to impose. At step six, the court makes any adjustment necessary to determine whether the sentence is 'just and proportionate' (see Sentencing Council, 2011). In addition, in 2012, the Sentencing Council issued a definitive guideline on totality. Apart from guidance from the Court of Appeal, this guideline represents the first attempt in this jurisdiction to structure judicial discretion with regards to multiple-offence sentencing. However, it falls short of providing comprehensive or detailed guidance on how to approach and determine sentence in such cases. Much is left to judicial discretion to resolve. Apart from general principles and rules on concurrency and consecutiveness, the guideline suggests ways of combining determinate and extended custodial sentences, fines and non-custodial sentences.

The guideline states that the principle of totality should be applied for offenders sentenced for multiple offences as well as for offenders serving an existing sentence. The document also states that the principle of totality involves two elements. First, it reflects the necessity of a just and proportionate total sentence, regardless of whether the separate sentences run concurrently or consecutively. Second, the guideline emphasises the importance of considering the individual offender: 'It is usually impossible to arrive at a just and proportionate sentence for multiple offending simply by adding together notional single sentences. It is necessary to address the offending behaviour, together with factors personal to the offender as a whole' (Sentencing Council, 2012, p. 5). Thus the court should be guided by the need for a proportionate total sentence.

The guideline identifies four steps that should be taken when making sentencing decisions on multiple determinate custodial sentences: (1) Establish separate sentences for each individual offence in the multiple-offence case; (2) Determine whether the case calls for concurrent or consecutive sentences ensuring that the sentences passed are just and proportionate; (3) Weigh the overall sentence(s) against the requirement that they be 'just and proportionate'; (4) Consider whether the sentence is structured in a way that will be best understood by all relevant parties. The guideline therefore reflects both limbs of the Totality principle: that the total sentence should be just and proportionate, and that due attention should be paid to the impact of the sentence on the offender (Thomas, 1979). In this sense, as with other guidelines issued by the Council, the guideline relating to sentencing for multiple crimes reflects judicial practice to date.

Research priorities

The primary task is to establish a firm measurement of the extent of multiple-offence cases in England and Wales. What proportion of sentenced cases involves multiple crimes? Beyond this basic question lie many more: For example, are there particular offences (or offender profiles) which are associated with particularly high volumes of multiple convictions? The next major task is to identify the factors and reasoning processes that influence sentencing decisions in multiple-offence cases. What factors do judges take into account when sentencing multiple conviction cases? What role do probation reports play in judges' decisions on multiple-offence cases? When judges reduce the total sentence, what are their rationales for doing so? To what degree do judges take offender's circumstances into consideration?

The degree of consistency across courts is also worthy of further investigation. To what extent do judges differ from each other in their sentencing decisions on multiple-offence cases? Are judges consistent across their own sentencing decisions? To what degree is their decision-making consistent with their articulated accounts of their approach? A fresh and comprehensive analysis of judgments, such as the one conducted by Thomas, would considerably enhance our understanding of sentencing practice with regard to multiple offending. In addition, a more thorough philosophical analysis of supporting principles would contribute significantly to the formation of practical guidelines. It would also be interesting to know whether the definitive guideline issued by the Council in 2011 has achieved its objective of promoting greater consistency in sentencing multiple-offence cases.

Finally, the Crown Court Sentencing Survey (CCSS; see Chapter 1) can play an important role in facilitating empirical research on this issue. The CCSS form (which judges are required to complete every time they impose a sentence) includes an item which notes whether totality was applied in the case. This permits exploration of the factors associated with the sentencing of multiple conviction cases. Such an exercise would mirror the use of the CCSS to explore the role that previous convictions play in the sentencing process (see Chapter 9 of this volume, and Roberts and Pina-Sanchez, 2015). Researchers would do well to exploit this new and unique source of information about sentencing in the Crown Court.

Notes

1. For example, in Home Office research, Moxon (1988) found that '36% of those convicted on one count received a custodial sentence, compared with 48% of

those convicted on two counts, 60% of those convicted of three offences and 68% of those convicted of four or more.'

2. The volume of cases involving multiple convictions is probably higher than these figures suggest, due to the fact that occasionally a court will sentence an offender for multiple convictions without noting on the CCSS return that totality was applied.
3. Data supplied to the author by the Sentencing Council.

References

Albrecht, H-J. (1994) *Strafzumessung bei schwerer Kriminalitat*. Berlin: Duncker and Humblot.

Ashworth, A. (2010) *Sentencing and Criminal Justice*, 5th ed. Cambridge: Cambridge University Press.

Bennett, C. (2012) Do multiple and repeat offenders pose a problem for retributive sentencing theory? In Tamburini, C. and Ryberg, J. (eds) *Recidivist Punishments: The Philosopher's View*. Lanham: Lexington Books.

Bottoms, A. (1998) Five puzzles in von Hirsch's Theory of Punishment. In A. Ashworth and M. Wasik, (eds) *Fundamentals of Sentencing Theory: Essays in Honour of Andrew von Hirsch*. Oxford: Clarendon Press.

Jareborg, N. (1998) Why bulk discount in sentencing? In A. Ashworth and M. Wasik (eds) *Fundamentals of Sentencing Theory: Essays in Honour of Andrew von Hirsch*. Oxford: Clarendon Press.

Lippke, (2011) Retributive sentencing, multiple offenders, and bulk discounts. In: M. White (ed.) *Retributivism*. New York: Oxford University Press.

Lovegrove, A. (2004) *Sentencing the Multiple Offender: Judicial Practice and Legal Principle*. Canberra: Australian Institute of Criminology.

——— (2008) *The Framework of Judicial Sentencing: A Study in Legal Decision Making*. Cambridge: Cambridge University Press.

Moxon, D. (1988) *Sentencing Practice in the Crown Court*. Home Office Research Study 103. London: Her Majesty's Stationary Office.

Reitz, K. (2010) The illusion of proportionality: desert and repeat offenders. In J.V. Roberts and A. von Hirsch (eds) *Previous Convictions at Sentencing: Theoretical and Applied Perspective*. Oxford: Hart Publishing.

Ryberg, J. (2005) Retributivism and Multiple Offending. *Res Publica*, 11: 213–233.

Sentencing Council (2010) *Consultation Stage Resource Assessment – Guidelines on Totality, TICs and Allocation*. London: Sentencing Council.

Sentencing Council (2011) *Assault. Definitive Guideline*. London: Sentencing Council.

Sentencing Council (2012) *Offences Taken into Account and Totality. Definitive Guideline*. London: Sentencing Council.

Sentencing Statistics Quarterly Brief, July–September (2010) *England and Wales*. London: Ministry of Justice.

Thomas, D. (1979) *Principles of Sentencing: The Sentencing Policy of the Court of Appeal Criminal Division*. London: Heinemann.

Vibla, N. (2014) *Sentencing for Multiple Offences: Towards a Conceptual Model within a Retributive Framework*. PhD diss., University of Cambridge.

Wasik, M. (2012) Concurrent and consecutive sentences revisited. In L. Zedner and J.V. Roberts (eds) *Principles and Values in Criminal Law and Criminal Justice*. Oxford: Oxford University Press.
Wells, M. (1992) *Sentencing for Multiple Offences in Western Australia*. University of Western Australia: Crime Research Centre.

13
Sentencing for Murder: Drawing Lessons from Research

Barry Mitchell and Julian V. Roberts

The literature on sentencing for murder falls into four categories. First, 'black letter' law sets out how the courts should punish convicted murderers and what should happen to them after conviction. Second, empirical research sheds light on the way that the sentencing provisions for murder determine the number of years served in custody prior to release on life licence. Third, a number of studies have documented what the public know or believe about sentencing for murder as well as how the public think murder ought to be punished (e.g., Mitchell and Roberts, 2012). Public opinion research is relevant to the sentencing for murder since public views are often employed to justify retention of a mandatory sentence (see Mitchell and Roberts, 2012). Fourth, there is a wealth of academic commentary advocating sentencing reform (e.g., House of Lords Select Committee, 1989; Committee on the Penalty for Homicide, 1993; Morris and Blom-Cooper, 2011; Mitchell and Roberts, 2013).

Overview

In this chapter, we explore the lessons from the limited empirical research in the field. We begin by noting recent trends in the minimum term imposed for murder and the time served prior to first release from prison. We then compare these data to public knowledge of sentencing for murder. After reviewing the research on public attitudes to sentencing murder, we identify some important priorities for further research. Our conclusion is that the highly emotional nature of sentencing in cases of murder should not prevent a more evidence-based approach to reforming the current law.

The mandatory nature of the sentence

The current law on the sentence for murder, which requires[1] the judge to impose life imprisonment (or equivalent[2]), was brought into effect nearly half a century ago. It represented the culmination of many attempts to abolish capital punishment, and it was widely assumed at the time that the overwhelming majority of the public supported such a sentence. Anything less (punitive), it was assumed, would precipitate a loss of public confidence in the criminal justice system. When passing sentence, the judge must state in open court the length of time that the offender must serve in prison before he or she can formally apply for release on licence.[3] This period, called the 'minimum term', is meant to reflect the needs of retribution and deterrence: the more serious cases should receive longer minimum terms of custody. The latest available statistics indicate that the average is about 20 years, but a small number of murders are regarded as so serious that no minimum term is identified, and the offender is likely to spend the rest of his or her natural life in prison. Even when the minimum term has expired, release on licence should only be granted if there is no unacceptable risk to public safety.

The fact that the judge is required to determine the minimum term, and that most offenders will be released on licence having served varying lengths of time in prison, clearly reflects a degree of judicial discretion. Persons convicted of murder are not all punished in precisely the same way, and one consequence of this is that the public may find the 'mandatory sentence' misleading. Indeed, participants in focus group research knew that 'life doesn't mean life' (Mitchell and Roberts, 2012, p, 86). They were aware that most offenders are released from prison – and to that extent were not misled – but were unaware of what happened to the offender on release. They were unaware that offenders on parole are required to observe various conditions, do not enjoy the same degree of freedom as other citizens, and may be recalled to prison. In other words, people were unaware of what in law, justifies labelling the sentence as mandatory.

The limited discretion given to judges obviously reflects the view in law that even within what might be thought of as a fairly narrow band of cases, some murders are more serious than others, and that is also the view taken by the public (Mitchell, 1998; 2000; Mitchell and Roberts, 2012). One of the crucial issues here, therefore, is whether the limited discretion allowed under the current law is adequate (as supporters of the status quo would claim), or whether some cases – most obviously those at the lower end of the seriousness spectrum – do not warrant the lifelong threat of imprisonment that inevitably characterizes the existing arrangements.

The current sentencing law – Schedule 21 of the Criminal Justice Act 2003

Parliament has sought to exert an unusually significant degree of legislative influence over the precise nature of each mandatory life sentence through the enactment of Schedule 21 of the Criminal Justice Act 2003. The sentencing judge 'must have regard to'[4] the principles set out in Schedule 21, which means that he or she must bear them in mind although need not follow them slavishly.[5] When determining the minimum term, the judge should assess the seriousness of the murder, and Schedule 21 identifies various 'starting points' for this purpose. In cases of 'exceptional seriousness' the starting point should be a whole life order (i.e., the offender should serve the rest of his natural life in prison). The schedule provides a non-exhaustive list of aggravating factors which reflect the kinds of murder that should fall into this category. Corresponding provision is then made for cases that are 'particularly serious' (which warrant a 30-year starting point), and for cases involving the use of knives (which warrant a 25-year starting point): in both instances lists of relevant factors are provided. In cases that do not fall within any of these three categories – that is, 'normal' murders – the starting point should be 15 or 12 years' imprisonment, depending on the offender's age at the time of committing the murder.[6]

Schedule 21 has been the subject of considerable criticism (see Thomas, 2008; Mitchell, 2012; Wasik, 2014). Serious concerns have been expressed about the lack of adequate opportunity for discussion and debate when the relevant provision in the Criminal Justice Bill (as it then was) was being considered in Parliament. One obvious concern is the size of the gaps between the starting points: the presence or absence of a single aggravating characteristic could double or halve the starting point and that might produce an unwarranted increase or decrease in the length of the minimum term. Although judges have to take account of other factors that aggravate or mitigate the seriousness of the murder, the starting point is likely to act as a kind of 'anchor' and thus have a significant impact on the minimum term that is set. This problem may be exacerbated by the distinction between adult and young offenders.

One might reasonably have expected to see a significant body of research evidence that would indicate how far and in precisely what ways these concerns are well founded. Yet there has been no detailed, systematic analysis of the operation of the current sentencing law. We have no reliable data showing just how influential – and in what way(s) – Schedule 21 actually is. We do not know the extent to which factors that are not listed in Schedule 21 are influential is the setting of minimum terms. Nor do we know how far judges are able to avoid setting inappropriate minimum terms notwithstanding the sizeable gaps in starting points.[7]

At this point, we turn to some findings from research on sentencing for murder.

(i) *Trends in minimum terms and in time served in custody*

How long do offenders convicted of murder and sentenced to life imprisonment in Britain actually spend in prison? This question may be answered by examining minimum terms imposed by courts, or by the number of years that mandatory life prisoners have served prior to their release on licence. Whereas minimum terms are determined by the needs of retribution and deterrence, release on licence depends on the assessment of risk to the public. We might expect the actual time served before release to be somewhat longer because some prisoners – for a variety of reasons – will be released later than their minimum term.

The average length of minimum terms imposed on mandatory life prisoners has been rising for many years. In the early 1970s, the average was in the region of 8 or 9 years: by the mid-1980s, it was about 10.5 years. In 2003, just before the relevant provisions in the Criminal Justice Act 2003 came into force (18 December 2003), it had gone up to 13.68 years. Table 13.1 shows the average minimum terms imposed over the last decade, from 2004 to 2013. As can be seen, the average minimum term imposed on offenders convicted of murder rose from 14.5 years in the first year after Schedule 21 was proclaimed, to 21.17 years in 2013, an increase of 46% in a decade.[8] The 2003 Act was intended to further increase the length of minimum terms,[9] and since 2004, the increase has clearly continued. Indeed, since 2010, it seems to have accelerated, and the latest figures reveal that between 1 January 2014 and 31 March 2014, the average minimum term was 20.25 years.[10]

Given the enormous increase in minimum terms over the last decade, the amount of time served in prison will continue to rise, and almost certainly at a greater rate than hitherto. Naturally, we wonder when these increases will end. What will sentences for murder look like by the time we know the full impact of Schedule 21? There is a real risk that not only will these increases in detention have significant financial consequences, but they are also likely to make the task of resettlement in the community on licence more difficult.

Schedule 21 appears to have had an impact on sentencing practice beyond murder, the implications of which call for further investigation. In *Appleby; Bryan and Roberts; and Cowles and Cowles,*[11] the Court of Appeal stressed that crimes resulting in human death should be regarded more seriously, and it has been argued that this is linked to Schedule 21 (Jeremy, 2010). Thus, sentences for manslaughter have also increased apparently in order to maintain a sense of proportionality in the punishment of that crime and murder. Table 13.2 provides some more limited data for sentencing manslaughter and two other non-murder

Table 13.1 Average minimum terms imposed on offenders convicted of murder, 2004–2013

Year	Average Minimum Term (in years)
2004	14.52
2005	16.14
2006	17.54
2007	15.91
2008	17.96
2009	17.54
2010	19.23
2011	19.35
2012	20.63
2013	21.17

Source: Data for 2004 to 2009 are drawn from Mitchell and Roberts (2012, Table 5.3); data for 2010 to 2013 were kindly supplied to the authors by the Analytical Services Directorate at the Ministry of Justice on 1 July 2014.

Table 13.2 Average custodial sentence length, selected offences, 2009–2013

	Manslaughter	Causing Death by Dangerous Driving	Causing Death by Careless Driving
2009	64.9	44.2	14.6
2010	74.0	49.1	15.4
2011	77.0	48.7	15.3
2012	88.1	49.5	13.7
2013	94.4	52.4	13.5
% increase, 2009–2013	+45%	+18%	–8%

Source: Adapted from Ministry of Justice data supplied to and available from the authors.

offences – causing death by dangerous driving and causing death by careless driving. In 2009, the average length of custodial sentences for manslaughter was 64.9 months, and by 2013, this had increased significantly to 94.4 months – a jump of 45%.[12] This is much greater even than the increase in the average minimum term for murder imposed over approximately the same four-year period (21%) and in excess of the increases for the two other offences.

The increase in the lengths of sentences for causing death by dangerous driving[13] is clearly much less, but in contrast, the sentences for causing death by careless driving generally decreased over this period. This latter crime is relatively new – created by the Road Safety Act 2006 – and it requires a relatively low level of culpability. It will be interesting to see whether Schedule 21 and the fact of human death appear to have greater influence on the sentencing of more serious homicides. We shall return to the issue of the wider-ranging impact of Schedule 21 in the conclusion to this essay.

It is worth comparing these official statistics to public estimates of the amount of time offenders convicted of murder spend in prison. First, however, it is worth noting public misperceptions about the trends in murder rates in this country.

(ii) *Public knowledge of murder sentencing trends*

Chapter 4 of this volume noted that most members of the public were misinformed about current sentencing practices for common offences such as burglary or robbery. Similar misperceptions and confusion exists with respect to sentencing for murder. A survey conducted in 2010 using a representative sample of the public posed two questions tapping public knowledge of sentencing trends for murder (see Mitchell and Roberts, 2012). Half the respondents in the survey were asked about the amount of time they believed convicted murderers actually serve in prison. Their responses are set out in Table 13.3, which reveals a clear tendency to underestimate how long offenders spend in prison. More than two-fifths of respondents thought that offenders convicted of murder are released after serving ten years in custody; just under half of the subgroup gave a broadly accurate response (which, at the time of the survey, was between 11 and 20 years).

The other half of the sample was asked how they thought the average time spent in prison by murderers in England and Wales compared

Table 13.3 Public estimates of number of years served in prison by offenders convicted of murder

Number of years offenders convicted of murder actually spend in prison	% of Respondents
1 to 5 years	3%
6 to 10 years	39%
11 to 20 years (correct answer)	48%
21 to 30 years	8%
More than 30 years	2%
	100%

Source: Adapted from Mitchell and Roberts (2012).

to other jurisdictions in the Western world. This is a difficult question because definitions of murder vary considerably between jurisdictions. One study conducted over a decade ago suggested that offenders in England and Wales spend longer than their counterparts elsewhere (Public Safety Canada, 2000): the average in that study was 14 years, which was significantly higher than many other jurisdictions. For example, the study reported that the average number of years served by life prisoners convicted of murder was 12 years in Sweden and Norway, 13 years in Belgium and Denmark, and 11 years in Ireland (ibid.). Moreover, as stated earlier, the average number of years served in prison prior to release on licence has increased over the past decade.

The correct answer to the second question we posed is most likely that offenders convicted of murder and sentenced to life imprisonment spend more time in prison in England and Wales, yet fully 61% of respondents incorrectly thought that offenders in this country spend *less* time in prison than in other Western jurisdictions. Sixteen percent thought there was no discernible difference between what happens in England and Wales and what happens elsewhere, and only 6% got the answer right.

These trends – demonstrating that the public misperceive the true severity of sentences for murder – set the context for research exploring public attitudes to sentencing for murder.

(iii) *Public attitudes towards sentencing for murder*

Survey research in England and Wales has produced apparently inconsistent results on public attitudes towards sentencing for murder. One weakness with the polling in this area is that respondents are asked their views of sentencing for murder generally, without providing any explanation of what constitutes murder or an outline of facts. For example a YouGov poll in 2013 asked about categories of murder such as 'murder of any child'. This methodology fails to provide an adequate test of levels of public support for the mandatory life sentence and also overstates the levels of public punitiveness (see discussion in Roberts and Hough, 2005). It is more appropriate to invite opinions in relation to specific cases (see discussion in Roberts, Feilzer, and Hough, 2011). We shall shortly discuss findings from a survey which did provide specific cases of murder for respondents to sentence. However, even findings from polls which ask about categories of murder suggest that the public vary their sentencing preferences according to the seriousness of the category of murder. For example, respondents were more supportive of a whole life sentence when the murder involved a child or a police officer (YouGov, 2013).

The first clear indication that public support for a sentence of life imprisonment in all cases of murder is much less than has traditionally been assumed came from two qualitative studies by Mitchell[14] (Law Commission 2004; 2005). Participants in both studies confirmed the earlier finding that the public recognize significant variations in seriousness in different cases of murder. The first of these small-scale studies, carried out in 2003, was based on 62 face-to-face interviews. Almost two-thirds of the interviewees said they did not support mandatory sentencing for murder, primarily because the sentencing judge needs to have sufficient discretion to accurately reflect the particular gravity of the case in hand. The second study, conducted in 2005, involved 56 participants from different areas of England. Each group met twice. In the first meeting, the groups again recognized variations in seriousness between different murder scenarios. A week later, the second meetings concentrated on the punishment for murder. Overall, about half the participants expressed support for mandatory sentencing, but when probed, they revealed they had different kinds of murders in mind. The main reasons for favouring a mandatory sentence were (a) the gravity of the offence, (b) a desire to guard against the judge having an off day and passing an unduly lenient sentence, and (c) a desire to avoid inconsistencies that might result from (too much) judicial discretion. Conversely, opponents of a mandatory sentence again highlighted the importance of reflecting the specific gravity of the facts of the case as warranting judicial discretion.[15] This research cast doubt on the assumption that the majority of the public are wedded to the mandatory life sentence for murder.

An explicit test of public support for a mandatory sentence was contained in questions contained in the 2010 survey (Mitchell and Roberts, 2012). Respondents were invited to give opinions across a range of murder scenarios,[16] the most serious of which was a murder in the course of a bank robbery where the offender was prepared to kill anyone who tried to prevent him. When asked to indicate their preferred sentence from a list of options including various fixed terms of imprisonment with release at some stage, or natural life imprisonment, only 52% chose the latter. This substantiates the public adherence to the principle of proportionality in sentencing.[17] It also suggests a degree of public support for a natural life sentence – at least for the most serious cases.

Murder in mitigating circumstances

A significant proportion of murder cases contain mitigating circumstances. Sometimes the law formally recognizes such circumstances as warranting conviction for a lesser crime (viz. manslaughter) – for example, where the offender had lost his self-control, suffered from a recognized abnormality of mental functioning, or killed in pursuance of a suicide pact – though in each case the court must be satisfied that various conditions have been fulfilled. Other cases, such as a killing under duress – that is, in order to avoid a threat of death or serious injury – are still regarded in law as murder.

Arguably, killing someone as an act of mercy, as where the victim is terminally ill and has (whilst of sound mind) clearly indicated a wish to die, provides one of the strongest forms of mitigation. Although the law reflects this (see Schedule 21, para 11), it does not recognize a defence or plea based on the killer's compassionate motive or 'good intentions' – assuming s/he killed because the victim had freely expressed a genuine desire to be delivered from their suffering – so that legal theory treats these cases as murder. In practice, however, the plea of diminished responsibility is sometimes stretched so that the killer is convicted of manslaughter and a mandatory life sentence is thereby avoided (Mitchell, 1997).

Yet some 'mercy' killings do result in conviction for murder and the imposition of a life sentence. In Inglis,[18] a woman took the life of her own son by injecting him with a fatal dose of heroin. He had suffered appalling head injuries and was severely incapacitated following a tragic accident. We used the following scenario describing a case in which a parent takes the life of his own child:

> Graham was 6 years old and suffered from a series of untreatable, extremely serious mental and physical disabilities. His mother, Jane, testified that she could not bear to see him suffer any more. One day she walked into a side ward in the hospital and disconnected the life-support machinery from Graham.

In response to this scenario, approximately two-thirds of respondents thought the offender should be sentenced to no more than 4 years' imprisonment, and a further 11% favoured 5 to 9 years. Only 4% suggested she should never be released from prison. This finding demonstrates that the public are sensitive to the characteristics of murder, and do not simply regard all cases as warranting imprisonment for life.

The acceptability of fixed terms instead of life imprisonment

The survey also tested public adherence to the mandatory life sentence by asking respondents to consider fixed terms of imprisonment as an alternative sanction. Respondents were randomly assigned to consider the sentence for one of three cases of murder. After each case description they were told the sentence imposed (life imprisonment), but were then asked whether they regarded a particular alternative sentence acceptable. The proposed alternative took the form of a fixed period of custody, followed by unconditional release – a fixed term sentence. The three murders described in the scenarios (Box 13.1 below) varied in relative seriousness, so different alternative sentences were provided for each case. The crucial question here was whether a fixed term alternative to a mandatory life sentence would be acceptable to members of the public; the specific value of the alternatives provided was thus relatively unimportant.[19]

Table 13.4 summarises public responses to the alternative sentences in the three cases. As can be seen, respondents in all three conditions were more likely than not to find the alternative fixed term sentence an acceptable substitute for life imprisonment. Thus, for the case of Stephen, the father who had been convicted of murder for killing his severely disabled infant daughter, fully 70% of the sample found the fixed term sentence 'definitely' or 'probably' acceptable to the life sentence. Over a third of the participants who considered this case responded that the alternative sentence would definitely be acceptable. There was less support for the alternative sentences in the other two cases – reflecting their higher perceived seriousness – but for both

Box 13.1 Murder cases used in alternative sanctions component

Case 1: Margaret
Please consider the following case. Margaret and her husband Richard had financial difficulties. Richard told her he had just spent a lot of money on a new car, and she became very angry. During a furious row, and Margaret picked up a very heavy ashtray and hit him over the head with it. Richard died shortly afterwards. Margaret was convicted of murder and sentenced to life imprisonment and required to serve 12 years before being released on licence.

Question: How would you react if instead of imposing the life imprisonment sentence the court imposed a sentence of 20 years custody? After serving all 20 years, Margaret would be released from prison without being on licence.

Case 2: Stephen
Sue was 12 years old and severely disabled. She had the mental age of a 4-month-old baby and suffered frequent fits. She was in frequent pain and faced the prospect of further major surgery with no guarantee of any improvement. Her father Stephen testified that he could not bear to see her suffer any more. One day he decided it was in her best interests that she should die, and he overdosed her medication so that she died peacefully. Stephen was convicted of murder and sentenced to life imprisonment and required to serve 8 years in prison before being released on licence.

How would you react if instead of imposing the life imprisonment sentence the court imposed a sentence of 10 years custody? After serving all 10 years, Stephen would be released from prison without any further conditions.

Case 3: Sarah
Sarah had been looking after her Uncle Max for 10 years. He suffered severely from dementia, and was also bad-tempered and regularly criticised her. One day, Sarah decided she couldn't stand it any longer. While her uncle was asleep, Sarah smothered him with a pillow, and he died. She was sentenced to life imprisonment and required to serve 10 years in prison before being released on licence.

How would you react if instead of imposing the life imprisonment sentence the court imposed a sentence of 15 years custody? After serving all 15 years, Sarah would be released from prison without any further conditions.

murders a majority of the respondents found the alternative sentence acceptable. Clearly, for each of the three scenarios, most respondents thought the alternative fixed term sentence would definitely or probably constitute an acceptable alternative to life imprisonment. Taken together, these findings suggest that the public does not support the mandatory life sentence for murder, since they favour fixed sentences in many cases, and are sensitive to murder where significant mitigation is present.

Table 13.4 Public acceptance of fixed term alternative to life imprisonment

	Case 1 (Margaret): 20 year alternative	Case 2 (Stephen): 10 year alternative	Case 3 (Sarah): 15 year alternative
This sentence would definitely or probably be acceptable as a substitute sentence.	55%	70%[20]	56%
This sentence would definitely or probably *not* be acceptable as a substitute sentence.	45%	30%	44%
Total	*100%*	*100%*	*100%*

Source: Adapted from Mitchell and Roberts (2012).

Conclusions and future research

To summarise, as a result of Schedule 21 (and possibly other causes), sentencing for murder has become more severe over the past decade. The average minimum term to be served prior to release on licence has increased significantly. In addition, there is evidence that sentencing for other homicide offences, specifically manslaughter, have also been affected. An interesting research project would address the question of whether a similar increase can be detected in the punishment of other criminal homicides. In any event, further research is also needed to see whether Schedule 21 is distorting proportionality in sentencing, if crimes such as manslaughter are being punished too severely when compared with other serious crimes such as robbery or rape.

The danger of Parliament legislating sentences for one specific offence, or category of offending, without due regard to the overall architecture of the sentencing regime for all crimes of violence, is that proportionality will be compromised. It is for this reason that we advocate a thorough review of the sentencing provisions for murder in the context of all forms of serious criminal violence. An independent body should conduct such a review, and the Sentencing Council of England and Wales or the Law Commission are obvious candidates for this task.

We need to understand much more about the way in which the current law – especially Schedule 21 – operates. Schedule 21 is obviously intended to play an important role in the determination of minimum terms, but there has been a conspicuous dearth of research to indicate how Schedule 21 works in practice. How frequently does it actually influence judges' sentencing decisions? Courts must have regard to the schedule but need not follow it slavishly. How frequently are their decisions influenced by factors *not* specified in Schedule 21? Are the gaps between starting points causing difficulties in determining minimum terms and, if so, how are judges dealing with it? How are they interpreting the ambiguous language in Schedule 21? There is a steadily growing body of case law decisions of the Court of Appeal – but it deals with specific aspects of the law, whereas what is needed is a systematic analysis of a significant sample of cases that would provide a detailed picture of the influence that the schedule exerts.

Public views

Although less empirical research has been undertaken on the operation of the mandatory life sentence in England and Wales than might have been expected, some useful lessons have been learned about public views on how convicted murderers ought to be sentenced. A significant proportion of the population underestimate the length of time offenders spend in prison before being released on licence, and they incorrectly believe that offenders in other Western societies serve more time in prison than their English counterparts. The findings from the 2010 survey cast serious doubt about the assumption that the overwhelming majority of the public support the current sentence for murder, namely a mandatory sentence of life imprisonment. This is strongly indicated by responses to a range of murder scenarios and the fact that many members of the public found determinate sentences to represent an acceptable alternative.

Perceived public opinion on the sentencing of murder is very likely to remain a significant influence on penal policy on the subject for the foreseeable future. Policymakers will surely want further survey evidence so that they can be confident about the state of public opinion. Ideally, we need to determine more clearly and precisely the extent to which the way in the public constructs seriousness in homicides and how far their approach mirrors that of the law. How far does their concept of (what we currently call) murder mirror the legal definition? Only then will we be able to assess the exact nature of the relationship between community views and legal practice.

Applied to sentencing, it would be worth exploring the question of whether the divergent starting points in Schedule 21 reflect clear distinctions in terms of community reaction. For example, an offender convicted of murder who used a hammer blow to kill attracts a starting point of 15 years. If he uses a knife, this jumps to 25, and if a gun was used in the murder, the starting point doubles to 30 years. Do these huge differences in punitiveness reflect distinctions in terms of perceived harm or culpability? Careful, case-based public opinion research may provide some interesting answers. Some insight can be gleaned from recent YouGov data. In the wake of government proposals to legislate a whole life sentence for the murder of a police officer, respondents were asked to choose from a range of sentencing options for murders involving different weapons. The public's sentencing preferences were the same, regardless of the weapon used.[21] This is further reason to question Parliament's decision to legislate starting points for different kinds of murder.

Notes

This chapter draws upon material originally published in Mitchell and Roberts (2012).

1. By making the sentence mandatory, the law seems to reflect the view that there is something 'special' or 'different' about murder; when sentencing for the vast majority of crimes, the judge has much more discretion in determining the appropriate punishment.
2. Life imprisonment is the mandatory sentence for those aged at least 21 years at the date of conviction (Section 1(1) Murder (Abolition of Death Penalty) Act 1965. Offenders aged under 21 years must be sentenced to 'custody for life' (Section 93 Powers of Criminal Courts (Sentencing) Act 2000*)*, though offenders aged under 18 years must be sentenced 'to be detained at Her Majesty's pleasure' (section 90 Powers of Criminal Courts (Sentencing) Act 2000*)*.
3. Section 270(1) Criminal Justice Act 2003.
4. Section 269(5) Criminal Justice Act 2003.
5. *Sullivan and others* [2004] EWCA Crim 1762.
6. If the defendant was aged 18 years or more at the time of committing the murder, the 'normal??? starting-point is 15 years; for those under 18, it is 12 years.
7. Clearly, it would be wholly inadequate to rely on the Court of Appeal to remedy any injustice that would otherwise ensue.
8. See Table A3.4 https://www.gov.uk/government/publications/offender-management-statistics-quarterly-october-december-2013-and-annual.
9. See House of Commons, Hansard, Debates for 20 May 2003, cols. 869–871.
10. Government statistics indicate that from 2004 to 2013, the average length of time served in prison for murder before first release on licence rose from 14 to 17 years. At first sight, this seems to reflect a gentler increase than that in minimum terms, but many of the offenders to whom the figures on the time served relate were sentenced before the Criminal Justice Act 2003 came into force. *Source*: Freedom of Information Request, Reference 90964; 19 June 2014.
11. [2009] EWCA Crim 2693, at 22.

12. We are grateful to Keir Irwin-Rogers for supplying these sentencing statistics derived from the Ministry database. Further details are available from the authors.
13. The increase in severity for this offence may also be a consequence of the fact that the maximum penalty for causing death by dangerous driving was increased from 10 to 14 years' imprisonment by section 285 of the Criminal Justice Act 2003.
14. The relatively small numbers of participants means that the findings from these studies cannot be generalised to the population of England and Wales as a whole. They did not explore the issue in detail: for example, they did not consider how far any alternate determinate sentences might be preferred.
15. Some participants thought that there should be maximum and minimum custodial limits within which judges should have to specify the particular term of imprisonment.
16. All the scenarios were based on the facts of real cases which had resulted in a murder conviction.
17. The responses to the scenarios showed wide variation, demonstrating the extent to which they were sensitive to characteristics of the case. The percentage of responses falling into the least punitive range (up to nine years imprisonment) ranged from only 1% for a killing of a bank employee during the course of a robbery to 79% for a parent killing a critically ill child. Similarly, at the opposite end of the severity spectrum, the proportion of respondents endorsing imprisonment for the offender's natural life varied from only 4% in the parent-child killing to 52% in a robbery homicide.
18. [2010] EWCA Crim 2637.
19. Whether a 20-year fixed term sentence is the 'appropriate' alternative to life imprisonment for murder is a separate question, which raises other issues such as the role of parole or whether some form of early release would need to be clarified.
20. More than a third of those who considered this scenario regarded the alternate sentence as definitely acceptable.
21. Thus 27% favoured a life sentence with the possibility of parole for murder with a knife, 26% for murder with a gun (YouGov, 2013).

References

Committee on the Penalty for Homicide (1993) *Report*. London: Prison Reform Trust.

House of Lords Select Committee (1989) *Murder and Life Imprisonment*. London: HMSO.

Jeremy, D. (2010) Sentencing Policy or Short-term Expediency? *Criminal Law Review*, 8: 593–607.

Law Commission of England and Wales (2004) *Partial Defences to Murder*. Law Commission Report No 290. London: The Stationery Office.

Law Commission of England and Wales (2005) *A New Homicide Act for England and Wales? A Consultation Paper*, Consultation Paper No 177. London: The Stationery Office.

Law Commission for England and Wales (2006) *Murder, Manslaughter and Infanticide*. Law Com No 304. London: The Stationery Office.

Mitchell, B.J. (1997) Putting Diminished Responsibility Law into Practice: A Forensic Psychiatric Perspective, *Journal of Forensic Psychiatry*, 8: 620–634.

——— (1998) Public Perceptions of Homicide and Criminal Justice. *British Journal of Criminology*, 38: 453–472.

——— (2000) 'Further Evidence of the Relationship Between Legal and Public Opinion on the Law of Homicide, *Criminal Law Review*, 814–827.

——— (2013) Sentencing guidelines for murder: from political schedule to principled guidelines. In: A. Ashworth and J.V. Roberts (eds) *Sentencing Guidelines: Exploring the English Model*. Oxford: Oxford University Press.

——— and Roberts, J.V. (2012) *Exploring the Mandatory Life Sentence for Murder*. Oxford: Hart Publishing.

———(2013) Bringing Principles and Fairness Sentencing for murder. *Criminal Law Forum*, 24: 501–526.

Morris, T. and Blom-Cooper, L. (2011) *Fine Lines and Distinctions: Murder, Manslaughter and the Unlawful Taking of Human Life*. Hook: Waterside Press.

Public Safety Canada (2000) *Comparative Murder Provisions*. Unpublished manuscript available from authors. Ottawa: Public Safety Canada.

Roberts, J.V., Feilzer, M. and Hough, M. (2011) Measuring public attitudes to criminal justice. In: D. Gadd, S. Karstedt and S. Messner (eds) *Handbook of Criminological Research Methods*. London: Sage Publications.

Roberts, J.V. and Hough, M. (2005) *Understanding Public Attitudes to Criminal Justice*. Maidenhead: Open University Press.

Thomas, D. (2008) Commentary [on R.v. Bonelli]. *Criminal Law Review*, 11: 905–906.

Wasik, M. (2014) Sentencing – The Last Ten Years. *Criminal Law Review*, 7: 477–491.

YouGov (2013) Survey Results Fieldwork May 2013. https://d25d2506sfb94s.cloudfront.net/cumulus_uploads/document/viwh311g5h/YG-Archive-prison-sentence-results-160513-life-sentences-death-penalities.pdf.

14
Sentencing Young Offenders

Max Lowenstein

The judicial approach to sentencing young offenders has evolved as society has developed. Statutes and case law now coexist with youth sentencing guidelines in England. Beyond this, government policy, academic research, media and public perceptions have also influenced youth courts. A number of themes recur in the youth sentencing debate in terms of how much priority is to be attached to the sentencing principles and interventions. For example, to what extent should youth court sentencing reflect deterrence, punishment and the protection of the public from harm? Should it reflect (to a greater degree than at the adult level) the promotion of offender welfare through rehabilitative programs? Which sentence types (or combination of interventions) can most effectively reduce youthful reoffending? There are few easy answers to such challenging questions.

Justifications for separate sentencing provisions for young offenders

Some members of the public believe that young offenders should be treated the same as adults – if they are convicted of the same offence. 'A crime is a crime' seems to capture this perspective; if you have been mugged, the shock and loss of money is no different if the mugger happens to be 17 rather than 27. The crime – in terms of its impact on the victim – may be the same, but this analysis fails to consider the second principal determinant of the sentence: the offender's blameworthiness. There are several reasons why we would blame young people less than adults convicted of the same crime – and therefore punish them more leniently. First, adolescents and young adults do not have the same life experience as mature adults, and this raises questions about the levels of culpability. A 15-year-old can reasonably claim that he did not fully appreciate the wrongfulness of the crime, a claim that is much harder for a mature adult to make.

The second reason for sentencing young offenders differently relates to their life stage. Penalties should be appropriate to the offender as well as the offence. Some adult penalties are particularly inappropriate for juveniles, and custody is the obvious example. Depriving an individual of his liberty has many serious consequences – on his employment, for example. A 12-month prison sentence will be much harder for a 15-year-old than a 30-year-old: a 15-year-old may never have been away from home before, whilst a sustained period of detention could have a deleterious effect on their education. For these reasons, criminal justice systems attempt to use imprisonment very sparingly for young offenders, resorting to detention only when it is absolutely necessary (see von Hirsch et al., 2009, chapter 7 for further readings on youth court sentencing).

Some recent trends

In terms of the volume of youth court cases appearing for sentencing, the latest statistics from England and Wales (Ministry of Justice, 2014b) show that in 2012 to 2013

- 43,601 young people (ages 10–17) in total were sentenced, which represented a 28% fall from 2011 to 2012.
- 2,780 young people (ages 10–17) in total were sentenced to immediate custody, which represented a 31% fall from 2011 to 2012 and a 61% fall from 2002 to 2003.

The Ministry of Justice and the Youth Justice Board publish sentencing data for offence categories, sentencing options/outcomes, age ranges, gender and ethnicity for young people (ages 10–17), young adults (18–20) and adults (21+). The data allows us to consider: 1) the profile of offenders broken down by offence category, 2) representation in custody, 3) reoffending rates, and 4) offender needs. For all offence categories, young people sentenced for indictable offences represented only 9% of the total numbers sentenced in 2012 to 2013. Young adults (18–20) represented 11%, and adults (21+) represented the remaining 80% of the total numbers sentenced in 2012 to 2013. Young people (10–17) represented only 16% of first-time entrants to the criminal justice system in 2012 to 2013, compared to adults (18+), who represented 84% of first-time entrants (Ministry of Justice, 2013a, p. 57). Young people (15–17) in custody represented only 1.5% of the total custodial population in June 2013, down from 3.7% in June 2003 (ibid., p. 58).

Finally, recent reoffending rates were higher for young people: 35.8% (young offenders, 10–17), 30.6% for young adults (18–20) and 24.4% for adults (21+) in 2011 to 2012 (ibid, p. 59). The higher reoffending rate for these offenders may suggest that a targeting of resources at the youngest is an important consideration in the battle to reduce recidivism (ibid, p. 60).

Youth court procedures and powers

Whilst the sentencing principles within section 142A of the Criminal Justice Act (2003) have remained prospective, youth courts continue to be primarily focused on the prevention of youth offending under section 37(1) of the Crime and Disorder Act (1998). Despite this, the long established principle of preserving youth welfare under section 44 of the Children and Young Persons Act (1933) has retained its importance. Youth welfare incorporates various societal, family, community, individual and situational elements (Morrell et al., 2011). These welfare elements only hint at the complexities facing youth court judges working with Youth Offending Teams (YOTs) as they attempt to divert young offenders away from custody (Allen, 2011). According to sections 65–66 of the Crime and Disorder Act (1998), diversion from court is attempted via police reprimands and warnings. Under section 65(4), the police are encouraged to warn rather than reprimand, depending on the seriousness of the offence. Under section 66, youth offending team referrals are supported so that more time can be spent with youth offenders in order to better understand individual welfare needs. It is important that this information via a pre-sentence report, which includes important forms of mitigation, is reported back to the youth court. The District Judge or the magistrates' panel sitting in the youth court are then required to consider the most suitable method of dealing with the offender. If there is insufficient information about the offender, the court may adjourn their sentencing until such information is provided (Moore, Rahman and Rendell, 2010).

The Criminal Justice and Immigration Act (2008) provides a range of youth sentencing options including youth rehabilitation orders (YRO), referral orders (RO) and detention and training orders (DTO). The youth court may also need to consider if the youth offender has committed a grave or dangerous offence. Section 174 of the Criminal Justice Act (2003) requires youth judges to provide reasons and to explain the impact of the sentence imposed. The explanation to a young offender should be responsive to the young person's chronological age and level of psychological maturity (Moore, Rahman and Rendell, 2010). With respect to the sentencing option thresholds, there is a requirement upon youth courts, under section 148 of the Criminal Justice Act (2003), to not pass a community sentence on a young offender unless the offence or combined offences are serious enough and such a sentence is the most suitable.

Youth sentencing guidelines

Section 125 (1) of the Coroners and Justice Act (2009) provides that every court must follow any relevant guideline, unless the court is satisfied that it would be contrary to the interests of justice to do so. At the adult level, courts apply the offence-specific guidelines issued by the Sentencing Council and its predecessors. Youth courts do not have the benefit of a set of offence-specific guidelines applicable to the sentencing of young offenders. However, there is a stand-alone guideline which provides guidance across offences. In 2009, the Sentencing Guidelines Council issued a definitive guideline to assist courts in sentencing young offenders. This guideline – which contains 'overarching principles' for sentencing youths – remains in effect until such time as it is revised or is replaced by the current statutory authority, the Sentencing Council of England and Wales.

The youth sentencing principles advocated prescribe an individualistic and flexible judicial approach. The support that is provided identifies a series of factors that affect the decision making towards young people (see Sentencing Guidelines Council, 2009, pp. 7–8). These are followed by four key elements to consider when determining the appropriateness of sentence in a case involving a youth:

- the age of the offender (both chronological and emotional);
- the seriousness of the offence;
- the likelihood of further offences being committed; and
- the extent of harm likely to result from those offences.

Young offenders are considered unlikely to have the same experience and capacity as an adult to understand the effect of their actions. Whether in fact a lack of individual experience, empathy and understanding can fully explain the propensity of a young person to offend or reoffend is too complex for the guideline to answer. Instead, it simply acknowledges that each individual young person is to be left to the judges to understand. There is no list of aggravating factors beyond previous convictions, and mitigating factors beyond an offender's maturity level and personal mitigation. Pre-sentence reports and advocates' representations are relevant when considering the relevance of maturity, reoffending risk, and the extent to which societal reintegration may be possible (Sentencing Guidelines Council, 2009).

When considering the welfare interests of young offenders, the youth guideline endorses a sentencing approach which incorporates detailed welfare information about the young person. The guideline lists relevant youth factors such as: 1) mental health conditions, 2) learning and communication difficulties, 3) youth stigmatization in court, 4) increased suggestibility, 5) adolescent angst, and 6) abuse (ibid., pp. 5–6). It also lists common factors in youthful offending such as: low family income, poor housing and employment records, low educational attainment, early experience of offending, violence or abuse by role models, and the misuse of drugs (ibid, p. 7). The sentencing approach advocated in the guideline supports the early recognition of young people's problems and the value of intervention, particularly in the lower age bracket of 10–14.

Beyond this detailed yet generic guideline, which applies to all offences, the offence-specific approach applicable to the sentencing of adult offenders (18+) has relevance for youth sentencing practices. When youth judges consider the seriousness of offences committed by young offenders under 18, some aspects of offence harm and offender culpability can assist them. This can include young offenders being considered as potentially vulnerable victims whose offending reflects a lower level of culpability (Sentencing Guidelines Council, 2004). When a young offender enters a guilty plea, the adult guideline can apply, with modification, in the youth court (Sentencing Guidelines Council, 2007). For young offenders receiving an antisocial behavior order (ASBO), principles have been provided in order to assist sentencing. In particular, whilst the assessment of the seriousness of an ASBO breach for adult offenders applies equally to young offenders, the different intellectual and emotional maturity levels of young people may affect their perceptions of time between imposition and breach (Sentencing Guidelines Council, 2008).

The definitive guideline for robbery contains a separate section which provides for factors to be taken into account at sentencing when the offender is a youth. Adult and young offenders involved in robbery may have different characteristics which are relevant to sentencing considerations. In particular, the age, maturity and reaction to group or peer pressure may vary between young offenders and adults (Sentencing Guidelines Council, 2006). Finally, there is reference to the sentencing of youthful offenders in the new guidelines for sexual offences. Whilst the sentencing of adults convicted of sexual offences follows a definitive guideline (Sentencing Council, 2014), those sentencing young offenders are currently referred to part 7 of the Council's sexual offences guideline, which list six specified offences. This will remain in force until the Sentencing Council produces more comprehensive guidelines for sentencing youths.

Approaching the youth custody threshold

Where the custody threshold lies for young offenders can be complex, depending on the seriousness of the offence and the risk posed to the public. Box 14.1 provides a typical example of the challenging cases confronting a youth sentencing court. It illustrates the complexity of youth court sentencing, particularly with respect to the youth custody threshold.

Box 14.1

The youth court is faced with sentencing a young 14-year-old male convicted of grievous bodily harm (GBH) and theft contrary to section 20 of the Offences against the Person Act (1861) and section 1 of the Theft Act (1968). He has low intelligence and is currently within a residential center (non-secure) due to his persistent offending and lack of parental control. The vulnerable young victim of the GBH, a 14-year-old male, has suffered a fractured skull and jaw from being viciously and repeatedly beaten about the head. He has been left psychologically traumatized, and his current depression and anxiety problems have been exacerbated. This victim also had his new smart phone stolen. The convicted young offender says he is sorry and has pleaded guilty. According to the pre-sentence report, the risk factors include a dysfunctional family background, limited interpersonal social skills, learning difficulties, substance abuse, and a proclivity for violent outbursts. Psychological testing reveals high impulsivity, suggestibility and psychopathic tendencies. His remorse for the offence appears to be more based on a fear of imprisonment rather than on the harm caused. In social situations, he is inept, threatens others in the community and chooses to exclude himself. The youth offender has received numerous police reprimands and cautions for past antisocial behavior. This then escalated to the use of YRO's. There is one previous conviction for GBH, 5 for assault occasioning actual bodily harm, and over 15 for minor thefts and cannabis possession offences.

When sentencing, there are a number of considerations that are applicable when determining the custody threshold in this case. Custody, if deemed appropriate, would consist of one of the three secure estates: a secure children's home, secure training centre, or a young offender institution. The detention training (community supervision) order (DTO) is the most common custodial sentence and may be applicable in this case. In recent years, there has been a decline in youth custody usage overall (Allen, 2011; Ministry of Justice, 2014a). A DTO is regarded as a last resort when a YRO, RO or a fine is not appropriate, and it may last from four months to two years. The order is split between a young person spending the first half of the order in custody and the second half released on license. If they reoffend whilst on license they may be returned to custody. There is a test to be applied to a 12- to 14-year-old persistent offender as in this example: Is the offence of such gravity that a sentence substantially beyond the 2-year maximum for a DTO is a realistic possibility? (Judicial Studies Board, 2013).

If custody is to be imposed, there would need to be a significant risk of serious harm to the public from the young offender committing further similar offences. The court needs to determine whether a sentence of 4 years detention would be appropriate for the current GBH and theft offences, and whether as a dangerous offender, it would be more appropriate for him to be sentenced in the Crown Court (ibid.). In determining where the threshold lies, the seriousness of the crime is determinative, and this includes offender culpability and offence harm. There is a strong presumption against youth court judges sending cases to the Crown Court unless it is the appropriate forum (*R v Wirral Borough Magistrates' court, ex parte K, 2002*).

Referring to the youth sentencing example in Box 14.1, GBH falls within the 2-year DTO maximum penalty, but could tip into the Crown Court, as the maximum penalty for GBH is 5 years detention (Judicial Studies Board, 2013). For GBH youth offenders under 18, the assault guideline does not appear to apply (Sentencing Council, 2011). Under section 100(2) of the Powers of Criminal Courts (Sentencing) Act (2000), a DTO can only be applied to persistent offenders under the age of 15. Persistence has been defined widely in case law with a focus on the established sentencing principles of offender welfare through mitigating factors and prevention from reoffending/public protection through aggravating factors (R v L 2012). It involves an offence that is regularly repeated which depends on the case facts, offence type and time gaps in offending behavior (R v M 2008). All offences may be relevant to establishing persistence, but the threshold appears to be high with convictions for the same offence and cautions required (R v TTG 2004) and (R v D 2001). Where there are no applicable offence specific guidelines, the court must look to the sentence that may have been appropriate for an adult offender convicted of the same offence (Judicial Studies Board, 2013).

Current youth sentencing concerns

Recent research sheds light on the ways that youth courts have responded to changes in youth sentencing law and policy. Between 1992 and 1997, a 40% increase in the use of custody for 10- to 17-year-olds, followed by a decline from 2001 to 2003, with the 10–14 age group particularly increasing was noted in the Ministry of Justice statistical bulletins (Audit Commission, 2004). This appears to be based upon the more punitive approach in the early 1990s of the Conservatives, which gave way to the political consensus of supporting a more engaging and costly model of intervention under New Labour from 1997 to 2010. More recent statistics recorded a peak in 2006, although the overall level came down from 2007 to 2010 (National Audit Office, 2010). Since 2010, the coalition government has endorsed alternatives to custody through rehabilitative youth programs and expanding victim access to restorative justice conferences (Ministry of Justice, 2012b).

According to Smith (2014a) three principal youth sentencing concerns emerge from the recent empirical trends: (1) ethnicity discrimination; (2) the sentencing of young rioters from 2011 (such as *R v Blackshaw and others 2011*); and (3) the decline in YOT prevention services due to public funding cuts since 2010 (House of Commons Justice Committee, 2013). In terms of the second concern, the public condemnation and blame of youth crime requires an understanding of the communication nexus between the judiciary, the public and the media. Most youthful offending is relatively minor and more common amongst children and young adults, peaking at 19 for males and 21–24 for females. Furthermore, 85% of detected offending was from adults over 21 in 2012 (Bateman, 2013, pp. 9–10). Despite these statistics, which suggest youth crime is not prolific, the public misperceive youth crime trends. It has been found that 75% of the public misperceive youth crime levels as rising (Hough and Roberts, 2004, p. 17). Such public misperceptions are a result of media reporting, which negatively reflects upon the minority of persistent or grave crime young offenders rather than the majority (Mattinson and Mirrlees-Black, 2000). In terms of the third concern, there is evidence of Black and Asian overrepresentation in remand and custodial populations (Feilzer and Hood, 2004). These differences do not appear to be fully explained by offence characteristics or past offending history (May et al., 2009). However, at sentencing, the evidence for discrimination against males at the custody threshold is not apparent when the detailed case facts are considered (Feilzer and Hood, 2004).

Overall, the current picture for youth custody suggests a continuing downward trend from 2005 to 2014, regardless of ethnicity (Ministry of Justice, 2014a). Young people from a black ethnic background have the highest reoffending rate (42.5%), compared to those of white at 35.8% and Asian at 30.2% (Ministry of Justice, 2013a). These latest figures suggest that ethnicity remains an important factor in the reduction of reoffending debate. The extent to which youth court judges can themselves reduce these reoffending rates is limited. However, courts can provide independent judicial oversight and ensure youth offenders are treated fairly through fully informed sentencing decisions.

Future of guidelines for youth

It may be that youth sentencing, like adult sentencing, will become subject to offence-specific guidelines. It remains to be seen whether the Sentencing Council pursues this route, creating separate guidelines for young offenders, or whether courts will be required to merely discount the sentencing ranges applicable to the sentencing of adult offenders. If the Sentencing Council decides that separate offence-specific guidelines are necessary in relation to youths, will more transparency, consistency and fairness in sentencing practice necessarily result? Can offence-specific guidelines enhance the current efforts of the judiciary operating in the youth courts to effectively engage with the most troubled and at risk young offenders? In other words, before we provide further sentencing guidelines, do we currently know enough about how best to gain the participation, trust and acceptance of young offenders whose complicated needs, if left unaddressed, may worsen as they progress towards adulthood? Perhaps we should be more concerned with the current effectiveness of the various noncustodial sentencing options which seek to reduce and prevent future youth offending. A clear priority for research at the youth court level is to determine which of the various disposals are most effective.

Research should address these questions in order to better inform youth sentencing practices. The answer to youth crime may lie in more effective pre-trial diversion or post-trial community and custodial options. Youth courts will continue to require access to detailed youth offender information, via pre-sentence and other expert witness reports. These reports can help to ensure that the problems and potential solutions for young offenders are fully understood. Targeting research and funding on the youngest offenders (ages 10–14) could reveal important insights into the etiology of youthful offending. Furthermore, research focused on the small number of severely maladjusted young offenders in custody currently appears important. Finally, by exploring the experiences and perceptions of youth court actors, future researchers can expand our understanding of youth court team work, which is crucial to delivering proportionate and effective youth sentencing.

Legislation Cited

Children and Young Persons Act (1933)
Crime and Disorder Act (1998)
Criminal Justice Act (2003)
Criminal Justice and Immigration Act (2008)
Coroners and Justice Act (2009)
Firearms Act (1968)
Offences against the Person Act (1861)
Powers of Criminal Courts (Sentencing) Act (2000)
Theft Act (1968)

Cases Cited

C & D v Sheffield Youth Court [2003] EWHC Admin 35
R (on the application of H, A and O) v Southampton Youth Court [2004] EWHC 2912 Admin
R v Blackshaw and others [2011] EWCA Crim 2312
R v D [2001] 165 J.P. 1
R v L [2012] EWCA Crim 1336
R v M [2008] EWCA Crim 3329
R v MW [2012] EWCA Crim 2314
R v Tom & Billy Thomas [2012] EWCA Crim 2983
R v TTG [2004] EXCA Crim 3086
R v Wirral Borough Magistrates' court, ex parte K [2002] EWHC 1640

References

Allen, R. (2011) *Last Resort? Exploring the Reduction in Child Imprisonment 2008–11.* London: Prison Reform Trust.
Audit Commission (2004) *Youth Justice 2004.* London: Audit Commission.
Bateman, T. (2013) *Children in Conflict with the Law: An Overview of Trends and Developments – 2012.* National Association for Youth Justice. 1–27. Accessed 20 December 2013. http://thenayj.org.uk/wp-content/files_mf/nayjbriefingchildreninconflictwiththelaw1.pdf
Bryman, A. (2012) *Social Research Methods.* 4th ed. Oxford: Oxford University Press.
CPS (2014) Youth Offenders: Legal Guidance. The Crown Prosecution Service. Accessed 6 March 2014. http://www.cps.gov.uk/legal/v_to_z/youth_offenders/.
Feilzer, M. and Hood, R. (2004) *Differences or Discrimination?* London: Youth Justice Board.

Hough, M. and Roberts, J. (2004) *Youth Crime and Youth Justice.* Bristol: The Policy Press.
House of Commons Justice Committee. (2013) *Youth Justice Seventh Report of Session 2012–13*, Volume I, HC 339. London: House of Commons.
Judicial Studies Board. (2013) *Youth Court Bench Book.* London: Judicial Studies Board.
Lowenstein, M. (2013) Towards an Understanding of Judicial Denunciation – Relating Theory to Practice by Comparing the Perceptions of English and Danish Lower Court Judges When Sentencing Minor Theft Offenders. *Criminology & Criminal Justice*, 13: 21–35.
Mattinson, J. and Mirrlees-Black, C. (2000) *Attitudes to Crime and Criminal Justice: Findings from the 1998 British Crime Survey.* London: Home Office.
Ministry of Justice. (2012a) *Youth Offences Resulting in a Disposal by Region, 2010/11.* London: Ministry of Justice.
——— (2012b) *Restorative Justice Action Plan for the Criminal Justice System*, London: Ministry of Justice.
——— (2013a) *Youth Justice Statistics 2011/12 – England and Wales.* London: Ministry of Justice.
——— (2013b) *Criminal Justice Statistics Quarterly Update to June 2013 – England and Wales.* London: Ministry of Justice.
——— (2014a) *Monthly Youth Custody Report – November 2013* (Jan. update). Youth Justice Statistics Collection. London: Ministry of Justice.
——— (2014b) *Youth Justice Statistics 2012/13 – England and Wales.* London: Ministry of Justice.
Moore, T., Rahman, P. and Rendell, T. (2010) *Youth Court Guide.* (4th ed.) Haywards Heath: Bloomsbury Professional.
Morrell, G., Scott, S., McNeish, D. and Webster, S. (2011) *The August Riots in England, Understanding the Involvement of Young People.* London: National Centre for Social Research.
Muncie, J. (2004) *Youth and Crime.* (2nd ed.) London: Sage.
National Audit Office. (2010) *The Youth Justice System in England and Wales: Reducing Offending by Young People.* Report by the Controller and Auditor General, HC 663 Session 2010–11. London: The Stationary Office.
Sentencing Guidelines Council. (2004) *Overarching Principles: Seriousness.* London: Sentencing Council.
——— (2006) *Robbery.* London: Sentencing Council.
——— (2007) *Reduction in Sentencing for a Guilty Plea.* London: Sentencing Council.
——— (2008) *Breach of an Anti-Social Behavior Order.* London: Sentencing Council.
——— (2009) *Overarching Principles – Sentencing Youths.* London: Sentencing Council.
Sentencing Council. (2011) *Assault, Definitive Guideline.* London: Sentencing Council.
——— (2014) *Sexual Offences, Definitive Guideline.* London: Sentencing Council.
Smith, R. (2014a) *Youth Justice: Ideas, Policy, Practice.* London: Routledge.
Smith, D. (2014b) Wider and Deeper: The Future of Criminology in Europe. *European Journal of Criminology*, 11: 3–22.

von Hirsch, A., Ashworth, A. and Roberts, J.V. (eds) (2009) *Principled Sentencing. Readings*
on Theory and Policy. (3rd ed.). Oxford: Hart Publishing.
Weijers, I. (2004) Requirements for Communication in the Courtroom: A Comparative Perspective on the Youth Court in England/Wales and the Netherlands. *Youth Justice*, 4: 22–31.
Youth Justice Board. (2013) *Annual Report & Accounts 2012/13*. HC 520. London: The Stationary Office.
Youth Justice Board. (2012a) *Statistics Bulletin: Offence Classification Numbers Used for Court Proceedings, 2011*. London: Ministry of Justice.
Youth Justice Board. (2012b) *Statistics Bulletin, Use of Custody by Region, 2010/11*. London: Ministry of Justice.

Index

Lightning Source UK Ltd.
Milton Keynes UK
UKOW07n1027240215

246777UK00002B/11/P

9 781137 390394